TWENTY MINUTES PRESS

Dear Readers:

If you are reading this book because it came to you directly, it is because you fall into one of three categories:

• You are a Senior in Computer Science at one of the 18 universities that *U.S. News & World Report* named as those with the best undergraduate Computer Science departments.

• You are a professional in the computer industry, and subscribe to industry publications, such as *Dr. Dobb's Journal* or *Web Techniques* magazine.

• You are a representative of one of the companies profiled in the enclosed book.

The Best Computer Jobs in America is the first national edition of a popular regional job guide for techies. It is designed to help you in one of several ways:

• If you are looking for your first job, these corporate profiles will give you the context you need to understand what company recruiters look for.

• If you are an experienced professional, here is the corporate research that allows you to find and compare companies in normalized profiles. Whether you are looking for a job, finding colleagues and companies using similar tools to find best practices, or strategizing the direction of your industry, these profiles will help.

• If you are profiled in this guide, you will attract the most appropriate talent for your environment.

Corporate research has never been so easy or so detailed. Enjoy this gift!

Sincerely,

Carol L. Covin, President
Twenty Minutes from Home

12510 Izaak Walton Rd.   Bristow, VA 20136   phone: (703) 367-9506   fax: (703) 367-9509
Web: http://www.20minutesfromhome.com

Also by the author:

Vandamere Press

Washington Area Computer Job Guide
New England Computer Job Guide
Midwest Computer Job Guide
Southeast Computer Job Guide

THE BEST COMPUTER JOBS IN AMERICA:

Twenty Minutes from Home

CAROL L. COVIN

Published by
Twenty Minutes Press
A Division of Twenty Minutes from Home
12510 Izaak Walton Rd.
Bristow, VA 20136
http://www.twentyminutesfromhome.com
carol.covin@20minutesfromhome.com

Copyright 2002 by Twenty Minutes Press

ISBN 0-9717846-0-4

Book cover design by Victor Weaver
http://www.victorweaver.com

Manufactured in the United States of America. This book is set in Palatino and Optima and was prepared on a Macintosh PowerBook G3, using Microsoft Word. Composition was done in QuarkXPress.

Table of Contents

Acknowledgements

My thanks to Jim Grogan, President and founder of Marketing By Innovation, who conceived the business model for this, the first, in a new series of job guides for computer professionals. Molly Tomlinson, a linguist and Senior Product Representative for Rational Software, provided editing support and a current perspective on computer skills. Tony Mazella, at Sheridan Books, sustained interest in this project during the long gestation period. Thanks to Art Brown, founder of Vandamere Press, publisher of the earlier series of Covin's Guides, who taught me the business of publishing. And, as always, thanks to my husband, Dave Covin, who first got me interested in programming and now patiently supports me while I write about the companies that do it.

Foreword

Covin's series of job guides for technical professionals began with *The Computer Professional's Job Guide for the Washington, D.C. Area* (Vandamere Press, 1989). It grew out of a realization that if commuters were traveling in equal numbers both directions across a bridge near Washington, D.C., then there must be an equal number of jobs on both sides of the bridge!

Why weren't people working near home? And, if they wanted to, how would they find jobs near home? Computer professionals have specialized skills that are only applicable in the appropriate software or hardware environment. If they were going to try to find all the jobs requiring, for example, Oracle expertise, how would they find them?

This was in the days before the Internet. The Internet, now the preferred marketplace for job seekers and employers alike, still did not solve all the problems of finding a job. Further, it added the problem of too much information and information that was not geographically-relevant. A search for Oracle jobs in Washington, D.C. yields hundreds of hits at each of several sites. Even a single employer's site can give hundreds of hits, and most request that candidates reply to each specific job opening.

Covin's Guide addresses this problem by providing techies with a source for corporate research. A series of company profiles are available at our web site (http://www.20minutesfromhome.com) and selected profiles have been included in this Guide. Stripping away the hype found in most company literature, Covin's Guide describes a company's internal technical environment. This is, after all, the main thing techies want to know about a company. Both through extensive interviews with companies, and carefully targeted research, Covin's Guide provides an overview of companies specifically aimed at technical professionals.

The Long and the Short of It

Covin's Guide consists of two types of profiles, long and short. Long profiles were developed through extensive interviews with hiring managers at the companies. Companies paid a fee for these profiles. Short profiles were developed through publicly-available information on the Internet and at the companies' sites.

What is the advantage to readers? Long profiles include an in-depth view of a company's technical environment. They include a description of a sample project, new technology the company is investigating, how technology is used in various business units, and a listing of all the major software being used. They include a description of the business and where and how techies support the business. They include an overview of the company's current technical staff—their average level of experience and education. And they include the company's hiring expectations—tangible and intangible qualities they look for and where they find candidates. They also include an overview of the company's culture—hours worked, dress code, travel requirements, benefits, and freebies.

Short profiles are a condensed version of this information. Sample job listings were picked that show a range of the technical tools used in the company. Geographic locations show where various skills are required. Readers gain insight into the career path at a company from the years of experience and educational requirements shown for different professional levels. Facts such as revenues, number of employees, and date founded show the size and maturity of a company. The industry the company is in helps candidates zero in on appropriate target companies and compare companies within an industry. Awards the company has won show why this company is considered a technical or business leader.

A Guide to the Guide

The profiles in this guide are divided into two chapters. Chapter Two, On the Profit Line, focuses on companies that are in the technology industry. These include hardware and software vendors, consulting/professional services companies, telecommunications companies, and retail or wholesale companies that specialize in selling computers, software packages, supplies, and peripherals. The first profiles in the chapter are the long profiles. These are followed by the short profiles. Chapter Three, On the Bottom Line, focuses on companies that use technology to further another business. Each of the four sets of profiles is alphabetical within the set. Chapter Four evaluates the various options for job-hunting, with pros and cons. Chapter Five helps entry-level professionals by describing entry-points into the industry. Chapter Six describes the top on-line sites for job hunters.

Appendix A describes the methodology used for preparing this guide. Additional Appendices are provided for cross-referencing companies by computer hardware or software (Appendix B), industry (Appendix C), state (Appendix D) and a simple alphabetic list (Index). Appendix E names the vendors that provide products listed in this guide. Appendix F lists articles used in research.

Summary

Covin's Guide provides a series of road maps designed specifically for techies. It provides a road map to a company's organization, to its technical environment, to its career path, and to the skills its hiring managers are looking for.

Although a further discussion of the methodology used is provided in a separate appendix, the essential criteria used to select the profiled companies is that they were named by well-known publications as the best to work for or the best managed. The author's assumption is that the best companies have the best jobs.

Further, companies say the best candidates are those who come into an interview well-prepared, having researched the company in advance. And, their number one criteria for hiring—candidates must be smart. This guide is designed to put you out in front in your search for the best company.

Good luck in your job search!

Carol L. Covin
Bristow, Virginia
January, 2002

About the Author

A recovering techie, Carol L. Covin's career has ranged from programming room-sized mainframes with 1MB of memory to documenting voice interfaces for two-pound wearable computers with a 1GB hard drive. Ms. Covin has taught programming in Petersburg, Virginia and programming instructors in Katmandhu, Nepal. She has designed imaging systems for $1 billion legal cases and databases for tracking the multi-million dollar electronic and communications gear on-board U. S. Navy ships. She has hired and managed techies for and been hired by both users and vendors. In Beijing, she introduced herself in Chinese, before, to the amusement and relief of her audience, admitting that the rest of her technical seminar would be in English, which was then translated by a local guide.

If prompted, Ms. Covin will tell her story involving cows and fences from the 60 hours she logged as a private pilot in Argentina, and another involving a tri-wheeler and wind changes from her one-time stint as an air-traffic controller. A confirmed suburban brat, Ms. Covin recently moved to a home on a creek, with 12 chickens, two dogs, and a half-mile driveway, which she shares with her husband of 34 years.

Chapter One

Geeks And Their Toys

Internet millionaires. 70-hour work weeks. Until the dot-com craze, most techies were simply in it for the fun, the technical challenge of finding a missing semi-colon, an over-written spot in core, an endless loop, real data that did not match a user's description—logic made real in software and hardware. And the pay was good.

Add the possibility of retiring by 30, signing bonuses, stock options, benefits that included on-site fitness centers, massages, balloons, and M&Ms and the profession started attracting much more attention. Techies were coddled during the Internet boom. But, then, not everybody enjoys staring at a computer screen for hours on end. Not everyone is interested in the arcane language and logic of computers. And, if Federal Reserve Chairman Alan Greenspan is right, computers are responsible for significant productivity gains. Techies have always been respected, even awed, so have generally been able to pick employers based on how cool their projects were. With the Internet boom and bust, techies are now relearning the importance of working for companies that last. A tight labor market pushed the salaries of Cisco-certified engineers into the $200,000 range. This tight labor market was also largely responsible for companies' aggressive recruiting and retention techniques over the last few years. The Y2K scare made companies realize that computer people were not interchangeable. It was cheaper to hang on to the ones you had than to try to find and train new ones.

Enter the new age: post September 11, 2001. The 2001 recession was accelerated by the tragic events on that day and since. Companies that had slowed their recruiting during the summer or laid off thousands of workers, are now being even more cautious. Technical professionals that have kept their jobs are staying put, for the most part, cutting the turnover rate significantly. The tens of thousands caught in the recession are having to look harder and longer for new jobs. Recruiters and hiring managers report some of the best resumes and candidates they have seen in years.

Jobs Overview—Not Post-Today, Gone-Tomorrow

This guide is designed to match employers and candidates. Where job listings can be considered a microview of an organization and its technology, these profiles are a macroview of companies and their technical environments. Instead of a comprehensive list of available job openings today, this guide provides a representative sample of the jobs each company offers. Where possible, it shows representative jobs in a sample career path. It also shows the awards each company has won that qualified them for inclusion in the guide.

Detailed profiles are provided for those companies that agreed to in-depth interviews with their highest technology executives and hiring managers. Companies paid a fee for this exposure, with the assumption that their hiring costs would be reduced with this opportunity to describe in detail the kind of candidates they look for. Hiring managers were interviewed with a detailed questionnaire. The questions in the survey were collected from techies in response to the query: "If you could ask a hiring manager anything you wanted, what would you ask?" The survey included questions that might be asked in a typical interview:

- Describe a sample project.
- What is the technical environment?
- What business units do techies support?

The profiles also include answers to questions that could not be asked by candidates in a typical interview:

- What are your layoff policies?
- What is the career path?
- What are your benefits?
- What are the real hours?
- Is travel a requirement?
- How far do people typically commute?
- What is your dress code?

Who Is In This Guide?

The companies profiled, with either short or in-depth descriptions, include all those American-based companies identified as the best by the following magazines and trade publications.

- *Computerworld*: 100 Best Places to Work in IT
- *Fortune*: 100 Best Companies to Work for in America
- *Industry Week*: 100 Best Managed Companies

The underlying assumption is that excellent companies have excellent jobs. A few profiled companies were included from a wider range of top companies interviewed in earlier research in 2000. They were named by magazines such as *PC Magazine*, *Red Herring*, and *Interactive Week*. For a more in-depth description of our methodology, see Appendix A, Methodology.

Who Should Read this Guide?

This guide is a service to techies. It is designed to provide information to jobseekers that is not available publicly. We asked companies to describe their technical environment in detail. Some of this information is typically not available to candidates until the interview. Much of the information is not available until you work for the company. This process is designed to accelerate your ability to learn about a company before you go through the time-consuming process of interviewing there and to enable you to ask specific questions from an informed background.

Finally, we asked hiring managers what is important to them when interviewing—the tangible and intangible qualities that set a candidate apart.

- Is a college degree important? A graduate degree?
- Do you look for candidates who are well rounded?
- Is there a need for good communication skills in this environment? Teamwork?
- Are your current employees, on average, very young, or very experienced?

A Techie Road Map

This book is a road map. It is not just a road map to companies and jobs, but a road map to the organization itself and where techies fit in.

- It is a road map to the organization's business units.
- It is a road map to the career path for techies.
- It is a road map to the company's technical environment.

This is the information you need to go into an interview prepared. If your favorite company is not profiled, these profiles will still give you a benchmark for an industry or a technology that will help in your search and evaluation.

Hiring managers almost universally said their number one requirement for techies is that they be smart. But, they were hard to pin down on how they decide if someone is smart or not. The bottom line was, "Smart people know smart people."

They are talking about you. They are looking for you. Stand out by being informed!

Chapter Two

On the Profit Line

This chapter includes companies that are in the technology business. They range from Internet companies to software vendors, hardware manufacturers, professional services firms, and telecommunications companies. Technical professionals working at these companies know that their contributions drive the company's success. This is important for several reasons:

- Salaries are typically higher than in non-technical industries.
- Career paths typically lead into the executive ranks.
- Budgets favor the mainline business.
- Retrenchments affect the core of a company last.

Career Paths

Career paths at product and services vendors differ significantly from those at non-technical companies. The main paths are in these functional areas:

- Product development
- Customer Support
- Pre- and Post-Sales Support
- Training
- Technical Writing
- Consulting Services.

It is important to understand these options, because different skills are required. Product development typically involves little contact with a customer, but requires deep technical skills. Product developers are responsible for anticipating or leading technical trends. The closer you are to a customer, the more important it is to be able to communicate in non-technical language. Jobs such as customer support, pre- and post-sales support, and consulting services all require the ability to speak to non-technical people in clear terms. These jobs also require the ability to adapt to new technical environments quickly. Training and technical documentation require the ability to remember or imagine what it was like not to understand your company's product so as to explain it to people for whom it is new. Finally, the more involved you are in consulting services or customer solutions, the more important it is to have business and project management skills to supplement technical expertise.

While the ability to interact with customers varies depending on the position, virtually all positions at a technology vendor have a sales component. Technical expertise may be called on at trade shows, in presenting papers at conferences, or interacting with a customer's technical experts before, during, and after a sale. Techies consider it a point of personal and professional pride to present the facts about technology and this can be in conflict with marketing or sales, which typically provide a context that favors their company's product. Balancing these points of view is essential for techies at product firms.

As they move up in their careers, techies may switch between working in the technical industry itself and working for customers who buy technical products. In fact, experience at a vendor is often an excellent reference for working at one of that vendor's customers. Techies may be surprised to find, however, that customers often have a deeper knowledge of their products than the vendors themselves. However, when you consider that customers use the product in real world environments, under circumstances that may never have been envisioned by the product's developers, this seeming anomaly makes sense. You will read more about customer companies in Chapter Three.

For now, enjoy reading about companies leading the technology industry and the career opportunities there!

BV SOLUTIONS GROUP, Inc.

"We look for critical skills like e-commerce, workflow, document management, Internet, and networking."
– Brad Vaughan
– Chief Operations Officer

- IBM SP mainframes, RS/6000s, Sun servers -
- C, C++, XML, WAP, Java, Oracle -
- Professional services - Large shop -

E-business, communications, and knowledge management with engineering precision. BV Solutions Group (BVSG) has learned a few things about managing complex projects from its experience with its parent company, Black & Veatch, one of the world's largest engineering and construction firms. They have learned the importance of rigorous processes. Documentation, an afterthought for most projects, is considered integral at BVSG. You would expect this from a company used to dealing with hundreds of sub-contractors and vendors. BVSG understands the value of coordinating communications with everyone on the team, whether it is through a common repository of documents and database, or a network that keeps everyone connected throughout the project's life cycle.

BVSG is leveraging its disciplined engineering approach and project management experience with a host of Fortune 1000 companies and Internet start-ups alike. This experience includes integrating legacy systems, integrating supply chains, supporting multiple interfaces, and adding new applications to existing infrastructure.

Surprise company event: a Halloween costume party for employees' children.

Fast Facts	Revenues: $50M (1999)
	Employees: 520 (1999)
	Founded: 1999
	Professional services; computer consulting
	Private; wholly-owned subsidiary of Black & Veatch
Awards	Information Week: Top 500 Technology Innovators (2000)
	Engineering News-Record: Excellence for Engineering Innovation (1999)
	Information Week: Top 100 E-Business Innovators (1999)
	CIO: Enterprise Value Award (1998)
Headquarters	10950 Grandview Drive
	Overland Park, KS 66210-1414
	(877) 287-6588
	www.bvsg.com

Business

BV Solutions Group was the Information Technology (IT) arm of Black & Veatch until it became an independent business unit in 1999. Since the 1980s, the organization has been providing IT support to Black & Veatch. In 1989, the division began soliciting work from outside the organization. Its staff grew to more than 200 by 1997. The company's client list reflects the variety of industries it serves: Sprint, Time Warner, Williams Communications, Caterpillar, General Motors, Hallmark Cards, Merck and Blue Cross/Blue Shield.

Black and Veatch is a private $2.15B engineering and construction firm with more than 8,000 professionals, based in Kansas City, Missouri. E.B. Black and N. T. Veatch founded the company in 1915. Black & Veatch is one of the largest and most diversified engineering and construction firms in the world. It has completed more than 35,000 projects for some 6,500 clients in the areas of information technology, power, infrastructure, petrochemical, telecommunications, and high-tech facilities.

Its roots as an information technology provider can perhaps be traced to an engineer's love of detail and organization. Twenty years ago, Black & Veatch allocated $30 million for the development of a computer automated power plant design and project management system. POWRTRAK redefined the approach to engineering by creating a set of common codes to identify categories of equipment such as pipes, valves, and fittings to replace the patchwork then in place in which suppliers each used their own codes and part numbers.

BVSG is the largest IT services provider in the Midwest, emphasizing its proprietary engineering approach as a competitive edge over competitors such as Andersen Consulting and EDS. In an industry where more than 85 percent of IT projects reportedly fail or are abandoned, a strict project methodology can be key in successful projects. Says Vaughan, "We follow a systematic, repeatable process to define the scope and establish the objectives for each project." As a result, BVSG's projects are completed on spec, on budget, and on schedule.

BVSG applies this disciplined engineering approach to projects ranging from communications to e-business and knowledge management, fault management and root cause analysis, configuration management, asset management, and security. BVSG projects have included development of a business strategy, site design, and technology selection and implementation for call centers, billing, outage management, messaging solutions, relocations, and disaster recovery applications. Knowledge management projects range from data warehousing to data mining, electronic document management, and decision support systems.

Technology

BVSG's hardware includes IBM SP mainframes, RS/6000 AIX systems, Sun workstations and 400 servers from Sun, HP, and Compaq. Alan Richardson, VP, Client Services, emphasizes the company's focus on high availability database servers, "Several of our locations have dual processors and triple-mirrored hard drives." Programming is typically in C or C++, although most other languages are supported for both internal projects and client work, including Visual Basic, XML, Java, and web-based and e-commerce development tools.

Additional software used includes databases like Oracle, Informix, and Ingres, as well as systems software like IBM's Tivoli and Computer Associates' tools. Additional packages include vendor-specific applications software, such as Oracle Financials, Oracle Project, and PeopleSoft. Naturally, the company also uses engineering drawing and document management software, including AutoCAD, Documentum, and FileNet.

BVSG's communications infrastructure reveals its devotion to tight communications with its worldwide clientele. It has a dedicated circuit Wide Area Network (WAN) that is a frame relay, ISDN network and a Virtual Private Network (VPN) using TCP/IP. Communications equipment includes that from Cisco, as well as satellite communications for coordinating with remote project sites. Its Metro Area Network (MAN) combines wireless, infrared, RF, and satellite technologies. BVSG has 9,000 PCs, including 1,000 print and file servers. Five thousand of these are at corporate headquarters, the rest disbursed worldwide.

Culture

BVSG offices are in a suburban setting. Dress is business casual. Core hours are from 9:00 AM to 4:00 PM. A 40-hour workweek is standard. Overtime is rare, but is paid. Flextime, telecommuting, and part-time work are all options. Travel requirements vary, with most staff, including client services, traveling about five percent of the time and managers 20 percent.

Benefits include Preferred Provider (PPO) and Health Maintenance (HMO) options. The company pays for life insurance, business travel accident, and short-term disability. The company also contributes to a profit-sharing plan, in which contributions are used to purchase company stock and employees are fully vested after seven years. The company observes 8 1/2 holidays, including a floating holiday, and offers two weeks of vacation to start, increasing to four weeks after 14 years. There is a tuition reimbursement program; eligible employees receive a 100-percent tuition and books reimbursement for graduate courses. There has never been a layoff at BVSG.

Company-sponsored teams for softball, basketball, hockey, soccer, bowling, tennis, skeet shooting, and golf are available, as well as discounts on professional sports and performing arts events. Company-based teams participate in community activities for the United Way, Bloodmobile, Christmas in October, and other volunteer programs. Social activities include a winter holiday event and a summer picnic.

Candidates

Four hundred eighty of BVSG's staff is at corporate headquarters in Kansas City. Technical staff members have an average of six years of experience and a Bachelor's degree. Explains Vaughan, "We don't look for years of experience [in a critical skill] because it is changing so fast. We do look for functional experience, like workflow and document management, and domain experience in our target industries, including telecommunications, utilities, finance, and health care." Vaughn continues, "We look for utility players who can go into our specialized markets, like outsourcing, e-commerce, and telecommunications. We have 230 developers." Specific experience with client software, such as Oracle and PeopleSoft can be very helpful. Job titles follow the Mercer code standard: Programmer 1-3, Programmer Analyst, Business Analyst, and executive management. There are dual technical and management career paths.

BVSG does hire entry-level professionals. A four-year college degree is preferred, but a two-year technical degree is also accepted. Technical staff members are organized in a project matrix style. Teamwork, the ability to plan and organize, and collaboration skills are key traits.

The company hired 170 technical professionals in the last year, of which 50 to 60 were for entry-level positions. They expect to hire 230 in the next year. Entry-level candidates are found through local technical schools and universities. Experienced candidates are found through job fairs, online recruiting (monster.com), and employee referrals (there is a bonus). Turnover is 11 percent.

Recent Job Listings

Job Title	Education	Experience	Skills	Location
Software Analyst 5	BS+ CS	2–3 years	Oracle, SQL Server, ETT/ETL, OLAP, data mining	Overland Park, KS
Software Analyst 4	BS CS	3–5 years	EJB, J2EE, SCP, Web Logic, Oracle, iAS, Websphere, Documentum, Lotus Notes, Domino.doc	Overland Park, KS
Software Analyst 4	BS CS	3–5 years	Data warehousing, security, MS Project, Primavera3	Detroit, MI
Microcomputer Specialist 2	HS or equivalent, A+ certification	1–2 years	Novell 4.3, NT server, Maestro NFS	Raleigh, NC
Applications Support Specialist 3	HDA certification		PCs, laptops, MS Office, NT Workstation	Overland Park, KS

Contact

Web: www.bvsg.com
Email: vaughanpb@bvsg.com (Brad Vaughan, COO)
Email: nashdk@bvsg.com(David Nash, HR Recruiter)
Include "Source: Covin's Guide" on your resume and in your cover letter.

CANDLE Corporation

"The most important thing is not the languages someone knows, but his or her attitude."
　　　　　　　　　　　　　　　　　　　　　　　　– James Nguyen
　　　　　　　　　　　　　　　　　– Director of Research & Development

• Sun, HP, UNIX, AIX, NT, Linux •
• C++, Java, C, Visual Age, PHP, XML, JavaScript •
• Application management and e-Business software developer •
• Large shop •

Measuring performance. Clickstream analysis. Applying the robust tools and experience from large-scale legacy systems to the needs of high-performance networks. Candle cut its teeth on high-performance systems and is today one of the world's largest, private software vendors. Its flagship product, OMEGAMON®, is still one of the company's premier products, but is now one of nearly 200 system tools. It provides application tracing for performance monitoring for MVS, DB2, and IMS; DASD analysis; and it supports web analysis for CICS. It is this strength in systems software for high-end transaction processing on mainframes that has given Candle the experience to extend its performance monitoring skills to new areas in the Internet world.

ETEWatch™ provides segmentation of network response versus application response and client response time in a given web transaction. IntelliWatch provides a performance profile of system, mail, and database performance for Lotus Notes applications. eBA* ServiceMonitor™ measures Web page speed from the user's side and tracks a user's path through a Web site, helping companies identify bottlenecks in their processing, including the tracking of dynamic HTML pages, with a Java applet. eBusiness Assurance Network™ (eBAN) provides Web-based reporting of Web-response time data that has been loaded into a data warehouse, ready for OLAP-based analytical processing, to find navigation bottlenecks, reactions to specific pages, and load balancing requirements. CandleNet™ eBusiness Platform (eBP™), powered by Roma™ technology, uses XML and a common set of interfaces Candle developed to help disparate applications—legacy, custom, and third party—collaborate. Robust software built on 24 years of experience monitoring systems and applications, applied to e-business and the Internet world.

Surprise company social event: tour of MGM Studios.

Fast Facts	Revenues: $340.5M (2000)
	Employees: 1,757 (2000)
	Founded: 1976
	Software; applications management and e-Business integration
	Private
Awards	American Express: Supplier Excellence (2000)
	Network Computing: Flying Colors (1999)

Headquarters
IEC: Best of e-Commerce (1999)
PC Week: Enterprise Excellence (1998)
201 N. Douglas Street
El Segundo, CA 90245
(310) 535-3600
www.candle.com

Business

Candle's major divisions include administrative functions like Communications, Legal, Finance, Human Resources, and Sales, as well as its more technically-oriented divisions, Enterprise Business Group (EBG), Information Technology (IT), Research and Development, Business Integration and Solutions (BIS), and Consulting and Services. EBG focuses on helping companies accelerate their business-to-business (B2B) e-business with products like those in the CandleNet family, which provide user response performance monitoring.

Five hundred twenty-eight of the company's employees work at corporate headquarters. Aubrey Chernick, founder of Candle, is still its Chairman and Chief Executive Officer. Chernick revolutionized the business of selling in the computer industry by spending two years telemarketing the company's early products—the first time high-end mainframe software had been sold over the phone. Chernick developed OMEGA-MON, diagnostic software for mainframes, to help customers better understand and manage their systems. All the company's suite of tools are designed to help customers integrate, manage, and monitor the performance and effectiveness of their systems from the customer's perspective at the Web, on the desktop, and in legacy systems. As Chernick explains, "The enemy in e-business is the second hand on a clock."

Technology

Candle's technical environment includes mid-range Sun, HP, and IBM hardware with operating systems from UNIX to AIX. They have approximately 2,000 PCs, mostly running NT, with a few on Linux. Development languages include C++, Java, C, Visual Basic, Microsoft C++, and IBM's Visual Age. For Web development, Java Script, Personal Home Page (PHP), HTML, and XML are common. On the infrastructure side, the technical staff uses COBOL and PeopleSoft for applications development and Web servers Netscape and IBM's Websphere. The company uses its own tools for network analysis, such as J-Builder, a development tool, and Purify for profiling code for C++. Third party tools include Sun's Java Test and a tool from Parasoft. The communications environment includes Cisco routers, electronic switches, gateways, and firewall.

There are two kinds of projects on the product development team: long-term, 12-month projects for a major product release, and short-term, 3-month projects for quarterly version releases. A short-term project might include a team of three or four people who develop a prototype and release it to selected customers for feedback before release to the general public. Long-term projects typically involve ten to twenty people and adhere to a more structured methodology from feasibility study through product launch and follow-up.

Development of the Advanced File Transfer Network Facility is an example of a short-term project. This is a B2B feature that allows customers to transfer files, transforming the data from one format to another. Security features might be added, like reconstructing files if a connection is broken, for files that would be sent over an MQ series network.

A long-term project is represented by the company's recent CandleNet BP product release. This product is a tool that lets applications like PeopleSoft on one machine and a custom application on another platform collaborate through XML. Standard software connectors are available for the market-leading Enterprise Resource Planning (ERP) applications like SAP. Says Nguyen, "This tool allows companies to integrate applications in weeks instead of years because the standardized interfaces are already in place."

Culture

Everyone at Candle, including the owner, works at workstations with 64-inch high panels. Managers have 10-foot square cubicles, with a table; everyone else has 8-foot square spaces. Electrical connections are designed into side panels, so staff members may face their desks and ergonomically-designed chairs in any direction

Dress is business casual; jeans are ok, but are seen more often on Fridays. Official hours are 37 1/2 hours. Technical professionals typically work around 50 hours a week, with flextime. Travel requirements range between five and ten percent. Telecommuting extends to employees working from home in Florida, Utah, New Hampshire, Maine, and Ireland. Turnover is typical of the high-tech marketplace at 24 percent.

Benefits include both HMO and point-of-service medical plans. Says Terri Shomohara, Senior Director of Compensation and Benefits, "We have very competitive benefits. The company pays for an HMO for its employees and their families." This company-paid benefit extends to dental, accidental death, and life insurance, and most of the cost of a vision plan. There are 12 holidays and 10 sick days. Vacations start at three weeks, and go to four weeks after six years. Employees may sell back vacation days, but must take at least five days a year. Supplemental benefits include a dependent care information resource, an employee assistance program, tuition reimbursement, and domestic partner benefits. The company contributes to a 401(k) plan and a profit-sharing program. There is a fitness center at corporate headquarters, a cafeteria on-site, and some concierge services, like dry cleaning pickup. There have been layoffs, generally when offices were consolidated, or the company re-oriented its business. Severance packages are based on years of service, and include COBRA extended medical benefits and outplacement services.

There is free coffee, tea, chocolate, and filtered water. Bagels and fruit are available for free every Thursday. Social activities include ski trips, ball games, whale watching, summer picnics, a Halloween party with costume contest for employees' children, and a formal winter holiday dinner.

Candidates

Candle has about 400 technical professionals, including 250 in its facilities in El Segundo and Agoura Hills, California. Additional sites include several other laboratories in California, and sites in Minnesota; White Plains, New York; and England. Most developers have a Bachelor's degree and an average of eight to twelve years of experience. Nguyen looks for "the ability to learn something new—capability, not just what someone knows already." Effective communications are critical, as is the ability to work well on a team. Says Nguyen, "I have somewhat of an accent, so if people are patient enough to try to understand me, I know they will work well with others." Says Steve Orzeck,

Director of Recruitment, "Of course our developers and infrastructure staff are technical, but even our sales and marketing people are highly technical."

New candidates are found through online recruiting (50 percent; monster.com, hotjobs.com, dice.com), employee referrals (30 percent), personal networking (10 percent), advertisements (5 percent), and employment agencies (5 percent). Last year Candle hired more than 300 technical professionals worldwide, including entry-level positions.

There is a dual technical/management career path. Job titles include Associate Software Developer, Software Developer, Senior Software Developer/Manager, Advisory Developer/Senior Manager, Consulting Software Developer/Director, Senior Director, Assistant Vice President, and Vice President.

Recent Job Listings

Job Title	Education	Experience	Skills	Group	Location
No technical positions currently posted. Sample jobs from earlier listings are shown below.					
Bus. Architect	BS technical, MBA preferred	10 years	Thin-client, EIS, Data Warehousing	Consulting & Svcs.	McLean, VA
Instrumentation Consultant	BS technical or equivalent	3-10 years	DHTML, Java, Citrix, Cognos, SAS	Consulting & Svcs.	White Plains, NY
Product Mgr.	BA/BS	3-5 years	e-finance, Java, EDI, XML, Vitria, STC, Neon, WebMethods	eBusiness Applications	El Segundo, CA
Soft. Developer			Level 2 support, NT, UNIX	Enterprise Computing Group	Portland, ME
Sr. Programmer Analyst	BA/BS MIS, CS, Business	2 years	PeopleSoft Financials, SQL, Oracle, DB2, UNIX	Information Technology	El Segundo, CA

Contact

Web: www.candle.com
Fax: (310) 727-7050 Attn: Recruitment Dept.
Include "Source: Covin's Guide" on your resume and in your cover letter.

EARTHLINK, Inc.

"Our data center is backed up by a huge generator, in case of a brown-out. The system goes straight to the UPS while the generator starts up automatically. It could give power to 25 city blocks. We also have enough diesel fuel to run 3 days straight."

– Paul Schnee
– Senior Technical Recruiter

- **• Sun SPARCs, Solaris, UNIX •**
- **• C++, Visual Basic, Oracle, Vantive •**
- **• Internet Service Provider • Large shop •**

Set up your Internet connection in ten minutes. Not 80 hours, as Sky Dayton did when he first signed up for Internet access. Owner of a coffeehouse, Dayton envisioned the Internet as a worldwide, virtual, real-time coffeehouse. But, not if it was too hard to get in/on. Dayton started EarthLink as the answer to consumers, not geeks, who wanted to surf. Now there are real surfboards at EarthLink's former Pasadena, California headquarters. Similar frustrations prompted Charles Brewer to start MindSpring in Atlanta the same year Dayton started EarthLink. Technical support 24 hours a day, with a live representative. Easy installation and user interface. The merger of former competitors and equals was initiated in 1999 and completed in February, 2000.

A set monthly fee. No longer than five minute's wait for a live person to answer the phone to help walk customers through any problems. The separate companies earned awards for growth and leadership in the ISP industry. EarthLink's initiation of a flat monthly fee for Internet access forced all other ISPs to adopt the new pricing scheme. The combined companies now have more than 4.8 million customers. Shy of America Online's 32 million, but competing on round-the-clock customer service and ease of installation and use. Now, it is Digital Subscriber Lines (DSL), broadband and high-speed access, that is forcing others to keep up.

Surprise company event: paint ball wars.

Fast Facts	Revenues: $986.6M (2000)
	Employees: 7,377 (2000)
	Founded: 1994
	Internet Service Provider (ISP)
	Public: ELNK (Nasdaq)
Awards	Interactive Week: The Internet 500 (2000)
	CNet: Editor's Choice (2001)
	Mobile Computing: First Class (2001)
	PC World: Best ISP (2000)
	Fortune: e-50 Internet Index (1999)
Headquarters	1375 Peachtree Street, 7 North
	Atlanta, GA 30309
	(404) 815-0770
	www.earthlink.net

Business

Two companies with the same vision, started on opposite ends of the country, merged as equals. The combined company kept the name and stock ticker symbol from Earth-Link, the headquarters and core values and beliefs from MindSpring. These core values and beliefs include respect for the individual, integrity, keeping commitments, competition brings out the best in people, frugality, best efforts even when that leads to mistakes, clarity in communication, friendly and fair dealings, a sense of urgency, and work should be fun.

Both companies initially targeted consumers looking for a user-friendly interface and round-the-clock customer support. EarthLink now also offers a shopping mall, and a combination of email, personal web page, personalized start page and chat capabilities. The company has recently initiated services for small businesses looking for web hosting.

Aggressively targeting competitors' subscribers, EarthLink highlights the advantages they offer. Their "Get out of AOL free" campaign and eBay auction targeted users who were unhappy with interruptions in service and long wait times for technical support. With the recent "Opt-Out of AOL" program, a donation in the new user's name to the Electronic Privacy Information Center underscores EarthLink's policy to keep member information private, rather than selling it to advertisers, as some competitors do.

Partnerships have long marked EarthLink's expansion. Its alliance with Sprint, a part owner in EarthLink, gives Sprint subscribers additional discounts and immediately added Sprint's 130,000 Internet customers to EarthLink's customer base.

Technology

A client-server environment based on Sun SPARCs, running on Solaris and UNIX, with HPs, DEC Alphas, and Compaq servers, and Dell clients, makes up the hardware suite for EarthLink, with 2,600 PCs as workstations and servers in Pasadena and Sacramento. Development is in C++ and C under NT, along with Visual Basic, SQL, and Oracle. Application software includes Vantive's call center software. The communications environment includes Cisco routers, Lucent telephony, OC48 and OC12 connections, and T1 and T3 lines.

Senior technical positions are found in the System Software Department for Pasadena and Atlanta, in the Product Management Department/Portal Group, the Information Technology and Engineering group, and the Broadband group. There are also support positions in EarthLink's other major offices, including Dallas, Harrisburg, Phoenix, San Jose, and Seattle, and call center positions, which require an understanding of PCs and the Internet. EarthLink's Research and Development group is testing wireless technologies.

Culture

EarthLink's office buildings house a secure Network Operations Center, which, as Schnee describes it, "looks like the control room of a starship." Ergonomics have been incorporated at the call centers, with 17 to 19-inch monitors, ergonomic keyboard and mouse, anti-glare screens, keyboard drawer, and telephone headsets.

The company pays for medical coverage for employees who select an HMO plan, and partial coverage for the several other medical insurance options available, including alternative medical benefits coverage, such as for acupuncture, as well as disability, dental, vision, and life insurance programs. They offer tuition reimbursement for job-related courses. The company observes seven holidays, with an additional three floating holidays. They offer two weeks of vacation and two weeks of sick leave. Stock options are available for most employees. There is an annual bonus plan for all employees, tied to the company's performance. And there is a 401(k) plan.

The company pays, on a sliding scale, expenses for van pooling. One-third of its Pasadena employees van pool. For five people in a pool, gas and upkeep are company-paid. For six people, the van is free. For more than 6 people in a van, the company pays $25 to $50 a month to each person in the pool.

EarthLink has a number of social events, including a year-end dinner. Discounted tickets are available for baseball and hockey games. Other company-sponsored events have included deep-sea fishing and ballroom dancing. They have never had a layoff, but expect that there may be some overlapping functions and adjustments in the recent merger.

Dress is very casual; jean, shorts and t-shirts are fine. As their web site says, "However you dress is your dress code." Official hours for the company are 9:00 AM to 6:00 PM. Call center operations cover a 24/7/365 schedule, with three shifts. When there is a queue, employees are authorized to work paid overtime, in order to keep the wait time down to the company's three-to-five minute goal. IT staff typically work 50 hours a week or more, with negotiated compensatory time and occasional spot bonuses. Travel is extensive for a portion of each department as new call centers are opened, with incentives for staff to relocate to the new center.

EarthLink's growth offers its technical professionals substantial opportunities for career advancement. Their ability to attract top technical talent, such as some of the Internet co-founders and one of the world's top network security people, combined with their active internal training program, provide an atmosphere for technical growth.

Candidates

Seventy percent of EarthLink's staff members are customer service personnel in the call centers. Most entry-level technical positions are in the call center. Approximately 15 percent of the staff account for more senior technical positions, such as LAN/WAN Engineers, Systems Analysts, Software Developers, and HTML Programmers. Says Schnee, "The people we target for entry-level positions are the technical power users. Geeks that go home and tear a machine apart to put in a CD-ROM and more memory and reformat the hard drive." EarthLink is proactive in hiring professionals with disabilities and has armed itself with adaptive technologies, such as screen readers for the blind.

Candidates are found through a variety of recruiting methods. These include company-hosted job fairs (EarthLink Mania), third-party job fairs, online recruiting (LA Times web site), cold calls based on online searches with spiders to locate candidates working at competitors, employment agencies, college recruiting, and networking through technical and educational boards. In 1999, EarthLink hired 2,020 employees; 80 percent of these were for entry-level positions. Top schools for recruiting include Pepperdine, USC/Malibu, UCLA, Pasadena City, and ITT Technical. Turnover in senior technical positions is 12 percent. For call center positions, turnover is 35 percent, half the industry average.

Recent Job Listings

Job Title	Education	Experience	Skills	Location
Sr. Network Access Engineering Designer	BS Engineering	5+ years	PPPOE, PPPOA, l2, TP Tunneling, DSL, Redback, Unisphere, Larscom	Atlanta, GA
Research Engineer		10–12 years	XML, WAP, cryptography, UNIX/NT kernel, finance, economics, law	Atlanta, GA
Sr. Data Acquisition Developer	BA/BS CS	2–4 years	Informatica, ETL Crystal, Business Objects	Pasadena, CA
Information Systems Analyst	BA/BS CS	1–2 years	Oracle PL/SQL, ETL, Crystal Reports	Pasadena, CA
Sr. Applications Analyst	BA/BS CS, IT, IS	4–5 years	SQR, PL/SQL, HR, Payroll, Financial systems	Pasadena, CA
Sr. Product Manager, Portal Products	BA/BS Engineering, Business, MBA preferred	5–7 years	Regional cable or broadband providers experience	Pasadena, CA
Java Developer	BS CS	1+ years	Java, Corba, XML, Perl, C, C++	Harrisburg, PA

Contact

Web: www.earthlink.net/about/jobs
Email: jobs@earthlink.net
         itcareer@earthlink.net
Include "Source: Covin's Guide" on your resume and in your cover letter.

INTERWOVEN, Inc.

"We provide the soft assembly line for web site production."

– Jack Jia
– Vice President, Engineering

- • **Sun Solaris, UNIX, Windows NT** •
- • **C++, Java, JavaScript, XML, DHTML, Perl** •
- • **Software developer** • **Large shop** •

Web to the max. Interwoven creates the content management system companies need to coordinate and collaborate in developing content for their web initiatives. Their client list reads like the Fortune 100: American Airlines, General Electric, Proctor & Gamble, BellSouth, and Xerox. Throw in a few more high tech companies like Cisco, Novell, Tivoli, Ask Jeeves, and Monster.com, mix with some name-brand companies on the web, like Martha Stewart Living, Nickelodeon, and Red Herring, and you see where the techies go to get their web tools.

To create products used by companies with the largest B2B and B2C web sites in the world, you need to find supurb employees. You have to find a lot of them to fuel an exploding company's growth (IPO in October, 1999; 2-for-1 stock split in July, 2000; all employees have stock options). Interwoven has an aggressive recruiting program. For several months in 2000, they threw in a free 3-year license to the BMW Z3 of choice for every engineer hired.

The company's I-Fit program includes an on-staff personal fitness trainer, himself a world-class triathlete. The company's Gift of Time program includes dry cleaning, concierge services, and on-site massages. Its Stop and Smell the Roses program includes white-water rafting trips. The company's culture of open communications includes an all hands meeting with the CEO every Friday. Their technical environment touches every kind of software development, from web-centric technologies such as Java, XML, and DHTML, to traditional client-server architecture and object-oriented design, to the die-hard operating system kernel work. It's the techies' idea of paradise—developing a foundation system that powers the web, and time to enjoy it.

Surprise benefit: after two years of service—free house cleaning.

Fast Facts	Revenues: $132.1M (2000)
	Employees: 888 (2000)
	Founded: 1995
	Software developer; web content management tools
	Public: IWOV (Nasdaq)
Awards	Upside: E-Biz 150 (2000)
	Open System Advisors: CrossRoads A-List (1999, 2000)
	Red Herring: Top 100 (1999)
	Upside: Hot 100 (1999)

Headquarters   1195 W. Fremont Ave.
                      Sunnyvale, CA 94087-3825
                      (408) 774-2000
                      www.interwoven.com

Business

Says Giga Information Group, "Interwoven leads the pack in content management." Interwoven has created a suite of tools specifically designed for managing data content on an enterprise's web site, content which may be drawn from disparate platforms, in varied formats. Jack Jia, Vice President of Engineering, summarizes the product's functionality," We provide a production environment where a lot of people can work together on a common body of web content. Hundreds to thousands of people working together on thousands to millions of files, application code, and databases can work collaboratively to produce new versions of a web site quickly."

The company's flagship product, TeamSite, is designed to track versions and manage all web content. It allows both technical and non-technical contributors to help build and contribute content to a web site. Key to this product are ease-of-use, scalability and an open systems architecture. Says Jia, "This is about scaling an operation from one person creating a web site to many people collaborating. Companies can use any of their own content creation tools since [Interwoven's products] work with all of them, whether they are from Microsoft, IBM, or Netscape." Interwoven licenses the software and provides training and consulting services.

Interwoven differentiates itself from its competitors, companies like Vignette, by being the only company to focus exclusively on content management software. As a result, Interwoven is free to partner with a number of companies that complement its software. Asera, for example, provides software to help companies manage marketing, selling, and product support across distribution channels. Earthweb is an online marketplace for technical products and services. GlobalSight, Idiom, eTranslate, LUZ, SDL, and Uniscape provide globalization and localization services that complement TeamSite's latest release, which supports multi-byte characters, facilitating web site translations into French, German, and Japanese. 2Roam is a wireless web Application Service Provider (ASP) that will help Interwoven's customers move selected pieces of their web site onto wireless web devices.

Technology

Development is on Sun Solaris, Windows NT and 2000, HP/UX, Linux, and variants of UNIX. Software is written in C++, Java, XML, DHTML, Perl, JavaScript, C and some Assembly language. The company's main product, TeamSite, works with all the major database management systems, including Oracle, Sybase, and Informix. It also works with major e-commerce applications software, including ATG's Dynamo, Broadvision, Microsoft's Commerce Server, IBM's WebSphere, and BEA Systems' Weblogic.

A typical project would be the development of a new version of TeamSite, such as the recent release of Version 4.5, which introduced Java and XML-based templating to simplify data entry. Projects generally range from 3 months to 9 months.

When asked what new technology the company was investigating, Jia responded,

"We are creating leading edge technologies to solve content management challenges in B2B, B2C, and wireless markets."

Culture

Interwoven's main office is in the mild climate of Silicon Valley, in a suburban campus office building, in a serene setting surrounded by trees, complemented by a fountain with patio tables and chairs. Staff members work in a combination of cubicles and offices.

The company provides major medical, dental, and vision insurance, along with life, accidental death, and short and long-term disability insurance. It also offers a 401(k) plan, a stock purchase plan, incentive bonuses, and generous stock options. Further benefits include a "Stop and Smell the Roses" program that organizes a monthly activity for employees. "One afternoon," says Gary Wimp, Vice President of Human Resources, "a bus showed up and took everyone to the circus." Other activities have included a family barbecue on the patio and the afternoon off for all employees to play baseball.

Business dress is very casual; jeans and shorts are ok. Hours are flexible. Travel is limited. Interwoven has offices in Chicago, Austin, Atlanta, and metropolitan Washington, D.C. There has never been a layoff. The Engineering team had zero percent turnover in the past year.

Interwoven's culture can best be summarized by statements from CEO Martin Brauns, who said to new employees at their full-day orientation, "I promise to keep, teach, and uphold the essential Interwoven values. These include open, honest, straight-forward communication, respect for colleagues, a laser focus on results, and a commitment to making our customers wildly happy."

Candidates

Interwoven's 90 engineers and 30 technical support professionals are rapidly being supplemented by hiring that has more than doubled the company's staff every year. Interwoven expects to double again in 2001. Almost 50 percent of Interwoven's candidates come from employee referrals. Another 20 percent come from employment agencies. The balance come from online and other sources.

The career path for engineers starts at Member of Technical Staff (MTS), then Staff Engineer, Principal Engineer, Director of Engineering, Vice President, and Senior Vice President. In addition, the consulting and training divisions have paths for technical consultants, technical account managers, and sales engineers. Current engineers on staff have, on average, a Masters degree in CS or EE and five to eight years of experience.

Jia looks for "two very simple things—smart people and nice people." On the technical side, candidates should know more than one system if they are working on integration. If they are working on the client or server side, they "need to know how to build a scalable server or sexy user interface." Jia seeks out candidates who learn quickly and have excellent analytical and trouble-shooting skills. Further, "[being] team-oriented, flexible, and focused are very important personality traits."

Interwoven does hire entry-level professionals. Wimp says that in a typical interview, a problem will be presented "to assess problem-solving skills and how to navigate through unknowns."

Recent Job Listings

Job Title	Education	Experience	Skills	Location
Staff Engineer		5+ years	Java, C, C++, XML, HTTP, TCP/IP, J2EE, Servlet, JSP	Sunnyvale, CA
Member of Technical Staff	BS EE, CS, MS preferred	5 years	C, C++, Perl, Gmake, gdb, Visual Studio, AIX	Sunnyvale, CA
Sustaining Engineer	BS CS	2 years	Perl, XML, COM, Java, C++	Austin, TX
Sr. QA Engineer	MS CS	2–4 years	XML, HTML, Perl, C++, CGI, Java servlets, white box testing	Sunnyvale, CA; San Francisco, CA; Austin, TX
Devnet Developer	BS CS, EE	4+ years	Perl, CGI, DHTML, JavaScript, Apache, IIS, AGT, ColdFusion, Broadvision, Verity	Sunnyvale, CA

Contact

Email: hr@interwoven.com
or
Email: Jobs@interwoven.com
Include "Source: Covin's Guide" on your resume and in your cover letter.

KELLY SERVICES, Inc.

"Kelly Services offers dynamic opportunities for IT professionals at the corporate level and also for contract employees who are ready to join a team that applies leading-edge information technology solutions to the benefit of our customers worldwide."

– Tommi White,
– Executive Vice President, Chief Administration and Technology Officer

"We offer not only outstanding IT opportunities, but they are with some of the best companies in the world. We get to place people in just about every hardware and software environment there is."

– Mike Shebak
– Vice President, Kelly IT Resources (KITR)

- **Sun servers, Dell clients (Kelly)** •
- **Uniface, Oracle (Kelly)** •
- **Temporary staffing** • **Large shop** •

Try before you buy. Try the job. Try the person. Kelly invented the modern temporary staffing business. Kelly started in 1946 as a business with an inventory of business equipment—calculators and typewriters, and the staff to use them. Kelly first brought customers' work to its own offices. Then, customers started asking for the people and equipment to come to them. Finally, customers asked for just the people, and the temporary staffing business was born.

Today, the four billion dollar firm is a global staffing services provider, with more than 2,200 company owned and operated offices in 26 countries. It has expanded its services far beyond its initial offering of clerical duties to include legal, accounting, light industrial, marketing, and information technology services. This has led to technical challenges. Providing just-in-time service to global companies and ensuring consistency of reporting required an integrated technical environment, just as Y2K was heating up. Kelly realigned their business processes on a global scale, inventoried and fixed application software, and introduced a risk assessment strategy and risk abatement approach that is now used on all projects.

Surprise benefit: IT employees can buy extra training with overtime hours.

Fast Facts	Revenues: $4.27B (1999)
	Employees: 6,500 Full-Time
	750,000 Temporary(1999)
	Founded: 1946
	Temporary Staffing
	Public: KELA (Nasdaq)
Awards	Fortune 500 (#374) 1999
	Information Week: 500 Most Innovative IT Providers (2000)
	Fortune: Most Admired Companies (1999)
	Web Awards: Outstanding Website (1999)

Headquarters   999 W. Big Beaver Rd.
                     Troy, MI 48084
                     (248) 362-4444
                     www.kellyservices.com

Business

Kelly provides temporary staffing for accounting, call centers, teaching, engineering, health care, information technology, legal, manufacturing, marketing, office, and scientific services. Its professionals include accountants, auditors, nurses, programmers, database administrators, lawyers, biologists, chemists, and physicists. On an annual basis, it employs more than 770,000 temporary staff. On an average day, 150,000 staff members are deployed, including 3,500 IT professionals.

Kelly's services include on-site management of vendors, a "super-contractor" or master vendor role, as well as managing departments such as payroll, accounts payable, and shipping. Kelly's temporary-to-full-time option, sometimes called temp-to-hire, with no fee or penalty, gives customers and staff members a reciprocal opportunity to evaluate the skills and fit between employee and job.

Kelly IT Resources (KITR) is the division responsible for temporary information technology assignments. Initially a response to customers' requests for PC technicians in the 1980s, the services requested expanded into database administration, call center and help desk outsourcing, and e-commerce initiatives. KITR was established as a separate division in 1999.

Kelly is the second largest staffing company in the United States, after Manpower, and the third largest in the world, after Adecco. It differentiates itself from its competitors with its ability to standardize reporting and processes across all offices, internationally, and thirty years of experience managing other vendor relationships for its customers.

Technology

There are two technical environments at Kelly, the internal, corporate environment, and the environment of the customers served by KITR.

Kelly's internal environment is run on Sun Solaris and UNIX Enterprise 4000, 5000, and 6000 servers, along with NT-based Dell desktops and laptops. Kelly has 6,000 PCs, including 1,000 at corporate headquarters. The development language used at Kelly is Uniface, Compuware's Enterprise Resource Planning (ERP) package. Oracle components used include Database Server, Financials, Human Resources, and Applications Implementation Methodology. One of Kelly's sample projects, StaffNet, keeps track of which people are available to be assigned to a given customer, and when they are coming off a project. The company's new online ordering service allows customers to order temporary help over the web. A third sample project was development of the Web-based resume database and search engine, the Kelly Career Network. These systems were developed using Oracle as the database and Uniface as the development tool. Kelly was one of the first users of the Web for job posting and recruiting.

KITR's environment spans that of its Fortune 500 and global client base, including a wide range of hardware and software platforms. One sample project includes providing network administration for Daimler Chrysler. KITR places people in all the large automotive companies, understandable given its roots in Detroit, but also has placed a number of people with Internet companies in Silicon Valley, in response to the need for quick ramp-ups. Job assignments range from network administration to web development, applications programming, and research.

Culture

Kelly corporate offices are in a suburban campus setting. Dress is casual at Kelly. Hours at Kelly are 8:00 AM to 5:00 PM. A 45-to-50 hour week is average. Hours over 50 a week are compensated with compensatory time, which may be cashed in or redeemed for additional training hours. Extra vacation hours, except for two weeks a year, may also be cashed in. Benefits include medical and dental coverage and a 401(k) plan.

Benefits are similar for KITR while on assignment, but overtime is paid. Salary and benefits do not continue between projects at KITR. Dress is business formal at KITR.

Candidates

Kelly has 250 technical staff members. The level of experience of current staff members ranges from zero to thirty years and averages five to seven years. Education levels range from an Associate's degree to Master's degree, with a Bachelor's degree the average.

Kelly expects to hire between 50 and 60 technical professionals in the next year. Turnover is less than 10 percent. White looks for candidates with relevant technical skills, but also for retail, services, or transaction processing business experience. Says White, "We are not writing systems for stamping out #2 pencils, and our products do not have bar codes on them. You have to be flexible because the service we provide is highly variable. It is like providing an electronic catalog that is unique for each customer. The skills are unique; the rates are unique; the way we get paid is different. We don't ship a bill of lading. We only get paid when the time card shows up at payroll. Candidates with credit card processing experience, for instance, will understand the high-volume transaction environment."

Candidates for Kelly are found through employee referrals, advertising, online recruiting, and employment agencies. Top colleges for recruiting include Oakland University, the University of Michigan, Michigan State University, and the University of Detroit. Kelly's career web site, under Full-Time Employee, includes IT positions both for its own, headquarters jobs, and for full-time positions it is filling as a recruiter for its customers. Kelly jobs are located in Troy, Michigan.

KITR has 2,500 technical staff members. KITR rarely hires entry-level professionals. The company has an extensive online training catalogue for staff members to upgrade their skills with new technologies. The largest number of jobs filled in KITR are for Help Desk Support, PC Technician, Programmer, Systems Analyst, System Engineer, System Administrator, Software Tester, Quality Analyst, Database Analyst, and Database Administrator. Mike Shebak, Vice President, KITR, says that while some customers are looking for someone who has done what they need in the last few years, others train temporary staff along with their own staff when they roll out a new technology. "It is important that candidates be able to move easily from one technology to another." Since staff members work at a customer's site, continues Shebak, "communication skills and enthusiasm are critical." Shebak looks for self-starters with a history of growing their skills consistently.

John Healy, National Business Development Manager with KITR, looks for opportunities for staffers to grow their skills throughout their career at KITR, "We had one client migrating from Macs to PCs. We provided all their desktop support technicians and network administrators. They took their staff and our staff through training."

Candidates for KITR are found through employee referrals, advertising, online recruiting, and employment agencies. KITR has more than one million resumes of technical staff members and these employees may also be offered or apply for positions within Kelly corporate IT. KITR links to Kelly's career web site. Positions are identified as Contract.

Recent Job Listings

Job Title	Education	Experience	Skills	Location
Sr. Middleware Engineer	BS CS, Industrial Engineering	2-4 years	Uniface, MyEureka, SQR, CC:Harvest, Endeavor	Troy, MI (employee)
CIO/CTO		10–15 years	$100M facility, mobile computing	Melville, NY (employee)
Software Engineer— Cartography	BA/BS	5 years	ESRI Arc/Info, ERDAS	Akron, OH (employee)
Sr. Design Engineer	BS CS	5–8 years	Ada, Rational Apex, Yourdon	Rochester, NY (employee)
e-Commerce Project Analyst	BA/BS preferred	10 years	Java, JavaScript, Vignette, JSP, DB2 Utilities	Warren, MI (contract)
Java, J2EE, JSP Developer		5+ years	JSO, EJB, XML, Oracle	New York, NY (contract)
Software Test Engineer			C++, WinRunner Test Direcctor	Carlsbad, CA (contract)
SQLServer DBA			Sybase, ASP, VB, perl	Reston, VA (contract)

Contact

Web: www.kellyservices.com (Kelly)
        www.kellyit.com (KITR)
Email: taffing@kellyservices.com (Kelly)
Fax: 1-800-522-9819 (Kelly)
Include "Covin's Guide" on your resume and cover letter.

NATIONAL SEMICONDUCTOR, Inc.

"I love to work here...it is great to be part of Silicon Valley."

– Ulrich Seif
– Vice President, Chief Information Officer

• IBM 9672, IBM AIXs, Dell servers •
• COBOL, CA-IDMS, Visual Basic, Silver Stream, SAP •
• Semiconductor manufacturer • Large shop •

Connecting digital to an analog world. Scanner-on-a-chip. DVD-on-a-chip. Information Appliance system-on-a-chip. One of the first companies to enter the market of mass-producing integrated circuits (ICs), National's products may be found in cellular phones, DVD players, laser printers, and fax modems. Its newest focus is on Internet Appliances, where it can leverage its expertise in integrating digital and analog data acquisition and conversion techniques for devices such as the WebPAD, a touch-screen portable Web access device, and America Online's new set-top box for Internet access through a television set.

National Semiconductor was launched in 1959 to manufacture transistors, largely for the military. Founded at the beginning of the industry that has transformed the U.S. economy, mass production of ICs, National soon became one of the largest companies in the semiconductor industry. Says Seif, "All the semiconductor companies are called 'Fair children.'" Fairchild Semiconductor's Robert Noyce and Jack Kilby, later founders of Intel, invented the integrated circuit, spawning the semiconductor industry.

National focuses on three major markets, home, wireless, and enterprise electronics. Its latest product is the Geode, its system-on-a-chip for Internet Appliances. The Geode provides streaming video, DVD playback, and video-on-demand. Says Seif, "We focus on the analog marketplace and interfaces between digital and analog. All the real world interfaces are analog. When you listen to music, an analog microphone captures the sound before it is converted into a digital signal. A digital tv has more analog parts than an analog tv."

Surprise benefit: onsite dental services.

Fast Facts	Revenues: $2.113B (2001)
	Employees: 10,300 (2001)
	Founded: 1959
	Manufacturer; semiconductors
	Public: NSM (NYSE)
Awards	Computerworld: Premier 100 IT Leaders (2000)
	Information Week: Top 500 Most Innovative (2000)
	CIO: WebBusiness 50/50 (1999)
	Network World: NW 200 (1998)
	PC Magazine: 100 Most Influential (1998)

Headquarters   2900 Semiconductor Drive
Santa Clara, CA 95052-8090
(408) 721-5000
www.national.com

Business

In 1959, eight engineers left Sperry Rand Corporation to found National Semiconductor in Danford, Connecticut. The company's first products were diffused silicon transistors. By 1962, their integrated circuits were being used in space vehicles, including the Mariner 10 Venus probe. In 1968, corporate headquarters was moved to Silicon Valley. Its chips found their way into fuel injection systems, seat belt locking devices, and anti-skid controls. Industry firsts included the first 16-bit single-card microprocessor, the first semiconductor absolute pressure transducer, the first single-chip 16-bit micro-processor, and the first single-chip data acquisition system. The industry's first one-volt analog integrated circuit and the first radio-frequency remote control circuit followed these.

In the 1980s, National introduced the first speech synthesizer and launched the fastest VLSI graphics engine in the industry. Its microprocessor was integrated into laser printers, and the company became the largest supplier of Ethernet controller chips. By the 1990s, its coding/decoding (codec) device was being used on approximately 200 million telephones and it partnered with Energizer Power Systems to develop "smart" batteries for notebook computers and cordless power tools. In 1999, National introduced the first high performance color scanner on a chip. National competes on the depth of its intellectual property portfolio and experience in designing custom and mass-market devices. Competitors include Texas Instruments, STMicroelectronics, Analog Devices, Linear Technology, and Maxim.

Technology

National has a dual technology environment. The Information Services (IS) division manages the company's internal infrastructure. The Engineering division creates its products. Hardware used in IS includes an IBM 9672, tens of IBM AIX systems and clusters of model 20 and 40 Dell servers. Application development on legacy systems is in COBOL and CA-ADSO. In the client server environment, development is in Visual Basic, with web enabling under SilverStream. Additional software used includes SAP, ISS (from Portal), and Ariba for purchasing goods used indirectly in the manufacturing process, such as office supplies. In addition, the company uses i2 for planning, and Workstream, a manufacturing execution system (MES), for tracking the movement of goods on the shop floor. The company also uses speech synthesis, like Lotus Notes' text-to-voice software, to read an employee's emails to them over the phone.

There are 7,400 PCs in the company, including 2,000 at corporate headquarters. Communication hardware comes from Bay Networks, Nortel, Nextlink, and Cirent. The company also supports Palm Pilots and laptops. As Seif says, "We are in Silicon Valley. Everyone who walks in comes in with a new gadget."

The recent implementation of Ariba is a representative project for IS. Twelve to fifteen staff members mapped business needs with the system's capabilities, using a structured design approach over a ten-week period. New technologies being investigated include wireless connectivity, combining voice and data networks, and design collaboration. Says Seif, "We want our customers' engineers to be able to use National's intellectual property to put a new product together, design it on a chip, and then we will manufacture it on their behalf."

Culture

Two thousand of the company's employees work at corporate headquarters. National has manufacturing sites in Maine and Texas, and in Scotland, Singapore, and Malaysia. There are technical professionals supporting each of these sites. Headquarters is located in a 10-building campus. All technical staff members in IS, including the CIO, work in private cubicles. Official hours are from 8:00 AM to 5:00 PM. Technical staff members work an average of forty to fifty hours a week, depending on the stage of a project. Travel requirements are dependent on the unit being supported. Those working on international projects may travel extensively. The company helps organize alternate commuting options. Dress ranges from business casual to very casual.

National pays the majority of costs for medical, dental, and vision insurance, and offers a range of HMO and point-of-service plans. The company pays for life insurance for employees and business travel accident insurance. Supplemental life insurance and long- and short-term disability insurance are available. National observes 11 holidays a year. Employees earn three weeks of vacation to start, increasing to four weeks after ten years. Employees get their birthday off. Coffee is free. The company contributes to employees' 401(k) plans and to a profit-sharing program when it meets performance goals. Employees may purchase stock at a 15 percent discount. The company organizes volunteer opportunities and matches employee contributions to schools, as well as offering cash contributions to organizations where employees volunteer their time. The company offers cash awards to employees who earn patents. They offer 100 percent tuition reimbursement and a scholarship program for employees' children. There is a company credit union and discounts on tickets to local amusement parks, such as Disneyland. The company offers employees onsite services that include dental appointments, car wash and oil changes, and laundry and dry cleaning pick-up and delivery.

There is an on-site gym, with personal fitness trainers available for a small fee, as well as exercise classes and on-site massages. The company park has soccer and baseball fields, volleyball and basketball courts, a picnic area, jogging trail, fountains, a lake, and an amphitheater. Social activities include an annual summer picnic (Dana Carvey was a featured entertainer at the Year 2000 picnic) and a winter holiday dinner. Company-sponsored sports teams include golf, softball, bowling, skiing, running, tennis, and white water rafting. The semiconductor business is a cyclical industry and National has had layoffs. They offer affected employees a severance package based on length of service with the company and provide outplacement services.

Candidates

IS has 397 technical professionals company-wide, including 225 at corporate headquarters. Current employees, on average, have a Bachelor's degree and fifteen years or more of experience. Experienced candidates have at least a Bachelor's degree and five years of experience. The company is currently recruiting for candidates with project management and web application development experience. In addition, says Seif, "We look for people who are creative. We look at problems as challenges, as opportunities, then it is way more fun." Adds Lorri Woodruff, Human Resources Business Partner, "Candidates should have good communication skills, a strong customer focus, and a team orientation." Additional technical skills being sought include database and systems administration experience. The company does hire entry-level candidates. They should have a Bachelor's or Master's degree, preferably above a 3.0 grade point average, and some intern experience. Says Seif, "We are willing to hire people with a business background and a good business sense. We have strong people who can train those with a business background in technical skills, but the reverse is harder."

Job titles include: Entry-level Programmer, Intermediate, Staff, Principal, and Member of the Technical Staff. There are similar paths for Analysts, Administrators, Network Engineers, and Factory Systems Engineers. There is a dual technical/management career path, with Entry-level, Intermediate, and Senior Managers. The executive level includes Manager, Director, and Vice President. The company hired 26 technical professionals in IS in the last year, including 14 for entry-level positions.

Top schools for recruiting entry-level candidates include Cal State Hayward, San Jose State, and Santa Clara. The company expects to hire 10 technical professionals in the next year, including three for entry-level positions. Candidates are found through college recruiting (21 percent), employee referrals (17 percent; there is a bonus), internal job postings (15 percent), unsolicited resumes (13 percent), online recruiting (12 percent; monster.com, jobtrak.com), temp-to-hire contractors (12 percent), re-hires (3 percent), job fairs (3 percent), employment agencies (2 percent), and advertisements (2 percent).

Recent Job Listings

Job Title	Education	Experience	Skills	Location
Application Engineer			Provide technical information to customers designing in National ICs	South Portland, ME
Software Application Engineer		5 years	C++, Continuous, GNU Tool Chain, Pantera SDK, Korean language a plus	Fremont, CT
Principal Software Engineer			NDIS 3, 4, 5, Linux	Longmont, CO
Systems Development Engineer	BA/BS or MA/MS	0 years	Computer architecture, peripherals, components, ICs, system design	Santa Clara, CA

Contact

Web: www.national.com
Email: jobs@nsc.com
Include "Source: Covin's Guide" on your resume and in your cover letter.

ROBERT HALF INTERNATIONAL, Inc.

"Ninety-seven percent of surveyed CIOs say that soft skills, such as the ability to communicate, work on a team, and understand the business, are critical when hiring IT candidates."

– Katherine Spencer Lee
– Executive Director, RHI Consulting

• **Varied hardware and software environments** •
• **Visual Basic, C++, Java, Perl** •
• **Temporary, contract, and full-time services** • **Large shop** •

Freedom. Freedom to explore new technologies. Freedom to try different environments. Freedom from office politics. Freedom to reject assignments. Robert Half International, and its arm for recruiting and consulting IT services, RHI Consulting (RHIC), provide contract services and IT job placement in a fluid environment that emphasizes short, focused projects, unlimited online training, and a career path that parallels that of a consulting firm.

With a try-before-you-buy approach, RHI Consulting places techies wherever they are most needed to supplement a company's staff. They offer professionals a choice of full-time placement, contract-to-hire arrangements, and consulting project assignments in a variety of industries, covering a wide array of technical environments. They offer companies seasoned professionals, with the experience needed to jump into an unfamiliar environment and the skill to leave some of their technical knowledge behind with the permanent staff.

In response to customer requests for PC support and network technicians from its other contracting arms, Robert Half started RHI Consulting in 1994. In six years it grew into a $340M division. The company's job openings read like a traditional and new economy career path, spanning IT and e-commerce positions alike. Technical support positions such as Email Specialist, Quality Assurance Associate, Network Administrator/engineer/manager, Help desk/tech support, and Hardware Technician represent 50 percent of the company's work. Development positions represent the balance, from Application Developer, to Business Analyst, Webmaster/data warehouse developer, Inter-/Intranet Developer, Database Developer, Project Leader/Manager, and Chief Information Officer.

Surprise benefit: 24/7 online Perl mentoring.

Fast Facts	Revenues: $2.699B (2000)
	Employees: 248,300 (2000)
	Founded: 1948
	Temporary and placement services
	Public: RHI (NYSE)
Awards	Fortune: America's Most Admired Companies (1999, 2000)

Headquarters   2884 Sand Hill Rd.
                     Menlo Park, CA 94025
                     (650) 234-6000
                     www.rhii.com

Business

Robert Half International, RHI Consulting's parent company, pioneered the specialized temporary services field. They are the oldest and largest financial recruiting firm in the world and the largest temporary accounting services business. Their services now include seven business areas. They deploy temporary staff, recruit full-time staff, and offer an in-between model that allows professionals to work in a contract-to-hire arrangement. Accountemps, Robert Half, and RHI Management Resources provide temporary, full-time, and project staff for accounting and finance positions. Office-Team provides temporary administrative staff. The Affiliates provides temporary and full-time legal personnel. The Creative Group provides advertising, marketing, and web design professionals. Robert Half has more than 280 offices around the world.

In its ongoing efforts to report on IT industry trends, RHI Consulting conducts regular surveys of CIOs and other technical professionals. Recent surveys include the Quarterly IT Hiring Index and the Hot Jobs Report for Information Technology. Competitors include Modis Professional Services, kforce, and Aerotek.

Technology

Hardware and software platforms range from mainframes to PCs, but most current assignments are client-server or web-based. Work is generally in an IBM, Sun, or HP environment. The most common languages used are Visual Basic, C++, Perl, and Java. Lee foresees an increasing demand for XML, web-based tools such as ColdFusion, and ASP development.

Application software most common on developer assignments includes SAP, PeopleSoft, Oracle, and Baan. A sample technical support assignment might call for workstation set-up and configuration of platforms like Compaq's iPAQ, or HPs installed in an NT or Novell network. Typical development projects last three to nine months and can include full-life cycle assignments from requirements analysis, to design, code, test, and implement. More often, consultants are brought in to supplement a client's staff with a particular skill set. On the technical support side, a common assignment is to provide a client with a large deployment team when they upgrade, for instance, from Windows 95 to Windows 2000, or to extend a help desk support team after a new installation, when a surge of inquiries are expected.

Culture

Benefits include paid vacation, holidays, and access to comprehensive medical benefits. Consultants also earn discounts on hardware and software at CompUSA.

Social activities include quarterly Consultant Appreciation Events (CAP). These often include technical presentations, contests, door prizes such as a Palm Pilot, and giveaways like T-shirts and frisbees. The company sponsors the Silicon Valley Marathon and promotes professional organizations like Women in Technology and the Help Desk

Institute. The company has sponsored the Waves to Wine bike ride up the California coast, a charitable event for Multiple Sclerosis research, for the last seven years.

One of RHI Consulting's key benefits is its commitment to training. The company has allied with SmartForce (formerly CBT Systems) for online courses, as well as CompUSA, New Horizons, and Prosoft I-Net Solutions for classroom training. Consultants are given the opportunity to earn certification in Microsoft Windows NT, Novell NetWare, Sun Java, and Cisco. There are more than 2,000 courses available over the Internet,with 24-hour online mentoring by experts who can answer questions and discuss progress.

RHI Consulting also offers a number of free resources to help consultants navigate their careers, including an IT Career Guide, a Salary Guide, tips on Interviewing and Preparing a Resume, and Quick Reference Guides for OracleDeveloper 2000, Java, and Linux. Just for fun, the company has compiled a list of resume bloopers, collected at their newest web site, www.resumania.com. Samples include, "I have eight arms and eight legs with excellent interpersonal skills," and "I need just enough money to have pizza every night."

Dress and office environment are determined by the client site. Overtime is paid. The average workweek is 40 to 50 hours. If more time is needed, on mission-critical projects, for instance, this is negotiated when the contract is signed. The only requirement for travel is to the client's site, and most clients are local.

Candidates

Consultants typically have one to three years of experience to start. The average consultant has between two and ten years of experience, with a bachelor's degree in MIS or CS. Technical support professionals generally have four-year technical degrees, or an associate's degree while working on a bachelor's.

While consultants are matched to the assignments that use their technical strengths, Lee emphasizes other traits that are important. "The most important skill for consultants is the ability to quickly assess, evaluate, and develop solutions." And, since this is a consulting environment, whether it is for technical support or for development, interpersonal skills are key.

Candidates are found primarily through the company's own Web site and from employee referrals (there is a bonus). The company also uses advertisements and participates in job fairs. RHI Consulting lists jobs for contract positions (Contract), positions in which an employee and employer may decide to make it permanent (Contract to Hire), and positions for which the company is recruiting employees for customers (Full-Time).

Recent Job Listings

Job Title	Education	Experience	Skills	Location
Java Developer			XML, JSP, Java Swing, Web Logic	San Jose, CA (Consulting)
Application Development			C++, Java, VB.Net	Saint Louis, MO (Consulting)

Job Title	Education	Experience	Skills	Location
PeopleSoft HRMS		2–4 years	Version 7.0+, PeopleTools, PeopleCode, User Security, Microfocus COBOL	Detroit, MI (Consulting)
Internet Application Developer			Linux, Apache, CGI, Perl, C++, PHP, mySQL	Tucson, AZ (Consulting)
Application Development Manager	PMP	5–8 years	Retail, evaluating software vendor proposals	Pittsburgh, PA (Contract to Hire)
Application Devlopment		2 years	Java, Java Script, Linux, XML, WebSphere, Oracle, OS390	Cedar Rapids, IA (Full Time)
Manager of Application Development			VB 6.0, ASP, Visual Interdev, Crystal Report 6.5, MS SQL/SVR	Earth City, MO (Full Time)
Sr. Developer J.D. Edwards OneWorld	BA/BS CS, Business	4+ years	OneWorld, CNC, financials, distribution, manufacturing	Irvine, CA (Consulting)
C++ Programmer		3 years	C++, PL/SQL, Oracle, education industry experience	Central Valley, CA (Direct Hire)
Software Engineer: Algorithms	BS CS, Software Engineering, EE, Math, MS preferred	5 years	C++, signal processing, statistics	Fremont, CA (Consulting)
Security Specialist	Graduate degree CS, Engineering	3–5 years	ISS, SNORT, Nessus, Sniffers, Snoop, L0pht, crack, DMZs, VPNs, Oracl	San Jose, CA (Consulting)
Software Engineer		4+ years	Visual C, C++, COM, ActiveX, cryptography	San Jose, CA (Full Time)

Contact

Web site: www.rhic.com
Include "Source: Covin's Guide" on your resume and cover letter.

3Com Corporation

Fast Facts   Revenues: $2.821B (2001) Employees: 8,165 (2001) Founded: 1979
                   Manufacturer; computer networking equipment Public: COMS
                       (Nasdaq)
Awards   Fortune: 100 Best Companies to Work For in America
                   Computerworld: 100 Best Places to Work in IS
Headquarters   5400 Bayfront Plaza
                   Santa Clara, CA 95052
                   (408) 326-5000
                   http://www.3com.com

Job Title	Education	Experience	Skills	Location
Manager, CRM Applications		10+ years	Siebel, Clarify, Business Objects	California
Sustaining Engineer	BS EE, CS		Embedded DSP code, Windows device drivers	Utah
Embedded Software Manager	BSEE or CS, MSEE preferred	8+ years	C, C++, SoftICE, ICE	California
Analog Design Engineer	BS/MS PhDEE	4 years	Cadence Analog Artist Design, SPICE, Matlab, Verilog	Pennsylvania
System Engineer	BS Engineering	5–10 years	5ESS/4ESS switches, SS7, IP, SIP, MIBs	Illinois

Acxiom Corporation

Fast Facts   Revenues: $1.01B (2001) Employees: 5,400 (2001) Founded: 1969
                   Databased marketing Public: ACXM (Nasdaq)
Awards   Fortune: 100 Best Companies to Work For in America
                   Computerworld: 100 Best Places to Work in IT
Headquarters   1 Information Way
                   Little Rock, AR 72203-8180
                   (501) 342-1000
                   http://www.acxiom.com

Job Title	Education	Experience	Skills	Location
Data Administrator			SAS, Syncsort, Multimatch	Conway, AR
Database Administrator		2 years	Oracle, UNIX, Ab Initio	Downers Grove, IL
Database Developer		3+ years	Oracle 7.x, SQL, PL/SQL, Pro C, Perl	Conway, AR

| Solutions Developer | | | TIE Commerce eVision Workbench, ROI Manage 2000 | Columbus, OH |
| Software Developer | BA/BS CS or certificate | 6 months | Pascal, PReS | Melville, NY |

Adobe Systems Incorporated

Fast Facts   Revenues: $1.266B (2000) Employees: 3,007 (2000) Founded: 1982
                    Software; desktop publishing Public: ADBE (Nasdaq)
Awards   Red Herring: 100 Top Companies of the Electronic Age
                    Fortune: 100 Best Companies to Work for in America
Headquarters   345 Park Avenue
                    San Jose, CA 95110-2704
                    (408) 536-6000
                    http://www.adobe.com

Job Title	Education	Experience	Skills	Location
Computer Scientist	BS CS or equivalent experience	3 years	C/C++, computer graphics	Minneapolis, MN
Computer Scientist, Audio	BS	3–5 years	QuickTime, DirectShow, C, C++	San Jose, CA
Electronic Software Distributor Computer Scientist	BS CS/EE/ Computer Engineering, MS preferred	5–7 years	C, C++, Perl, CGI, Oracle, installers	Seattle, WA
Localization Engineer	BS	1–3 years	MSDevStudio 6.0, Java, Perl, Vise Installer, CodeWarrior, AppleGlot	San Jose, CA
Senior Computer Scientist, Acrobat Security	BS	10+ years	IETF PKIX, XML DigSig, XKMS, SOAP, C, C++	San Jose, CA

Agilent Technologies, Inc.

Fast Facts   Revenues: $10.773B (2000) Employees: 47,000 (2000)
                    Founded: 1999 Manufacturer; test & measurement equipment Public:
                    A (NYSE)
Awards   Fortune: 100 Best Companies to Work for in America

Headquarters	395 Page Mill Rd., PO Box 10395
	Palo Alto, CA 94306
	(650) 752-5000
	http://www.agilent.com

Job Title	Education	Experience	Skills	Location
Digital IC Design Engineer	BS/MS/PhD EE		CMOS digital logic design, Verilog/VHDL	My-P-Bayan Lepas, Malasia
Analog IC Design Engineer	BS/MS/PhD EE		CMOS analog circuit design	My-P-Bayan Lepas, Malasia
Analytical Response Center Engineer	BS/MS MCSE certificate a plus	2 years	Remote analytical and IT post-sales support, French language	Netherlands
Application Engineer	BS Engineering or Applied Science		Product changes	My-P-Bayan Lepas, Malaysia
Associate Product Test Engineer	Technical diploma, Engineering		RF Microwave, test and repair, microcircuits	My-P-Bayan Lepas, Malaysia

American Management Systems, Inc.

Fast Facts	Revenues: $1.279B (2000) Employees: 8,500 (2000) Founded: 1970
	Professional services; large-scale integration Public: AMSY (Nasdaq)
Awards	Fortune: 100 Best Companies to Work for in America
	Computerworld: 100 Best Places to Work in IT
Headquarters	4050 Legato Road
	Fairfax, VA 22033
	(703) 267-8000
	www.ams.com

Job Title	Education	Experience	Skills	Location
Operations Research Analyst	BS Operations Research	5–10 years	Regression analysis, C++, Java, SQL, military background	Fairfax, VA
Calibration Programs Analyst	BS or MS Engineering		U.S. Navy ships engineering or combat systems	Fairfax, VA
Programmer Analyst		2 years	CRM, Arbor/BP, Clarify, Saville, Siebel, CICS, Dutch language a plus	The Hague, Netherlands

Database Professional	BA/BS CS, Engineering, Math, Physics, Business/IT	2 years	DB2, Oracle, Sybase	Dusseldorf, Germany
	BA/BS CS, Engineering, Math, Physics, Business/IT	Junior to Mid-level	Telecommunications, billing, German language a plus	Bern, Switzerland

Analog Devices, Incorporated

Fast Facts   Revenues: $2.578B (2000) Employees: 9,100 (2000) Founded: 1965
Manufacturer; integrated circuits Public: ADI (NYSE)

Awards   Computerworld: 100 Best Places to Work in IT
Information Week: Top 500 Technology Innovators

Headquarters   1 Technology Way
Norwood, MA 02062-9106
(781) 329-4700
http://www.analog.com

Job Title	Education	Experience	Skills	Location
Advanced Technology Deployment Designer	BS EE	3+ years	Semicustom IC design and layout, Verilog	Wilmington, MA
Analog Design Engineer	BS EE, MS EE preferred	10–15 years	Analog, CAD, Bipolar, BiCMOS	Greensboro, NC
CAD Engineer IV	MS EE, ME, CS or equivalent experience	4 years	UNIX, C++, IC CAD design tools, MEMS	Cambridge, MA
Senior Software Engineer	BS/MS CS, EE, Physics, Math	5 years	C, C++, Java, Solaris, Sun Forte, Clearcase	North Andover, MA
RF Systems Application Engineer	BS/MS EE	4–6 years	PCB layout, RF design, Othello	Aalborg, Denmark

Analysts International Corporation

Fast Facts   Revenues: $288.3M (2000) Employees: 4,800 (2000) Founded: 1966
Professional services; network design, conversion Public: ANLY
(Nasdaq)

Awards   Computerworld: 100 Best Places to Work in IT

Headquarters   3601 W. 76th Street
Minneapolis, MN 55435-3000
(952) 835-5900
http://www.analysts.com

Job Title	Education	Experience	Skills	Location
Senior Programmer Analyst		5+ years	Visual C++, SQL Server, COM/DCOM, ADO, UML	Minneapolis, MN
Testing Specialist		5+ years	Mercury Test Suite, Loadrunner	Minneapolis, MN
ATG Dynamo Developer		3 years	ATG Dynamo, XML, EJB, JSP	Minneapolis, MN
Algorithms Engineer	MS CS or Operations Research	0–5 years	Java, C++, XML	Dallas, TX
Programmer Analyst			FoxPro, Oracle	Hawaii

Andersen

Fast Facts   Revenues: $8.4B (2000) Employees: 77,000 (2000) Founded: 1900s
Professional services, accounting; Accenture; computer consulting
   Partnership

Awards   PC Week: Fast-Track 500
Fortune: 100 Best Companies to Work for in America

Headquarters   33 W. Monroe St.
Chicago, IL 60603
(312) 580-0033
http://www.arthurandersen.com

Job Title	Education	Experience	Skills	Location
E-Business Senior Architect		8+ years	Java, OOD, Oracle, XML	Chicago, IL
Practice Director, Retail IT Consulting		9+ years	RETEK, JDA, Island Pacific/SVI, SAP Retail	Atlanta, GA
JDEdwards Consultant		3+ years	CNC, OneWorld, AS/400	Chicago, IL
Hyperion Director		8–10 years	Hyperion Essbase, Cognos, SAS Analytics	Atlanta, GA
Oracle Consultant	BA/BS preferred		Oracle 11.3	London, UK

Apple Computer, Inc.

Fast Facts   Revenues: $7.983B (2000) Employees: 8,568 (2000) Founded: 1976
                    Manufacturer; personal computers (Macintosh, iMac) Public: AAPL
                        (Nasdaq)
Awards   Forbes ASAP: Dynamic 100
                    Computerworld: 100 Best Places to Work in IT
Headquarters   1 Infinite Loop
                    Cupertino, CA 95014
                    (408) 996-1010
                    http://www.apple.com

Job Title	Education	Experience	Skills	Location
AppleWorks Engineer		3 years	Mac OS SDK, Visual C++, BoundsChecker, CodeWarrior, Cocoa, QuickTime	Santa Clara, CA
Applications US Designer	BS/MS User Interface Design	5+ years	IMovie, Director, Lingo, Flash, C++	Santa Clara, CA
SAP SD Functional Analyst	BS CS, Info Mgt.	7–9 years	SAP R/3 SD, SIS, ATP	Santa Clara, CA
Lead Systems Integrator/ Hardware Design Engineer	BS/MS EE	5+ years	SDRAM, Flash, ATAPI, Bluetooth, Firewire	Santa Clara, CA
Developer Technical Support Engineer	BS CS or equivalent	4+ years	Shell scripting, Perl, C++, Chinese language	Beijing, China

Applied Materials, Inc.

Fast Facts   Revenues: $9.564B (2000) Employees: 19,220 (2000) Founded: 1967
                    Manufacturer; chip manufacturing equipment Public: AMAT
                        (Nasdaq)
Awards   Fortune: 100 Best Companies to Work for in America
                    Forbes ASAP: Dynamic 100
Headquarters   3050 Bowers Ave.
                    Santa Clara, CA 95054-3299
                    (408) 727-5555
                    http://www.appliedmaterials.com

Job Title	Education	Experience	Skills	Location
Engineer	BS/MS/PhD Engineering	Entry-level	GPA 3.0	Santa Clara, CA
Student Co-op	Pursuing degree, Industrial Engineering	N/A	Data collection, analyis	Austin, TX

Engineering Technician I	AA Applied Science, BS Laser/ Electro-Optics, military training	N/A	Calibration, trouble-shooting	Hillsboro, OR
Product Technology & Support	BSCS, BSEE, MS preferred	10+ years	ASKS, anti-virus	Santa Clara, CA
College Intern	Pursuing degree	N/A	Reduce number of electrical connections	Santa Clara, CA

Arrow Electronics, Inc.

Fast Facts	Revenues: $12.959B (2000) Employees: 12,200 (2000) Founded: 1956 Distributor; electronics Public: ARW (NYSE)
Awards	Fortune: 100 Best Companies to Work for in America Computerworld: 100 Best Places to Work in IT
Headquarters	25 Hub Drive Melville, NY 11747 (516) 391-1300 http://www.arrow.com

Job Title	Education	Experience	Skills	Location
Component Engineer	BSEE	3 years	Board level design, MS-Access	Denver, CO
Electrical Engineer	MSEE	1 year	ASIC design	Thousand Oaks, CA
Database Manager	BA/BS CS	5 years	DB2, Oracle	Denver, CO
RF Business Development Engineer	BSEE	5–10 years	RF/Microwave	Boston, MA
Technical Sales Engineer	BS	2 years	ASIC/LSI Logic	Irvine, CA

AT&T Corporation

Fast Facts	Revenues: $65.981B (2000) Employees: 166,000 (2000) Founded: 1875 Telephone services Public: T (NYSE)
Awards	Computerworld: 100 Best Places to Work in IT PC Magazine: 100 Most Influential
Headquarters	32 Avenue of the Americas New York, NY 10013-2412 (212) 387-5400 http://www.att.com

Job Title	Education	Experience	Skills	Location
Technical Manager, IT	Master's or equivalent	Senior	Tier 1/Tier 2 technical systems requirements	Middletown, NJ
Database Engineer	Bachelor's	5 years	Oracle, SQL Server, Java, Cold Fusion	Oakton, VA
Software Engineer	Bachelor's	5–10 years	C++, Java, Oracle, Solaris, TS clearance	Columbia, MD
System Architect	Master's	5 years	System Architect 2001, SIGINT, TSSCI clearance	Columbia, MD
Voice Administrator	Bachelor's	Experienced	Avaya PBX, Voice Mail, AMIS, OctelNet	Minnesota

@stake

Fast Facts	Founded: 2000 Private Professional services; IT security
Awards	Computerworld: 100 Best Places to Work in IT
Headquarters	196 Broadway
	Cambridge, MA 02139-1902
	(617) 621-3500
	http://www.atstake.com

Job Title	Education	Experience	Skills	Location
Project Manager			RFP response, lead projects	San Francisco, CA
Senior Security Architect			Firewall, DNS, Web Server	San Francisco, CA

Autodesk, Inc.

Fast Facts	Revenues: $936.3M (2001) Employees: 3,584 (2001) Founded: 1982
	Software; engineering design (CAD/CAM) Public: ADSK (Nasdaq)
Awards	PC Magazine: 100 Most Influential
	Fortune: 100 Best Companies to Work for in America
Headquarters	111 McInnis Parkway
	San Rafael, CA 94903
	(415) 507-5000
	http://www.autodesk.com

Job Title	Education	Experience	Skills	Location
Programmer/ Software Engineer III	BS CS or equivalent		C++, Java, Perl, SourceSafe, LISP	San Rafael, CA
Software Developer	BS CS, Math, Software Engineering	7+ years	C++, Gmax, 3ds max	San Francisco, CA
Software Developer/Build Engineer	BS CS	1 year	C++, Java, MFC, XML, ObjectARX	San Rafael, CA
Programmer/ Software Engineer	BS CS	5+ years	C++, Java, OpenGL, XGL, WinInet, Apache	Novi, MI
Senior Network Engineer			DMZ, EMEA, C CIE, Cisco VPN, VoIP, European language	Neuchatel, Switzerland

Avnet, Inc.

Fast Facts   Revenues: $12.814B (2001) Employees: 13,600 (2001)
Founded: 1955 Distributor; electronics Public: AVT (NYSE)
Awards   Forbes: Best of the Web
Computerworld: 100 Best Places to Work in IT
Headquarters   2211 S. 47th Street
Phoenix, AZ 85034
(480) 643-2000
http://www.avnet.com

Job Title	Education	Experience	Skills	Location
Web Developer	High School	2 years	ASP, VB Script, Oracle, DreamWeaver	Computer Marketing Group
Senior Systems Programmer	BA/BS CS	6 years	UNIX	Avnet corporate
Technical Consultant	BA/BS CS	2 years	Design, develop full life cycle solutions	Operational Process Group
Systems Application Engineer				Applied Computing Group
Business Technology Consultant				Computer Marketing Group

BellSouth Corporation

Fast Facts	Revenues: $26.151B (2000) Employees: 103,900 (2000) Founded: 1984 Local telephone services Public: BLS (NYSE)
Awards	Network World: NW 200 Computerworld: 100 Best Places to Work in IT
Headquarters	1155 Peachtree St. NE Atlanta, GA 30309-3610 (404) 249-2000 http://www.bellsouthcorp.com

Job Title	Education	Experience	Skills	Location
Senior Business Analyst			Analysis of PMAP benchmarks, SEEMS payments	Atlanta, GA
Network Analyst II	BS MIS, EE, CS, Systems Engineering	3–5 years	DSL, Fiber Optic, OSPF, BGP	Atlanta, GA
Senior Application Technology Manager			Enterprise database	Atlanta, GA
Software Developer			Oracle, PeopleSoft HRMS	Atlanta, GA
System Designer II			Pre-sales technical support	Birmingham, AL

BORN

Fast Facts	Revenues: $139M (2000) Employees: 900+ (2000) Founded: 1990 Professional services; computer consulting Private
Awards	Fortune: 100 Best Companies to Work for in America
Headquarters	301 Carlson Parkway Minnetonka, MN 55305 (952) 258-6000 http://www.born.com

Job Title	Education	Experience	Skills	Location
Consultant		1 year	JDEdwards Install/CNC, Sun, HP9000, RS/6000, AS/400, Oracle, DB2, EAI, Java	Minneapolis, MN

CDW Computer Centers, Inc.

Fast Facts	Revenues: $3.842B (2000) Employees: 2,700 (2000) Founded: 1982
	Retailer; catalog sales, computers Public: CDWC (Nasdaq)
Awards	Fortune: 100 Best Companies to Work for in America
	Computerworld: 100 Best Places to Work in IT
Headquarters	200 N. Milwaukee Avenue
	Vernon Hills, IL 60061
	(847) 465-6000
	http://www.cdw.com

Job Title	Education	Experience	Skills	Location
Senior Programmer/ Analyst	BA/BS or equivalent	5+ years	AS/400, SYNON/COOL2E	
Enterprise Reporting Analyst			ShowCase Strategy, Essbase/ NT	
SQL Database Administrator			MS SQL, Data Mirror	
Internet Design Manager	BS			
Senior Internet Developer	BS CS		ASP, VBScript, SQL 7, XSL, Site Server, IIS	

Cerner Corporation

Fast Facts	Revenues: $378M (2000) Employees: 3,104 (2000) Founded: 1979
	Software vendor; hospital systems Public: CERN (Nasdaq)
Awards	Fortune: 100 Best Companies to Work for in America
Headquarters	2800 Rockcreek Parkway
	Kansas City, MO 64117
	(816) 221-1024
	http://www.cerner.com

Job Title	Education	Experience	Skills	Location
Application Architect	BA/BS CIS, MIS, IS, CS, Engineering, Business	5 years	Design and code reviews	Kansas City, MO
ADS Database Administrator	BA/BS CS, IS	12 years	Oracle, VMS, AIX	Lee's Summit
Application Developer	BA/BS CIS, MIS, IS, CS, Engineering, Business	2 years	Actuate, PeopleTools, SQR, Oracle, SQL Server	Kansas City, MO

| Citrix Technical Consultant | BA/BS CIS, MIS, IS, CS, Engineering, Business | 3 years | Citrix Metaframe | Kansas City, MO |
| CCL Developer | BA/BS CIS, MIS, IS, CS, Engineering, Business | 2 years | Discern Explorer | Kansas City, MO |

Cisco Systems, Inc.

Fast Facts   Revenues: $22.293B (2001) Employees: 21,000 (2000)
Founded: 1984 Manufacturer; network components Public: CSCO
(Nasdaq)
Awards   Fortune: 100 Best Companies to Work for in America
Computerworld: 100 Best Places to Work in IT
Headquarters   170 W. Tasman Drive
San Jose, CA 95134-1706
(408) 526-4000
http://www.cisco.com

Job Title	Education	Experience	Skills	Location
Technical Leader I	BS EE, CS	10+ years	Java, LDAP, Active Directory	San Jose, CA
Hardware Engineer III	BS EE or equivalent, MS preferred	5+ years	ASIC development, Synopsis	San Jose, CA
Customer Solutions Manager II	BS/MS/PhD EE, CS, OR	10+ years	CLEC, UM, IP VPNS, VoIP	Edison, NJ
Manager, Software Development	BS CS, EE or MS	7 years	ASICs, diagnostic software	San Jose, CA
Systems Engineer II		5–8 years	X.25, ATM, SNA, Voici	Milano, Italy

Comark, Inc.

Fast Facts   Revenues: $1.56B (2000) Employees: 1,364 (2000) Founded: 1977
Distributor; computers, peripherals, and supplies Private
Awards   Computerworld: 100 Best Places to Work in IT
Headquarters   444 Scott Drive
Bloomingdale, IL 60108
(800) 888-5390
http://www.comark.com

Job Title	Education	Experience	Skills	Location
Sr. IS Business Analyst FI/CO	BA/BS, MBA desirable	5 years	SAP R/3, GL, AP, AR, ABAP	Bloomingdale, IL
IS Technical Analyst—BW	BA/BS, MBA desirable	4 years	SAP R/3, Business Warehouse	Bloomingdale, IL
Sr. SAP Basis Administrator	BA/BS, MBA desirable	6 years	SAP Basis, Oracle	Bloomingdale, IL
Engineering Resource Manager	BA/BS CS, Engineering, Business	3–5 years	P/L responsibility for staff	Bloomingdale, IL
Sr. Field Engineer	AA/AS, hardware and software certifications	3 years	IBM, Compaq, Apple maintenance and installation	Milwaukee, WI

Computer Associates International, Inc.

Fast Facts Revenues: $4.198B (2001) Employees: 21,000 (2001) Founded: 1976
Software; systems-level; professional services Public: CA (NYSE)

Awards Fortune: 100 Best Companies to Work for in America
Computerworld: 100 Best Places to Work in IT

Headquarters 1 Computer Associates Plaza
Islandia, NY 11749
(631) 342-5224
http://www.cai.com

Job Title	Education	Experience	Skills	Location
Systems Engineer	BA/BS or equivalent experience preferred	3 years	RMON, NAT, NFS, Java, Perl, CSH, Tcl/TK, Oracle	Islandia, NY

Dell Computer Corporation

Fast Facts Revenues: $31.888B (2001) Employees: 40,000 (2001)
Founded: 1984 Manufacturer; PCs, built-to-order Public: DELL
(Nasdaq)

Awards Fortune: 100 Best Companies to Work for in America
Computerworld: 100 Best Places to Work in IT

Headquarters 1 Dell Way
Round Rock, TX 78682-2222
(512) 338-4400
http://www.dell.com

Job Title	Education	Experience	Skills	Location
Web Developer	BA/BS or equivalent or MA/MS	5–10 years	C++, Java, Oracle, Perl	Austin, TX
Tandem Programmer	BA/BS	3–5 years	NonStop TS/MP, Kernel OS, COBOL	Austin, TX
Programmer Analyst	BA/BS or MA/MS	8–10 years	C++, Java, Tandem, Teradata, WebMethods	Austin, TX
Programmer Analyst IV-GPS	BA/BS IS or Business	3–5 years	Oracle Express data cubes	Austin, TX
DBA	AA or equivalent	3–5 years	Oracle, Tandem, ERWin	Austin, TX

Deloitte Touche Tohmatsu

Fast Facts   Revenues: $11.2B (2000) Employees: 90,000 (1999) Founded: 1893
Professional services, accounting; Deloitte Consulting, computers
    Partnership

Awards   Fortune: 100 Best Companies to Work for in America
Computerworld: 100 Best Places to Work in IT

Headquarters   1633 Broadway
New York, NY 10019-6754
(212) 492-4000
http://www.deloitte.com

Job Title	Education	Experience	Skills	Location
Administrative WAN Analyst	Nortel, CCNA, MSCE, CNE	4 years	50+ site network, ATM, RIP, OSPF	Hermitage, TN
Consultant, Data Quality and Integrity	BA/BS Business, CS, CA, CISA	1–3 years	Data conversion, accounting	Toronto, Canada
Knowledge Manager	MA/MS MIS	5–7 years	Organizational design, pharmaceutical industry	Chicago, IL
Manager, Data Quality and Integrity	BA/BS Business, CS, CA, CISA certification	5+ years	Data conversion	Toronto, Canada
Project Manager	BA, MBA preferred	5+ years	Banking roll out, network installations	Ljubljana, SI

Electronic Data Systems Corporation (EDS)

Fast Facts Revenues: $19.227B (2000) Employees: 122,000 (2000)
Founded: 1962 Professional services; outsourcing Public: EDS
(NYSE)

Awards Network World: NW 200
Computerworld: 100 Best Places to Work in IT

Headquarters 5400 Legacy Drive
Plano, TX 75024-3199
(972) 604-6000
www.eds.com

Job Title	Education	Experience	Skills	Location
Program Manager- Web Hosting	BS CS, EE, MCSE a plus	5 years	Java, D/HTML, Oracle, BEA Web Logic	Dallas, TX
Systems Programmer	BS CS or equivalent		IBM 3090, VTAM, NCP	Lowell, MA
Advanced C++ Developer	BA/BS CS	4+ years	Java, XML, DataStage	Louisville, KY
Object-Oriented Systems Analyst	BA/BS CS	5–7 years	UML, COM+, MTS, ASP, IIS, JavaScript	Manitoba, Canada
Senior Project Manager	BA/BS, PMP certification	15 years	Object-oriented methodologies	Manitoba, Canada

EMC Corporation

Fast Facts Revenues: $8.873B (2000) Employees: 24,100 (2000) Founded: 1979
Manufacturer; computer memory disks Public: EMC (NYSE)

Awards Information Week: Top 500 Technology Innovators
Computerworld: 100 Best Places to Work in IT

Headquarters 35 Parkwood Drive
Hopkinton, MA 01748-9103
(508) 435-1000
http://www.emc.com

Job Title	Education	Experience	Skills	Location
Senior Software Engineer, OS Internals/Device Driver			C++, Assembler, U-code	Cambridge, MA
Senior PCB Designer	BSET, BSEE	5–10 years	DFM, DFA, Specctra, Valor	Hopkinton, MA
Principal Design Engineer	BSEE	10+ years	Die bumping, flip chip	Hopkinton, MA

Job Title	Education	Experience	Skills	Location
Data Modeler	BS CS, MS a plus	7 years	Oracle, Informatica	Westboro, MA
Senior Assessment Consultant	BA/BS technical, MBA	10–15 years	Strategic information storage needs	Vienna, VA

EPIQ Systems, Inc.

Fast Facts	Revenues: $23.3M (2000) Employees: 120 (2000) Founded: 1988 Software; bankruptcy administration Public: EPIQ (Nasdaq)
Awards	Computerworld: 100 Best Places to Work in IT Forbes: 200 Best Small Companies
Headquarters	501 Kansas Avenue Kansas City, KS 66105-1300 (913) 621-9500 http://www.epiqsystems.com

Job Title	Education	Experience	Skills	Location
Client Services Representative— Chapter 7	AA	2 years	Directory structures, TCMS, Siebel	Kansas City, KS

Ernst & Young International

Fast Facts	Revenues: $9.55B (2000) Employees: 88,625 (2000) Founded: 1895 Professional services; accounting; Cap Gemini bought computer services arm Partnership
Awards	Computerworld: 100 Best Places to Work in IT Fortune: 100 Best Companies to Work for in America
Headquarters	787 Seventh Avenue New York, NY 10019 (212) 773-3000 www.eyi.com

Job Title	Education	Experience	Skills	Location
Data Mining Specialist	BS CS, Statistics, Computational Math, Actuarial Science		C++, Oracle, SAS, MARS, PL/SQL	New York, NY
Information Systems Risk Manager	BA/BS or MA/MS CS, IS, Engineering, Business, CPA	5 years	IT control and security	New York, NY
IT Risk Management Auditor	BA/BS, MA/MS, Business, CS	2 years	Audit IT business processes	Atlanta, GA

Mergers & Acquisitions Senior Manager—IT Operations	BA/BS CS, Accounting, Business, MBA a plus	8–10 years	Director of Technology, cash flow impact	New York, NY
Data Analysis Specialist	BA/BS, Engineering, Accounting, MIS, CS		SAS, Lotus Notes	Cleveland, OH

Forsythe Technology, Inc.

Fast Facts Revenues: $631.1M (2000) Employees: 550 (2000) Founded: 1970
Leasing; computer equipment; professional services Private

Awards Computerworld: 100 Best Places to Work in IT

Headquarters 7500 Frontage Road
Skokie, IL 60077
(847) 675-8000
http://www.forsythemca.com

Job Title	Education	Experience	Skills	Location

No technical positions currently available

Galileo International, Inc.

Fast Facts Revenues: $1.643.3B (2000) Employees: 3,300 (2000)
Founded: @1970 Software; reservations, Public: GLC (NYSE) (bought by Cendant)

Awards Computerworld: 100 Best Places to Work in IT

Headquarters 9700 W. Higgins Rd.
Rosemont, IL 60018-4796
(847) 518-4000
http://www.galileo.com

Job Title	Education	Experience	Skills	Location
WebSphere Administrator (Anticipated)	BA/BS CS	5 years	J2EE, VisualAge, ClearCase, OS/390, RACF	Denver, CO
Network Analyst (Anticipated)	BA/BS or equivalent	3 years	VLAN, Netbeui, DHCP, OC3	Denver, CO
Open Systems Planner/Engineer (Anticipated)	BA/BS CS, Math	5+ years	SAS, MVS, C++, Visio	Denver, Co

TPF Systems Performance Analyst (Anticipated)	BS CS	3–7 years	TPF	Denver, Co
Windows/UNIX System Adminstrator (Anticipated)	BS CS	7 years	Linux, X.25, Perl, Apache, WebSphere	Denver, CO

Gartner, Inc.

Fast Facts   Revenues: $858.7M (2000) Employees: 4,322 (2000) Founded: 1979
Publishing; market research, industry analysis Public: IT (NYSE)

Awards   PC Magazine: 100 Most Influential
Computerworld: 100 Best Places to Work in IT

Headquarters   56 Top Gallant Rd.
Stamford, CT 06904-2212
(203) 316-1111
http://www.gartner.com

Job Title	Education	Experience	Skills	Location
Senior Systems Analyst	BA/BS, MA/MS a plus	5+ years	Weblogic, Oracle Forms	Stamford, CT
Senior Database Administrator	BA/BS	6–8 years	Oracle, C, SQL/PL	Stamford, CT, moving to Trumbull, CT
Director, Consulting	BA/BS, MBA preferred	10 years	Strategic planning, CRM	Atlanta, GA
Research Director, Supply Chain Execution		10+ years	ERP, SCM, SAS, B2B	Stamford, CT
Research Director, Database & Systems	BA/BS	10+ years	BMC, Tivoli,	Stamford, CT

Gateway, Inc.

Fast Facts   Revenues: $9.601B (2000) Employees: 24,600 (2000) Founded: 1985
Manufacturer; personal computers Public: GTW (NYSE)

Awards   Industry Week: 100 Best Managed Companies
PC Magazine: 100 Most Influential

Headquarters   4545 Towne Centre Ct.
San Diego, CA 92121
(858) 799-3401
http://www.gateway.com

Job Title	Education	Experience	Skills	Location
Software Developer II	BA/BS CS	4 years	Broadbase BRIO, FoxPro	Beverly
Database Administrator	BA/BS	4 years	C++, SDLC	Denver, CO
NT Design Engineer	BS EE, ME	2 years	Assembly, C	Denver, CO
Security Engineer	BS CS	4 years	NT, AS/400, Novell, PBX	Denver, CO
EDI Developer	BS CS	5 years	Gentran, Visual C++, VAN	San Diego, CA

Genuity Inc.

Fast Facts	Revenues: $1.137B (2000) Employees: 4,832 (2000) Founded: 1948
	Internet access and web hosting; was BBN, developer of ARPANET,
	pre-cursor to Internet Public: GENU (Nasdaq)
Awards	Computerworld: 100 Best Places to Work in IT
Headquarters	225 Presidential Way
	Woburn, MA 01801
	(781) 865-2000
	http://www.genuity.com

Job Title	Education	Experience	Skills	Location
Senior Application Developer		4+ years	Oracle, Arbor billing system	Cambridge, MA
Business Analyst	BA/BS CS or equivalent		Relational database	Woburn, MA
Strategic Initiatives Manager	BS Engineering + MBA preferred	3–5 years	Partnerships	Burlington, MA
Telco Quoting Specialist	BS	1–3 years	DS3, OC-3, QTG, LATTIS, Vantive	Burlington, MA
Project Manager	BA/BS	1–3 years	MS-Project, risk management tools	Irving Williams Sq, TX

Hewlett-Packard Corporation

Fast Facts	Revenues: $48.782B (2000) Employees: 88,500 (2000)
	Founded: 1939 Manufacturer; mid-range, server computers Public:
	HWP (NYSE)
Awards	Industry Week: 100 Best Managed Companies
	Fortune: 100 Best Companies to Work for in America

Headquarters   3000 Hanover Street
                     Palo Alto, CA 94304
                     (650) 857-1501
                     http://www.hp.com

Job Title	Education	Experience	Skills	Location
IC Designer	MS, PhD EE	2 years	CMOS, analog design, MRAM	Boise, ID
Senior Hardware Engineer	BS, MS, PhD EE		Compact Flash, solid state memory	Boise, ID
Senior Software Engineer/ Scientist	BS, MS, PhD CS		Database, Secure Digital Storage	Boise, ID
Engineer/ Scientist	BS, MS CS or Engineering	5 years	Agent frameworks, fuzzy logic	France
Software Applications Specialist	BA/BS CS or Business with MIS	2 years	Oracle 8i, Brio, OLAP, Perl, COBOL	Guadalajara, Mexico

Honeywell International, Inc.

Fast Facts   Revenues: $25.023B (2000) Employees: 125,000 (2000)
                   Founded: 1921 Manufacturer; electronics and aerospace materials
                        Public: HON (NYSE)
Awards   Industry Week: 100 Best Managed Companies
                   Computerworld: 100 Best Places to Work in IT
Headquarters   101 Columbia Rd., PO. Box 4000
                   Morristown, NJ 07962-2497
                   (973) 455-2000
                   http://www.honeywell.com

Job Title	Education	Experience	Skills	Location
Senior Staff Engineer Software	BA/BS	Experienced	C++, Vs-Works OS, SEI Level 4	Teterboro, NJ
Technology Manager	PhD Engineering, Materials Science	10+ years	Wafer fabrication, CLC Phase Gate Reviews	
Web Content Engineer	BA/BS	3 years	DreamWeaver, Oracle	Morristown, NJ
Technical Services Team Member	BA/BS or MS IS or equivalent		SAP, ABAP	
Database Administrator	BA/BS CS or related		SQL, Six Sigma, Access	Tempe, AZ

International Business Machines Corporation (IBM)

Fast Facts Revenues: $88.396B (2000) Employees: 316,303 (2000)
Founded: 1911 Manufacturer; computers; software; professional
services Public: IBM (NYSE)

Awards PC Magazine: 100 Most Influential
Industry Week: 100 Best Managed Companies

Headquarters New Orchard Road
Armonk, NY 10504
(914) 499-1900
http://www.ibm.com

Job Title	Education	Experience	Skills	Location
Human Factors Engineer/ Scientist	MA/MS	2 years	User-Centered Design, Psychology	Endicott, NY
Hardware Development Engineer	BS or equivalent	0–18 months	C++, Java, Electrophotog- raphy	Boulder, CO
Advanced Software Engineer	BA/BS	3 years	Siebel	Atlanta, GA
CICS System Programmer	BA/BS	5+ years	DB2, CICS, MVS	Washington, DC
Computational Scientist	BA/BS	10 years	RS/6000 SP, MPI, Pthreads	Boulder, CO

Intel Corporation

Fast Facts Revenues: $33.726B (2000) Employees: 86,100 (2000)
Founded: 1968 Manufacturer; integrated circuits Public: INTC
(Nasdaq)

Awards Fortune: 100 Best Companies to Work for in America
Computerworld: 100 Best Places to Work in IT

Headquarters 2200 Mission College Blvd.
Santa Clara, CA 95052-8119
(408) 765-8080
http://www.intel.com

Job Title	Education	Experience	Skills	Location
ASIC Design Project Leader	BS/MS	6–8 years	VLSI, RTL, DFT	Hudson, MA
DSP Processor Architect	MS CE, CS	2–4 years	C/C++, VLSI, VHDL, Verilog	Fremont, CA
Mobile Wireless Hardware Architect	MS/PhD	7 years	Wireless product design	Santa Clara, CA

Job Title	Education	Experience	Skills	Location
Staff Compiler Engineer	MS/PhD	4 years	VPN, Codegen	San Jose, CA
Senior BIOS Software Engineer	BS CS, EE	5+ years	ITP, x86 assembly, PCI, LPC, PnP	Portland, OR

International Data Group (IDG)

Fast Facts	Revenues: $3.1B (2000) Employees: 13,400 (2000) Founded: 1964 Publisher; computer newspapers, market research, industry analysis Private
Awards	PC Magazine: 100 Most Influential Fortune: 100 Best Companies to Work for in America
Headquarters	1 Exeter Plaza Boston, MA 02116 (617) 534-1200 http://www.idg.com

Job Title	Education	Experience	Skills	Location
Research Analyst	BA/BS or equivalent	1–3 years	Analysis of information appliance and HDTV markets	Mountain View, CA
Senior Software Engineer	BA/BS	4–6 years	Java, Apache, Oracle, Perl, XSLT	San Mateo, CA
Network Administrator	High school	1–2 years	Win95/2000, Mac, HTML, ASP, SQL	Topsfield, MA

Kingston Technology Company

Fast Facts	Revenues: $1.6B (2000) Employees: 2,000 (2000) Founded: 1987 Manufacturer; computer memory Private
Awards	Fortune: 100 Best Companies to Work for in America PC Week: Fast-Track 500
Headquarters	17600 Newhope St. Fountain Valley, CA 92708 (714) 435-2600 http://www.kingston.com

Job Title	Education	Experience	Skills	Location

No job openings at this time

KPMG Consulting, Inc.

Fast Facts	Revenues: $2.856B (2001) Employees: 10,000 (2001) Founded: 1897 Professional services; computer consulting, KPMG Public: KCIN (Nasdaq)
Awards	Computerworld: Top Systems Integrators Computerworld: 100 Best Places to Work in IT
Headquarters	1676 International Dr. McLean, VA 22102 (703) 747-3000 http://www.kpmgconsulting.com

Job Title	Education	Experience	Skills	Location
Process Improvement Consultant	BA/BS, Junior military officer	2–4 years	Business Process Re-engineering	Washington, DC
Datawarehousing Project Lead	BA/BS		Oracle Warehouse Builder	New York, NY
Mainframe Developer	BA/BS MIS	0–3 years	COBOL, CICS, JCL, Endevor	Washington, DC
Functional Oracle Financials Consultant	BA/BS		Oracle Financials 11i, experience in university applications	Mountain View, CA
SAP Consulting Professional	BA/BS or equivalent		SAP, ABAP/4, Chinese language	China

Lexmark International Group, Inc.

Fast Facts	Revenues: $3.807B (2000) Employees: 13,000 (2000) Founded: 1991 Manufacturer; printers and supplies Public: LXK (NYSE)
Awards	Industry Week: 100 Best Managed Companies PC Magazine: 100 Most Influential
Headquarters	1 Lexmark Centre Dr. 740 W. New Circle Rd. Lexington, KY 40550 (859) 232-2000 http://www.lexmark.com

Job Title	Education	Experience	Skills	Location
Business Systems Analyst	BA/BS	10 years	Oracle, Discoverer, Customer Contracts	Lexington, KY
Web Project Manager	BS	1 year	Web, Internet programming	Lexington, KY
EBusiness Analyst	BS	5 years	Programmer, report writing	Lexington, KY

Lockheed Martin Corp.

Fast Facts   Revenues: $25.329B (2000) Employees: 126,000 (2000)
                   Founded: 1910 Manufacturer; military equipment; professional
                     services Public: LMT (NYSE)
Awards   Information Week: Top 500 Technology Innovators
                   Computerworld: 100 Best Places to Work in IT
Headquarters   6801 Rockledge Dr.
                   Bethesda, MD 20817-1877
                   (301) 897-6000
                   http://www.lockheedmartin.com

Job Title	Education	Experience	Skills	Location
Embedded Software Engineer	BA/BS related	2 years	Avionics, simulation, clearance	Ft. Worth, TX
Advanced Systems Engineer	BS/MS/PhD/JD	9–13 years	i2, SeeBeyond, EAI	Detroit, MI
Systems Engineer	BS EE, Math, Physics	5–8 years	U-2S sensor system, clearance	Palmdale, CA
Hardware Engineer	BA/BS related	5 years	Components engineering, CAD, clearance	Syracuse, NY
Computer Systems Analyst, Associate	BA/BS related	0 years/ Entry-level	LAN design, database management	Orlando, FL

Lockheed Martin Management & Data Systems

Fast Facts   Revenues: $25.329B Employees: 126,000 Founded: 1910
                   Professional services; satellite systems Subsidiary: Lockheed Martin
                     Corporation
Awards   Computerworld: 100 Best Places to Work in IT
Headquarters   P.O. Box 8048
                   Philadelphia, PA
                   (610) 531-7400
                   http://mds.external.lmco.com

Job Title	Education	Experience	Skills	Location
Database Analyst Senior	BA/BS related	5 years	Lotus Notes, clearance	Fairfax, VA
Software Engineering Senior Staff	BA/BS related	14 years	IBM S/390, UNIX System Services, ALC, clearance	McLean, VA
Software Engineering Senior Staff	BA/BS related	14 years	C++, Oracle, ISAPI extensions, clearance	Fairfax, VA

Systems Engineering Senior Staff	BA/BS related	14 years	Satellite communications, RF, clearance	Chantilly, VA
Embedded Software Engineer Associate	BA/BS related	0 years/ entry-level	JOVIAL, flight control,clearance	Goodyear, AZ

Lucent Technologies, Inc.

Fast Facts Revenues: $33.813B (2000) Employees: 87,000 (2001)
Founded: 1996 Manufacturer; telecommunications equipment, was Bell Labs Public: LU (NYSE)

Awards Fortune: 100 Best Companies to Work for in America
Computerworld: 100 Best Places to Work in IT

Headquarters 600 Mountain Avenue
Murray Hill, NJ 07974
(908) 582-8500
http://www.lucent.com

Job Title	Education	Experience	Skills	Location
Systems Engineer	MS or PhD EE, Physics	3 years	Optical fiber	Norcross, GA
Analog Circuit Design Engineer	BS or MS EE	5+ years	PWB, firmware, analog design	Somerset, NJ
IT Applications Programming	BS CS	3 years	PeopleSoft, Java, XML	Greensboro, NC
Portal Application/Web Developer	BS CS	2–3 years	JSP, servlets, DHTML, Peoplesoft, SEI	Warren, NJ
IT Technical Manager			Database, optical fiber	Somerset, NJ

Manugistics Group, Inc.

Fast Facts Revenues: $268M (2001) Employees: 1,451 (2001) Founded: 1969
Software; supply chain management Public: MANU (Nasdaq)

Awards Computerworld: 100 Best Places to Work in IT

Headquarters 2115 E. Jefferson St.
Rockville, MD 20852
(301) 984-5000
http://www.manugistics.com

Job Title	Education	Experience	Skills	Location
Vice President, Software Development	BS CS, Engineering, MBA preferred	10 years	Java, J2EE, UML, Corba, Oracle	Rockville, MD

Optimization Developer	BS CS, Engineering, Math	5–8 years	C++, Oracle, algorithm development	Rockville, MD
Business Consultant	BA/BS Logistics, OR	2–5 years	Measurement, supply chain	Chicago, IL
Principal Consultant		5–10+ years	Manugistics, CPFR, VMI, European languages	Bracknell, England
Application Support Consultant	BA/BS CS, MIS, Logistics	1+ years	3PLs, Oracle, Web Server, German, Polish, language	Ratingen, Germany

Mercury Interactive Corporation

Fast Facts Revenues: $307M (2000) Employees: 1,418 (2000) Founded: 1989
Software; performance testing Public: MERQ (Nasdaq)

Awards Computerworld: 100 Best Places to Work in IT
Fortune: America's Fastest Growing Companies

Headquarters 1325 Borregas Avenue
Sunnyvale, CA 94089
(408) 822-5200
http://www.merc-int.com

Job Title	Education	Experience	Skills	Location
Certification Program Manager	BA/BS preferred	3+ years	MS Office	Sunnyvale, CA
Cognos Developer	Training in CS, database certification	0 years	Decision Stream, PowerPlay, Upfront, Impromptu, Oracle 8i	Sunnyvale, CA
Systems Engineer	BS CS	3+ years	Performance monitoring	
Desktop Support Analyst	A+ certification	1–2 years	Ghost imaging, NT, Anti-virus	Sunnyvale, CA
Senior Product Marketing Manager	Technical degree or equivalent, MBA preferred		Testing/Tuning in production	Sunnyvale, CA

Microsoft Corporation

Fast Facts Revenues: $25.296B (2001) Employees: 39,100 (2001)
Founded: 1975 Software; PC applications, operating systems Public:
MSFT (Nasdaq)

Awards Fortune: 100 Best Companies to Work for in America
Forbes ASAP: Dynamic 100

Headquarters   1 Microsoft Way
Redmond, WA 98052-6399
(425) 882-8080
http://www.microsoft.com

Job Title	Education	Experience	Skills	Location
Architect	MS/PhD CS	10 years	Casbah, GPM, IIS, VS.NET	Redmond, WA
Program Manager	BA/BS or equivalent	2 years	SQL Server Engine, XML	Redmond, WA
Software Design Engineer Lead	BA/BS CS, Engineering MS preferred		OLEDB, URT, XML, Windows CE	Redmond, WA
Computational Linguist	MS+ Linguistics, CS		Natural language processing, native Spanish language	Redmond, WA
Senior Consultant II	BA/BS CS, MCSD	5+ years	VC++, SOAP, .NET, MSMQ	Bloomington, IL

MicroStrategy Incorporated

Fast Facts   Revenues: $102.05M (2000) Employees: 1,662 (1999)
Founded: 1989 Software; data mining Public: MSTR (Nasdaq)

Awards   Fortune: 100 Best Companies to Work for in America
Intelligent Enterprise: Most Influential Companies in IT

Headquarters   8000 Towers Crescent Drive
Vienna, VA 22182
(703) 848-8600
http://www.microstrategy.com

Job Title	Education	Experience	Skills	Location

No openings at this time.

Motorola, Inc.

Fast Facts   Revenues: $37.58B (2000) Employees: 147,000 (2000)
Founded: 1928 Manufacturer; communications equipment Public:
MOT (NYSE)

Awards   Industry Week: 100 Best Managed Companies
PC Magazine: 100 Most Influential Companies

Headquarters   1303 E. Algonquin Rd.
Schaumburg, IL 60196
(847) 576-5000
http://www.motorola.com

Job Title	Education	Experience	Skills	Location
Software Integration Engineer		5 years	J2ME, 3G multi-media	Libertyville, IL
Senior Microarchitect, PowerPC			Cache coherency, symmetric multiprocessor	Austin, TX
Senior Software Engineer	BS CS, EE, MS preferred	5 years	MAC/OSS Security, DOCSIS	Mansfield, MA
Senior Software Applications Engineer	BS CS	3 years	Embedded design, WAP	Hong Kong
Compiler Engineer	BS CS, EE	2+ years	RS232, C++, USB, CodeWarrior	Bucharest, Romania

National Instruments Corporation

Fast Facts	Revenues: $410.1M (2000) Employees: 2,511 (2000) Founded: 1976 Manufacturer; test and measurement equipment Public: NATI (Nasdaq)
Awards	Fortune: 100 Best Companies to Work for in America
Headquarters	11500 N. Mopac Expressway
	Austin, TX 78759-3504
	(512) 338-9119
	http://www.ni.com

Job Title	Education	Experience	Skills	Location
Analog Hardware Design Engineer	BS or MS EE	2 years	A/D, D/A converters	Austin, TX
Digital Design Engineer			VHDL, C, Assembly	Austin, TX
Senior Electrical Engineer	BS EE, CE	5 years	BIOS, C, analog design	Austin, TX
Software Engineer	BS CS, EE, CE		C/C++	Austin, TX

NCR Corporation

Fast Facts	Revenues: $5.959B (2000) Employees: 32,960 (2000) Founded: 1884 Manufacturer; financial systems equipment, ATMs Public: NCR (NYSE)
Awards	Computerworld: 100 Best Places to Work in IT
	CIO: Web Business 50/50
Headquarters	1700 S. Patterson Blvd.
	Dayton, OH 45479
	(937) 445-5000
	http://www.ncr.com

Job Title	Education	Experience	Skills	Location
Systems Integration Engineer	BS CS, Engineering, Business		IBM 4690	Raleigh, NC
Application Services—Senior Consultant		6+ years	NCR, Teradata, IBM, HP, Big 5	San Francisco, CA
IT Business Solutions Consultant	BA/BS Business, IT, Master's a plus	2–3 years	Oracle 11i, ERP	Dayton, OH
Program Manager		5 years	EBI, SCI clearance, Teradata	Rockville, MD

Network Appliance, Inc.

Fast Facts Revenues: $1.006B (2001) Employees: 1,469 (2000) Founded: 1992
Manufacturer; high-speed storage devices Public: NTAP (Nasdaq)

Awards Computerworld: 100 Best Places to Work in IT
Network World: NW 200

Headquarters 495 E. Java Drive
Sunnyvale, CA 94089
(408) 822-6000
http://www.netapp.com

Job Title	Education	Experience	Skills	Location

There are no open positions at this time.

Oracle Corporation

Fast Facts Revenues: $10.86B (2001) Employees: 42,927 (2001) Founded: 1977
Software; database management, tools Public: ORCL (Nasdaq)

Awards Industry Week: 100 Best Managed Companies
PC Magazine: 100 Most Influential

Headquarters 500 Oracle Parkway
Redwood City, CA 94065
(650) 506-7000
http://www.oracle.com

Job Title	Education	Experience	Skills	Location
Software Engineer	BS/MS CS, Engineering, Business		SQL, UNIX	Waltham, MA
Senior Applications Engineer		3+ years	JSP, XML, CRM, PL/SQL	Redwood Shores, CA

Job Title	Education	Experience	Skills	Location
Senior Application Developer			Oracle 8i, JSP, XML	Redwood Shores, CA
Senior Applications DBA/System Administrator	BS/MS IS, CS	4+ years	AOL, PL/SQL, Pro*C, JDeveloper	Redwood Shores, CA
Associate Consultant	MBA Finance	1–5 years	ERP Financials	Hyderabad, India

PRC, Inc.

Fast Facts   Revenues: $5.588B (2000) Employees: 40,300 (2000) Founded: 1954
Professional services; electronic warfare Subsidiary: Northrop
        Grumman

Awards   Computerworld: 100 Best Places to Work in IT
Information Week: Top 500 Technology Innovators

Headquarters 1500 PRC Drive
McLean, VA 22102-5050
(703) 556-1000
http://www.prc.com

Job Title	Education	Experience	Skills	Location
Application Developers			Java, Perl, Oracle, Bourne Shell, C++	Langley, McLean, or Reston, VA
Database Administrators			Informix, Lotus Notes	Langley, McLean, or Reston, VA
Computer Analysts			Lotus Notes, ARCVIEW	Langley, McLean, Reston, VA
Network Engineers			Spectrum, Cisco routers	Langley, McLean, or Reston, VA
Network Administrators			NT, UNIX, Banyan Vines	Columbia, MD

PricewaterhouseCoopers

Fast Facts   Revenues: $21.5B (2000) Employees: 150,000 (2000) Founded: 1890
Professional services; accounting; Management Consulting Services
        subsidiary, computer consulting Partnership

Awards   Computerworld: 100 Best Places to Work in IT
Information Week: Top 500 Technology Innovators

Headquarters 1301 Avenue of the Americas
New York, NY 10019
(646) 471-4000
http://www.pwcglobal.com

Job Title	Education	Experience	Skills	Location
SAP FI/CO Consultant	BA/BS	2–3 years	ASAP, A/R	Boston, MA
Principal Consultant—Strategy/ICE	MA/MS/MBA	8–15 years	Telecom, wireless	Atlanta, GA
Oracle Financials Team Lead	BA/BS	7–10 years	GL, AP, FA	Atlanta, GA
Siebel Technical Architect	Degree		Siebel	Melbourne, Australia
Information Systems Consultant	Honours degree	3 years	Oracle ERP, EDI, document management	Belfast, Ireland

QUALCOMM Incorporated

Fast Facts Revenues: $3.197B (2000) Employees: 6,300 (2000) Founded: 1985
Manufacturer; communications chips, software Public: QCOM
   (Nasdaq)

Awards Fortune: 100 Best Companies to Work for in America
Industry Week: 100 Best Managed Companies

Headquarters 5775 Morehouse Dr.
San Diego, CA 92121-1714
(858) 587-1121
http://www.qualcomm.com

Job Title	Education	Experience	Skills	Location
Digital Design Engineer (Board Level)	BSEE, CE		Microprocessor, wireless	San Diego, CA
VLSI/CAD Physical Design Methodology Engineer			C++, Cadence, Skills, Avanti	San Diego, CA
Systems Engineer (Physical Layer)	MS/PhD EE, CE		IS-95, GSM, Matlab, C++, queuing theory	San Diego, CA
Software Engineer	BS EE, CS	4 years	CDMA, SDL, 3G, GPRS	Farnborough, England
Software Engineer	BS CS, EE	1–3 years	COM, CDMA	Beijing, China

SAS Institute Inc.

Fast Facts	Revenues: $1.02B (1999) Employees: 6,400 (1999) Founded: 1976
	Software; statistical modeling, data mining Private
Awards	Intelligent Enterprise: Top 10 Companies to Work for
	Computerworld: 100 Best Places to Work in IT
Headquarters	SAS Campus Drive
	Cary, NC 27513-2414
	(919) 677-8000
	http://www.sas.com

Job Title	Education	Experience	Skills	Location
Systems Developer	BA/BS CS	5 years	JavaScript, JSP, JNDI	NC
Systems Engineer II	BA/BS CS, Business	5 years	SAS, HR Vision	NC
Systems Engineer	BA/BS CS, Business	3 years	SAS, e-Intelligence	CA, OR
Systems Application Developer	BA/BS CS	7 years	MVS, CMS, SQL, C	IL
Enterprise Performance Consultant	BA/BS	2 years	SAS IntreNET, SAS GRAPH, DataStep	TX, MO

Scientific-Atlanta, Inc.

Fast Facts	Revenues: $2.512B (2001) Employees: 10,227 (2000) Founded: 1974
	Manufacturer; telecommunications equipment, satellite, cable Public:
	SFA (NYSE)
Awards	Network World: NW 200
	Computerworld: 100 Best Places to Work in IT
Headquarters	5030 Sugarloaf Parkway
	Lawrenceville, GA 30044
	(770) 903-5000
	www.scientificatlanta.com

Job Title	Education	Experience	Skills	Location

No job openings at this time.

Silicon Graphics, Inc.

Fast Facts   Revenues: $1.854B (2001) Employees: 5,956 (2001) Founded: 1982
Manufacturer; servers, scientific/graphics workstations Public: SGI
(NYSE)

Awards   Computerworld: 100 Best Places to Work in IT
PC Magazine: 100 Most Influential

Headquarters   1600 Amphitheatre Parkway
Mountain View, CA 94043-1351
(650) 960-1980
http://www.sgi.com

Job Title	Education	Experience	Skills	Location
Engineering Department Manager II	BS/MS EE		3-D graphics, CAD-flow	Mountain View, CA
Technical Consultant II	BS CS, EE	5 years	Fortran, C, Gigabit Server Network	Chantilly, VA
MTS Design I	BS EE, CS		Chipbench/edit, Verilog, Tck/tl, Perl, Cadence	Chippewa Falls, WI
Senior MTS—Consulting Engineer	MS CS, EE	7–10 years	C, UNIX, Linux, Irix, Infinibank,	Eagan, MN
MTS Design II	MS/PhD EE, CS	3 years	ECAD, Perl, tcl, VLSI	Mountain View, CA

Solectron Corporation

Fast Facts   Revenues: $18.692B (2001) Employees: 65,273 (2000)
Founded: 1977 Manufacturer; contract electronics Public: SLR
(NYSE)

Awards   Industry Week: 100 Best Managed Companies
Forbes ASAP: Dynamic 100

Headquarters   777 Gibraltar Drive
Milpitas, CA 95035
(408) 957-8500
http://www.solectron.com

Job Title	Education	Experience	Skills	Location
Program Engineer	BS IE	3–5 years	System assembly	Memphis, TN

Sprint Corporation

Fast Facts   Revenues: $23.613B (2000) Employees: 84,100 (2000)
                   Founded: 1986 Telecomm.; local, long-distance Holding company
Awards   Computerworld: 100 Best Places to Work in IT
Headquarters   2330 Shawnee Mission Parkway
                   Westwood, KS 66205
                   (916) 624-3000
                   http://www.sprint.com

Job Title	Education	Experience	Skills	Location
Cisco Router Engineer	BS CS, EE	3–5 years	IP, IS-IS, DNS, DSU	Reston, VA
Network Design Engineer	BS CS, EE	5+ years	BGP-4, IS-IS, OSPF, EIGRP, SONET	Reston, VA
Software Engineer IV	MS CS	Experienced	WebLogic, Iplanet	Kansas City, MO
Oracle Developer	BA/BS or equivalent	3–5 years	PLSQL, VB, C++	Overland Park, KS
Technical Applications Consultant	BA/BS	Experienced	Data transport, voice application	Honolulu, Hawaii

SRA International, Inc.

Fast Facts   Revenues: $312M (2000) Employees: 1,709 (2000) Founded: 1978
                   Professional services; systems integration; software, data mining
                       Private
Awards   Fortune: 100 Best Companies to Work for in America
Headquarters   4350 Fair Lakes Court
                   Fairfax, VA 22033
                   (703) 803-1500
                   http://www.sra.com

Job Title	Education	Experience	Skills	Location
Sr. Data Analyst	BA/BS CS, Master's preferred	10 years	IDEF1X, ERWin, Visible Advantage	Arlington, VA
Sr. Telecom Security Specialist		5 years	Solaris, Cisco, HP OpenView, Perl, Oracle,	New Carrolton, MD
Sr. NetView Engineer		5 years	Tivoli, Cisco, Bay	New Carollton, MD
Computer Linguist	Degree, Linguistics, CS, with AI/NLP		Perl, speech recognition, information clustering	Fairfax, VA

Sun Microsystems, Inc.

Fast Facts   Revenues: $18.25B (2001) Employees: 38,900 (2001) Founded: 1982
Manufacturer; servers, ICs; software (Solaris, Java) Public: SUNW
(Nasdaq)

Awards   Computerworld: 100 Best Places to Work in IT
Fortune: 100 Best Companies to Work for in America

Headquarters   901 San Antonio Road
Palo Alto, CA 94303
(650) 960-1300
http://www.sun.com

Job Title	Education	Experience	Skills	Location
Pre-Sales Engineering Manager		10+ years	Sun E10K clustering, mirroring	Varies
Software Engineer	BA/BS, CS Intern experience a plus	Entry-level	UNIX, Solaris, Java, C	CA
Software Engineer	BA/BS MIS	Entry-level	Oracle, SAP, C, Java, SQL	CA
Hardware Engineer	BS EE	Entry-level	ASICs, board design, Verilog, Synopsis, C	CA

Systems & Computer Technology Corporation

Fast Facts   Revenues: $427.2M (2000) Employees: 3,400 (2000) Founded: 1968
Professional services; administrative software for universities Public:
SCTC (Nasdaq)

Awards   Computerworld: 100 Best Places to Work in IT

Headquarters   4 Country View Rd.
Malvern, PA 19355
(610) 647-5930
http://www.sctcorp.com

Job Title	Education	Experience	Skills	Location

No job listings online. Submit resume online.

TechieGold.com

Fast Facts   Revenues: $80.7M (2000/Stride) Employees: 345 (2000/Stride)
Founded: 2000 Online recruiting Private, subsidiary Stride &
Associates

Awards   Computerworld: 100 Best Places to Work in IT

Headquarters   206 Newbury Street, 3rd Floor
                      Boston, MA 02116
                      (617) 585-6500
                      http://www.techiegold.com

Job Title	Education	Experience	Skills	Location
Software Engineer			VC++, MFC, OO, embedded point-of-sale	Atlanta, GA
Senior Engineer			C/C++, MQ Series, Rational Rose, TIBCO	Harborside, NJ
Enterprise Solutions Architect		10+ years	EJB, UML, WebLogic, XML	New York, NY
Games Developer		2 years	C/C++, Playstation, XBOX	Los Angles, CA
Senior Realtime Software Engineer			C/C++, multi-threading, Solaris	Westchester, CT

Tellabs, Inc.

Fast Facts   Revenues: $3.387B (2000) Employees: 8,643 (2000) Founded: 1975
                    Telecommunications Public: TLAB (Nasdaq)
Awards   Fortune: 100 Best Places to Work in America
                    Computerworld: 100 Best Places to Work in IT
Headquarters   4951 Indiana Avenue
                    Lisle, IL 60532-1698
                    (630) 378-8800
                    http://www.tellabs.com

Job Title	Education	Experience	Skills	Location
No current IT jobs posted. Sample positions are shown below.				
Software Tools Developer	BS/MS CS, Computer Engineering	4+ years	Titan 5300, UNIX Shell, Perl, ClearCase	Lisle, IL
Systems Lead Engineer	BS CS, EE, MS preferred	10 years	CORBA, carrier telecom systems experience	Lisle, IL
Software Engineer	BS CS, MS preferred, 3.0 GPA	Entry-level	C, BGP, OSPF, ISIS, QOS, VPN	Wilmington, MA

Teradyne, Incorporated

Fast Facts Revenues: $3.044B (2000) Employees: 10,200 (2000) Founded: 1960
Manufacturer; automated test equipment for electronic gear Public:
TER (NYSE)

Awards Industry Week: 100 Best Managed Companies
PC Week: Fast-Track 500

Headquarters 321 Harrison Avenue
Boston, MA 02118
(617) 482-2700
http://www.teradyne.com

Job Title	Education	Experience	Skills	Location
Semiconductor Design Engineer	BS EE, MS preferred	3–7 years	Jaguar, Cadence, SiGe	Agoura Hills, CA
Manager Information Technology	BA/BS	6–10 years	Notes, Oracle, Web apps	Boston, MA
Hardware Engineer	BS EE	10 years	1+ GHz ATE, Analog ASIC	Agoura Hills, CA
Software Engineer	BS CS, EE or equivalent		VLSI, C++, Pascal, Bourne-Shell	Austin, TX
Field Application Engineer	BS EE		Visual Basic, UNIX, C, NT, Teradyne tester	Beijing, China

Texas Instruments, Incorporated

Fast Facts Revenues: $11.875B (2000) Employees: 42,400 (2000)
Founded: 1930s Manufacturer; integrated circuits Public: TXN
(NYSE)

Awards Computerworld: 100 Best Places to Work in IT
Fortune: 100 Best Companies to Work for in America

Headquarters 12500 TI Blvd.
Dallas, TX 75266-0199
(972) 995-3773
www.ti.com

Job Title	Education	Experience	Skills	Location
DSP Product Engineer	BS CE, EE	2 years	VLSI, ATE	Houston, TX
Wireless Applications Engineer	BS EE		3G wireless phone, real-time video streaming, C, Assembly	Dallas, TX

Wireless Embedded Systems Software Engineer	BS CS, EE	5 years	C++, DSP, EPOC, CSP/BIOS, Code Composer Studio	Dallas, TX
Programmer Analyst	BS CS	Experienced	Java, Oracle, CGI, ASP, finance	Dallas, TX
China Export Manager	BS EE, Business		TI products, Mandarin language preferred	TBD

TRW Systems and Information Technology Group

Fast Facts	TRW/Rev.: $16.969B (1999) Emp.: 122,000 (1999) Founded: 1901 Professional services; command and control systems Division of TRW, Inc.
Awards	Computerworld: 100 Best Places to Work in IT
Headquarters	12900 Federal Systems Park Drive Fairfax, VA 22033 (703) 968-1000 http://www.trw.com

Job Title	Education	Experience	Skills	Location
Software Engineer	BS CS, EE, Math	Entry-level	JDBC, ASP, Perl, XML, clearance	Fairfax, VA
Software Engineer	BA/BS Business, CS, Master's preferred	Mid-level	Oracle Financials, Joint Ineroperability Test Command	Alexandria, VA
Operations Research Analyst	BA/BS or equivalent experience	Mid-level	Electronic record-keeping, clearance	Chantilly, VA
Systems Engineer	BS CS, SE	4–6 years	Virtual knowledge database, clearance	Chantilly, VA
Computer Security Representative	BA/BS	Mid-level	Network risk analysis, clearance	Arlington, VA

Unisys Corporation

Fast Facts	Revenues: $6.885B (2000) Employees: 36,900 (2000) Founded: 1873 Manufacturer; servers; professional services; systems integration Public: UIS (NYSE)
Awards	Computerworld: 100 Best Places to Work in IT Information Week: The Top Technology Innovators

Headquarters   Unisys Way
Blue Bell, PA 19424
(215) 986-4011
http://www.unisys.com

Job Title	Education	Experience	Skills	Location
Integration Architect	BS CS, EE	10 years	SQL-Server, Oracle DBA	Malvern, PA
Network Design Engineer	BA/BS CS or equivalent experience	Experienced	FACCSM, CSRD, Sun LAN, clearance	Arlington, VA
Software Engineer		Experienced	Interdev, SourceSafe	St. Louis, MO
CICS Systems Programmer	BA/BS	Experienced	OS/390, Omegamon, DB2	Salt Lake City, UT
SAP ABAP Programmer		3 years	SAP ABAP, IDOC, ALE	Harrisburg, PA

Ventera Corporation

Fast Facts   Revenues: $8M est. (2000) Employees: 80 est. (2000)
Founded: 1996 Professional services; e-business consulting Private
Awards   Computerworld: 100 Best Places to Work in IT
Headquarters   1600 International Drive, Suite 100
McLean, VA 22102
(703) 760-4600
http://www.ventera.com

Job Title	Education	Experience	Skills	Location
Systems Architect	BA/BS CS, Engineering	Experienced	J2EE	
Database Administrator	BA/BS CS, Engineering	6 years	n-tier Internet application, SQL	
Senior Network Engineer	BA/BS CS, Engineering	Experienced	Firewall, intrusion detection, PKI	

WRQ, Incorporated

Fast Facts   Revenues: $150M (2000) Employees: 722 (2000) Founded: 1981
Software; integrate legacy, client-server, Internet platforms Private
Awards   Fortune: 100 Best Companies to Work for in America
Headquarters   1500 Dexter Avenue North
Seattle, WA 98109
(206) 217-7100
http://www.wrq.com

Job Title	Education	Experience	Skills	Location
Software Developer	BS CS or equivalent	5 years	UML, Java, C++, internationaliza-tion	Seattle, WA
Software Developer—X Windows/NFS			Reflection X, C++, networking security	Washington

Xilinx, Incorporated

Fast Facts   Revenues: $1.659B (2001) Employees: 2,678 (2001) Founded: 1984
Manufacturer; integrated circuits, FPGA Public: XLNX (Nasdaq)
Awards   Interactive Week: The Internet 500
Fortune: 100 Best Companies to Work for in America
Headquarters 2100 Logic Drive
San Jose, CA 95124
(408) 559-7778
http://www.xilinx.com

Job Title	Education	Experience	Skills	Location

No current openings. Accepting resumes.

Chapter Three

On the Bottom Line

This chapter profiles companies that buy and use computers to support another main-line business. They are customers for companies in the technical industry. Almost any company of any size in today's world depends on computers. Companies depend on computers to hold vital corporate information, such as customer, accounting, and product data. They use computers to help communicate with their customers and with their own employees. Most have added an online component to their business. Customer companies employ more technical professionals than the vendors that supply technology products, by almost two to one.

What does this mean for technical professionals when they are looking for jobs? It means that at some point in their careers, they are probably going to work for a company that buys and uses technology. These companies need experts to deploy, enhance, and integrate software, and to develop technical solutions to their business problems.

Career Path

In general, technical expertise is deeper at a customer company. There are two reasons for this. One, already mentioned in Chapter Two, is that customers, dealing with real world problems, have to wrestle with a generic product until it solves a problem. This may mean developing interfaces, patches, or separate code, but it rarely means changing the business to fit the product. Second, techies working in customer companies typically stay in technical positions longer, developing a deeper understanding of a product under a variety of conditions. While techies at vendor companies have to understand at a high-level how their product works with various hardware and software configurations, techies at customer companies must make technical products work reliably in their unique circumstances. Career satisfaction comes from stretching technology in new and interesting ways. Further, it is these discoveries that help drive product development as customers report back to vendors what the next generation should include.

The technical career path in a customer's environment is different from that in a vendor's environment. For one thing, companies have varying levels of commitment to the use of technology. Thus, while one company may invest a significant share of its revenues in technology, another may view technology as simply a cost. Companies also disagree on the level of technical expertise they need. Some have a dual technical/management career path. Others encourage techies to enter management ranks at the project or program level. The following list shows the typical career path for techies at a customer company:

- Functional expert (Programmer, Analyst, Specialist)
- Project Manager
- Program Manager
- Group Manager
- Vice President/Technical Fellow

Until recent layoffs dug deep into employee ranks, IT positions were typically protected during business downturns—in recognition of the critical nature of IT infrastructure.

Companies also recognize that in order to attract top technical talent they have to compete not just with interesting work, but with comparable salaries. Some companies have gone so far as to spin off their technical services division into a separate company, so as to pay competitive salaries while not disrupting salary conventions at the parent company.

Enjoy reading about companies that use technology to drive their business success and help define what the next generation of products will look like!

AFLAC, Inc.

"Our Open Image application, merging encrypted signatures with digital forms, is bleeding edge technology and we've had it for five years."

– Lynn Fry
– Vice President, Information Technology

• **IBM CMOS 9672/R46, Server farm with 160 NT-based Compaqs** •
• **COBOL, Visual Basic, ADABAS, SQL-Server** •
• **Insurance • Large shop** •

Technology to solve real-world business problems. Ahead of its time in developing imaging solutions integrating digital signatures with business forms, AFLAC has continued to roll out programs using advanced technology to support its leadership position in supplemental insurance. Integrated voice response (IVR), workflow processing, and imaging in a server farm/mainframe backend configuration supports a 4,000 strong field sales force.

What kind of person does it take to manage this dual role of advancing technology's limits while keeping a practical eye on business requirements? Fry answers, "We look for people with strong technical skills who are consensus builders. We want people who advocate change but are also able to work in a large organization and get things done." What is Fry's favorite Internet site? "Our intranet site has all our employees listed, with their phone numbers and photos, so if you see someone's name on a memo that you don't know, you can pull up their picture."

AFLAC is wild for the Atlanta Falcons, even offering special food in the company cafeteria during football season honoring their favorite team. Asked what their most successful recruiting event has been, Amy Cox, Senior Corporate Recruiter, responded, "We have lost a lot of employees to consulting firms. Now, they are coming back. We keep in touch with an active referral program."

Surprise benefit: a free balloon on your birthday.

Fast Facts	Revenues: $9.72B (2000)
	Employees: 5,015 (2000)
	Founded: 1955
	Supplementary insurance
	Public: AFL (NYSE)
Awards	Fortune 500 (#205)
	Computerworld: Best Companies to Work For in IT (2000)
	Fortune: Best Companies to Work for in America (1999, 2000)
	Information Week: e-Business 100 (1999)
	Latina: Best Companies for Latinas to Work For

Headquarters   1932 Wynnton Rd.
Columbus, GA 31999
(706) 323-3431
www.aflac.com

Business

AFLAC, Inc., a holding company for AFLAC (American Family Life Assurance Company of Columbus) offers supplemental insurance designed to provide its policyholders cash payments for expenses generally not covered by major medical insurance policies. This could include co-payment obligations, payment for the use of physicians outside a medical plan's coverage, travel expenses to reach treatment centers, continued salaries after medical coverage ends, nursing home or in-home care, even long-distance phone calls associated with care.

AFLAC was founded in 1955 and was among the first to offer an insurance policy for cancer treatment expenses. Brothers John, Paul, and Bill Amos started the company, offering insurance policies in Georgia and Alabama to start, then throughout the Southeastern United States. In 1974, AFLAC initiated service in Japan, introducing that country's first supplemental insurance policy for cancer expenses. Today, AFLAC leads the insurance industry in supplemental insurance coverage in the United States, typically through payroll deductions at employers' sites. It ranks first among foreign insurance companies in Japan, which accounts for 80 percent of its sales.

AFLAC's corporate presence can be felt in its commitment to a variety of organizations involved in efforts against cancer. A sample of community projects includes sponsorship for the Don Imus' Ranch for Children, the AFLAC Cancer Center at Children's Healthcare of Atlanta, endowment of a chair for cancer research at the USC/Norris Comprehensive Cancer Center in Los Angeles, and support for the Ronald McDonald House.

AFLAC has more than 5,000 employees, including 2,300 at corporate headquarters. It insures more than 40 million people. A favorite of both small investors and Wall Street, returns to investors have been at the average annual rate of 27.2% over the last ten years. Its management was recently described by The Wall Street Transcript as one of the best in the insurance industry. AFLAC recently bought two of its competitors, Colonial and Providence, and exceeds the market share of its other competitors, including UNUM, Conseco and Aon.

Technology

AFLAC's technical environment includes an IBM CMOS 9672/R476, 160 Compaq NT servers, and 2,000 PCs in a client-server environment. Development on the mainframe is generally in COBOL and a little Assembler, with CICS, TSO, ADABAS, Natural, and Easytrieve. Development on the client-server side is generally in Visual Basic or C++, using Microsoft's COMTI to access the mainframe with DNA architecture, in a distributed communications environment, that includes Cisco communications hardware. Additional software used includes Crystal Reports, a report generation tool; DMS GT, a screen mapper, SQL-Server, to manage the server plantation; and SQL-Time, for inventory. Additional tools used include Expediter and Visual Studio.

Four thousand Panasonic laptops are used to support the field sales force with automation tools like the Open Image application. Each laptop is connected to a pen tablet that collects digital signatures, encrypts them, and transmits them via modem to Open Image (from Eastman Imaging System), which resides on a host server. There, the signature is married to the appropriate form in an application. Additional sample projects include the development of an interactive voice response (IVR) system to let agents check on the status of new policies. This was developed using tools from Lucent Technology and Conversant. The company recently implemented a correspondence workflow system that scans and indexes incoming mail, integrating all correspondence from each policyholder. A link to the database retrieves policyholder coverage data, which is presented to a clerk answering the inquiry, along with the correspondence. Skills needed to answer the request are rated in a 7-point system on the way in and assigned to the correspondence, so it can be queued and routed to someone with the appropriate skills for processing. The screens for this application were developed in Visual Basic. Eastman imaging software was used for scanning and digitizing the correspondence. Robots were written in C++ to direct images, update the ADABAS database, connect to an SQL-Server backend, generate error reports, match up correspondence with error reports and re-introduce the correspondence into a queue for re-work. COBOL was used for development on the mainframe side. The project took 12 months and 14 people.

Culture

Corporate facilities include an onsite acute care clinic and daycare center as well as a wellness program. Employees can earn points toward prizes like water bottles and t-shirts through various health-oriented activities like using walking trails or getting a mammogram or blood pressure screening. The company has arranged a number of discount programs with local merchants for flowers, dry cleaning, movies, and cars. The company celebrates football Friday in honor of the Atlanta Falcons, inviting employees to wear Falcon memorabilia and go to a pep rally. The company sets aside one week a year as employee appreciation week, and offers treats throughout the year, like free popcorn and ice cream days. There is a formal Christmas party and company-sponsored teams for basketball, tennis, bowling, and volleyball. All employees are eligible for stock options.

As might be expected, AFLAC pays for supplemental insurance for its employees. It also offers the traditional menu of optional benefits that includes major medical, dental and vision, insurance, group life, accidental death, and disability insurance. There are 401(k) and profit-sharing plans, with the company contributing a portion to the 401(k). Ten company holidays are observed, and employees have a pool of 16 to 26 personal time off (PTO) days to cover needs for illness and vacation. There have never been any layoffs.

Dress is business casual during the week, and casual, with jeans and tennis shoes allowed, on Fridays. Employees work in cubicles, with Assistant Director and above claiming private offices. Official hours are 8:30 AM to 5:30 PM. A typical week is 45 hours or less, but could soar to 80 hours during critical projects. There is a rotation schedule for oncall duties. Travel requirements are limited. Telecommuting is an option, but with only 3 of 360 people invoking the privilege, it is still rare. Commuting, for most, however, is a short ten minutes.

Candidates

There are 360 technical professionals at AFLAC, all working in the Information Technology division, supporting applications for the company's other divisions, which include Marketing, Client Services, Claims, and Finance. The company has a dual technical/management career path. On the technical side, there are careers in both development and systems programming. The career path on the developer's track includes Programmer Trainee; Programmer; Programmer Analyst I, II; Senior Programmer Analyst; and Systems Consultant I, II, III. A Systems Consultant III is at the same level as Team Leader. The management path continues to Assistant Director, Director, Second Vice President, Vice President, and Senior Vice President/CIO.

AFLAC hired 100 technical professionals in the last year and expects to hire 110 in the next year, to sustain a 20 percent growth rate. Turnover is around 12 percent. They rarely hire entry-level professionals. Candidates are found through advertisements (25 percent), employment agencies (25 percent), contacts (20 percent; there is a bonus for employee referrals), unsolicited resumes (20 percent), online recruiting (5 percent), and college recruiting (5 percent). AFLAC has a few contract programmers on staff and occasionally out-sources a turnkey project, but, in general, most work is handled with its own staff.

Team players with a strong technical background and good interpersonal skills summarize AFLAC's requirements for technical professionals. A college degree is a benefit, but the focus is on technical skills. Current staff members have an average of seven years of experience and range in education from high school diplomas to Ph.D. degrees. Reflecting its emphasis on building highly technical solutions to real-world business problems, staff members must have the ability to communicate technical issues to a non-technical audience.

Recent Job Listings

Job Title	Education	Experience	Skills	Location
Programmer/ Analyst II	AA/AS CS	3 years	Visual Interdev, VB, ASP, SQL Server	Field Force Automation Development
Sr. Programmer Analyst	BA/BS	3 years	COBOL, Easytrieve, DB2, VSAM, JCL, Assembler	Corporate Systems Development
Technical Project Consultant	BA/BS CS	5 years	C++, COM/ DCOM, VB, SQL Server, MTS	Client Application Development
Systems Consultant	BA/BS	4 years	COBOL, Assembler, Easytrieve, DB2, CICS, Natural, Active X Components	ISD Marketing
Sr. Systems Consultant	BA/BS	6 years	SQL Server, SMS, SNA, ActiveX, MQ Series	NT Platform Services

Contact

Web: www.aflac.com
Job line: (800) 522-0011
Include "Source: Covin's Guide" on your resume and cover letter.

BOSE Corporation

"Honesty and integrity are non-negotiable."

– Rob Ramrath
– Director, Corporate Information Services

- HP servers and desktops, Windows NT, UNIX -
- SAP, Oracle, Microsoft IIS -
- Audio equipment manufacturer - Large shop -

It's the music. In the 1950s, Dr. Amar Bose, then a graduate student at MIT, decided to buy a new stereo system. He was disappointed to find that speakers with impressive technical specifications failed to produce the realism of a live performance. Puzzled, Bose began to study the problem, which led to an exhaustive research project into psychoacoustics, the relationship between actual sound and reproduced sound as perceived by the human ear. Bose eventually went on to become a professor at MIT, where he still teaches a course in acoustics. In 1964, he formed Bose® Corporation. The company began as a small research organization, and is now, thirty-six years later, a leading innovator in sound reproduction technology and a manufacturer of quality audio products.

Big sound in small packages. Simplicity and elegance of design. Easy-to-use. Bose applies these goals when it re-invests 100 percent of its profits back into research and development and growth.

A few highlights from the company's list of technology awards illustrate Bose's penchant for technical innovation:

- Technical Innovation Award from *Discover Magazine* for Auditioner® audio demonstration technology (1995)
- Inventor of the Year (1987) for Dr. Bose and Dr. William Short from the Intellectual Properties Owners Association for their acoustic waveguide technology.
- Best of What's New from *Popular Science*, for the Wave® radio.

Surprise address: The Mountain.

Fast Facts	Revenues: $1.1B (2000)
	Employees: 6,000 (2000)
	Founded: 1964
	Manufacturer; audio equipment
	Private
Awards	Forbes 500 (#220)
	Computerworld: 100 Best Places to Work in IT (2000)
	CIO: CIO 1000 (1994)
Headquarters	The Mountain
	Framingham, MA 01701-9168
	(508) 879-7330
	www.bose.com

Business

Bose sets itself apart from its competition by demonstrating excellence in innovation, setting standards in the audio industry with a number of breakthroughs. With a research and development staff that is proportionately the largest in the industry, Bose creates products that combine simplicity and small size.

Some of its innovative technologies and their associated products include:

- Delco-GM/Bose music system. This was the first system customized for the acoustics of an automobile.
- Acoustic waveguide technology incorporated in the Acoustic Wave® music system, the first complete high-fidelity stereo in one small, portable case. This technology is also included in the Wave radio.
- Acoustimass speaker technology incorporated in Virtually Invisible® speaker systems. These were the first systems, consisting of a bass module and cube speakers, that made the high fidelity component nearly invisible.
- Auditioner audio demonstration technology gives people the ability to hear what a space will sound like before it is built.
- Acoustic Noise-Cancelling® headset technology incorporated into a family of Bose aviation headsets. These are the first headsets that reproduce speech and music with high fidelity while reducing unwanted cabin noise in an airplane.

Products range from the company's original 901® Direct/Reflecting® speaker, which mimics the sound of a live concert by reflecting 89 percent of the sound off walls, to its Pro Loudspeakers, designed exclusively for professional musicians. Bose introduced factory-installed, customized car speakers in 1982, and now many of the world's luxury automobiles feature Bose speakers, including Mercedes Benz, Cadillac, and Corvette. In 1986, the company introduced speaker cube arrays to fill a room with sound and in 1989, its Acoustic Noise-Cancelling headsets for pilots and ground crew. The Auditioner demonstration system allows architects and engineers to test how a room will sound, from blueprints, before it is built. Bose sound systems can be found in stadiums and auditoriums, cars and spacecraft, on stage and at home. Its five divisions are the Home Audio Division, the Automotive Systems Division, the Professional Systems Division, the Noise Reduction Technology Group, and the Direct Marketing Group.

Technology

Hewlett Packard servers and desktops and Windows NT and UNIX operating systems are standard. Application packages and the development tools that come with them include SAP for Enterprise Resource Planning (ERP), PeopleSoft for Human Resources, i2 for factory planning, CA-MANMAN for factory floor production, Hyperion for reporting, Oracle and SQL for database management, HP OpenView for systems monitoring, and Ecotools for database monitoring.

The company has 2,500 PCs at corporate headquarters, and an additional 1,000 at various sites around the world. Communications gear includes Mytel and Lucent phone switches, Lucent Automated Call Distribution (ACD) and Octel's voice mail system.

Bose's recent expansion of its SAP system added general ledger, sales order management, and finished goods inventory functions. More than seventy Bose retail stores will use SAP's retail management component. Web site sales go directly to the SAP system, using Microsoft's COM/DCOM connector and Transaction Server to map distributed objects to SAP's Business Application Protocol Interface (BAPI). New technology being deployed or investigated includes a storage area network system (SAN) for SAP, Microsoft's Systems Management Service for centralized control and remote PC software installations, and the convergence of PC, telephone, and email systems.

Culture

The corporate headquarters of Bose is located on one of the highest elevations in the Framingham area, and affords a view of downtown Boston from the suburbs. There are four Bose buildings in the Framingham Technology Center, including a dedicated facility for research and development engineering, and a facility for manufacturing. Staff members work in private cubicles and private offices.

Benefits include various medical, dental, and vision plans, a fully funded retirement plan, a 401(k) plan with a company match, and credit union. Disability and life insurance are available, as well as employee assistance, adoption benefits, tuition reimbursement, and domestic partner programs. The company subsidizes memberships to fitness centers and offers employee discounts on all of its products, as well as discounts on products at partner companies for automobiles, personal computers, and Disney parks. Social activities include holiday parties, a summer outing, and golf and softball leagues. Recognition programs at both the corporate level and the department level reward employees for exemplary performance. Employees are reviewed annually and are eligible for merit increases and participation in the corporate bonus program.

Dress is business casual. The company's workday is 8:15 AM TO 5:00 PM. Flexible work hours, part-time work hours, telecommuting and alternate work schedules, such as 9/80 and 4/10 are options. A 45-hour workweek is average. Travel requirements depend on the position.

Candidates

Combining both a distributed and centralized information technology (IT) model, Bose employs130 information technology professionals at corporate headquarters, and another 60 worldwide. Channel-specific application areas, like the Direct Marketing Group, keep their own IT units. Developers generally have a Bachelor's or Master's degree and five to twenty years of experience. Job titles are casual, but there are specialists in networks, systems administration, SAP, data center operations, and database applications.

Bose hired 60 information systems professionals in the last year, plus an additional 15 software engineers. Five of these were for entry-level positions. They expect to hire 50 in the next year. Additional engineering positions include those for electrical, chemical, mechanical, and materials engineers. Candidates are found through employee referrals (30 percent; there is a bonus program for referrals), online recruiting (30 percent), employment agencies (30 percent), and unsolicited resumes (10 percent).

A minimum of a Bachelor's degree is typical for salaried positions and an interest in the industry is common. As Ramrath says, "This company is engineering driven. We have a passion for both excellence and innovation, as we continually seek to develop new technologies and products that bring benefits to consumers' lives." And, in a tribute to a company that has almost as many direct marketing awards as product awards, Bose looks for candidates who are very customer-focused.

Recent Job Listings

Job Title	Education	Experience	Skills	Location
Software Engineer	BS CS or eqivalent		Matlab, C, C++, DSP, Java, Perl, audio data acquisition	Framingham, MA
O/S Administrator II	BS CS	5+ years	HP 3000 MPE, HP 9000 UNIX	Framingham, MA
Siebel Configurator	BS CS	3–5 years	PL/SQL, C, C++, Siebel Tools E-Script, Java, Javascript, VBScript	Framingham, MA
Embedded Software Engineer	BS EE, CS	5 years	C, assembler for embedded real-time applications, C++, MPEG video encode/decode, digital audio, RISC, CISC	Framingham, MA
Embedded Software Engineer, Team Lead	BS EE, CS, Master's desirable	7–10 years	Project team leader	Framingham, MA

Contact

Web: www.bose.com/careers
Email: jobs@bose.com
Include "Source: CG0900" on your resume and cover letter.

CITIGROUP Inc.

"We operate a huge Sun network on the trading floor; we are one of Sun's largest clients and we have one of the largest IBM mainframe installations in the country."

– Mel Taub
– Senior Executive Vice President, Salomon Smith Barney
– CIO, Global Corporate and Investment Bank (GCIB)

"We look for people with scars on their backs, who have managed projects with substance, communicating across sophisticated disciplines."

– David Halpin
– Vice President, Global Information Systems
– Citigroup Business Services

- **IBM mainframes, HP UNIX, Suns** •
- **COBOL, DB2, UDB, C, C++, Java, Tivoli** •
- **Financial services** • **Large shop** •

Global financial network. Banking (Citibank). Insurance (Traveler's). Investment brokerage (Salomon Smith Barney). Mutual funds (Primerica Financial). Largest credit card issuer in the world (Mastercard, Diner's Club). First to introduce ATMs on a large scale. First to introduce compound interest to consumers. First to offer unsecured personal loans to consumers. And, it all rests on technology. Walter B. Wriston, President, then Chair, of Citibank from 1967 to 1984 believed, "The basis for wealth has evolved from land to labor to information. " Underlining this belief, Wriston said, "Information about money is as important as money itself." Citigroup's technological infrastructure supports this contention. The corporate banking unit alone has 8,500 MIPS in processing power, with a distributed environment that spans the largest IBM mainframes available, along with Compaq, HP, Digital, and Sun servers, and 75,000 PCs.

Wireless cell phone Internet ordering, with Diner's Club cards. Pilot the concept in Japan, where almost ten percent of the country's cell phones are Internet-enabled. Then roll it out globally. As the country's largest financial services company, Citigroup now serves 100 million clients in 100 countries, and it continues to rely on technology to extend its services.

Surprise benefit: Owns a volleyball court a block from its offices, right off Wall Street.

Fast Facts	Revenues: $111.826 (2000)
	Employees: 230,000 (1999)
	Founded: 1812
	Financial services; banking, insurance, credit cards, investment services
	Public: C (NYSE)
Awards	Fortune 500 (#7)
	Information Week: Top 500 (1998)
	Computerworld: Top 100 (1998)

Headquarters   153 E. 53rd Street
New York, NY 10043
(212) 559-1000
www.citigroup.com

Business

Citigroup's history began in 1812 with the founding of a new bank for the merchants and industrialists of New York City. With revolutionary programs to help small investors, like checking accounts with no minimum balance, and compounded interest savings accounts, Citibank was the largest bank in New York by 1893 and the largest in the United States by 1894. Its innovations were not only in financial services. In addition to its successful introduction of ATM technology, in 1985 the bank introduced Direct Access, linking its customers through their personal computers at home or in the office. A year later, it introduced touch-screen ATMs.

Some history may be helpful. Citibank bought Diner's Club in 1981. Primerica Financial, a mutual fund firm, bought Smith Barney in 1987 and combined it with Shearson Lehman in 1993. In 1993, Primerica also bought Traveler's Insurance. In 1997, it acquired Salomon, Inc., combining it with Smith Barney. In 1998, Traveler's and Citibank merged to become Citigroup. Competitors like Bank of America, Chase Manhattan, and Merrill Lynch in banking and brokerage services, or AIG in insurance, or American Express in credit cards, do not have the breadth of financial services that Citigroup offers, nor the geographic reach.

Technology

IBM mainframes support the company's technical infrastructure. HPs, Suns, DECs, and Compaqs represent the server side. The Business Services group has 70 NT servers and 600 workstations, connected over T3 lines. GCIB has 75,000 PCs, including 30,000 servers. Development in Business Services is in C, C++, COBOL, Java, Oracle, Sybase and OLAP products. GCIB uses these languages and tools, in a DB2 environment, along with Visual Basic, Active Server Pages (ASP), JavaScript, Visual Interdev, Java Swing, and Universal Database (UDB). Additional packages used in Business Services include McCormack and Dodge, Flexi, Essbase, Cognos, and Powerplay.

The company was an early adopter of wireless email systems such as the Blackberry. It has connected Palm Pilots and video servers for daily information broadcasts and training to the desktops of its 11,000 financial consultants in 5,000 offices. Business Services' current technology initiatives center around web portals and single-point authentication. GCIB has installed an IBM text-to-voice system for its visually impaired financial consultants and is installing imaging technology so its overseas clients can review and track documents, such as a letter of credit, scanned in at another branch.

A sample project for Business Services includes the 500,000 lines of code toolkit that re-engineered all regulatory filings for Y2K. This was written in C, using Crystal Reports, the ERWin data modeling tool, and Oracle. A GCIB sample project involves managing the employee stock option program for Microsoft's employees who have an icon on their screens that shows them the value of their options, how many are vested, and a button to exercise them and send a check to their bank account. On another project, the company's retail investors can access a web site, which now has 8 million hits a day, to view real and virtual portfolios, get research, communicate with their financial consultant, buy and sell equities and mutual funds, and do option trading. For this application, staff members are porting the software from IBM S7As (AIX) to IBM mainframes for the backend and Sun web servers on the front end, under DB2.

Culture

In New York City, technical professionals work at 399 Park Avenue 10022 (212-559-1000). In Tampa, Florida, where Business Services is based, offices are at 3800 Citibank Way, 33607. In New York city, offices are in a high-rise building. Outside of New York, offices are typically in campus settings. As Halpin notes, "I am looking at palm trees." Technical staff members at all sites typically work in private cubicles. Dress, for the most part, is business casual, although for some groups in New York with more client interface, dress is business formal. New Yorkers average 40 hours a week, peaking to 50 as needed, with flextime and PCs at home. Outside New York, the workweek averages 50 hours a week, also with PCs at home. Travel represents 15 to 20 percent of a staff member's time. A twenty-minute commute in Florida is average, while an hour in New York is common.

Benefits include medical and dental plans and a wealth-building program with stock options for all employees. Citigroup announced a 4-for-3 stock split in August, 2000.The company observes 10 holidays and offers 12 sick days. Social activities include company-sponsored basketball and soccer teams, as well as volunteer walks for juvenile diabetes and MS. In 1998, as part of the merger with Traveler's, Citigroup laid off 10,000 employees. They were given two weeks of severance for each year of service and outplacement services, such as help in resume writing and interviewing.

Candidates

Citigroup has 5,000 technical professionals worldwide. This includes 3,000 in New York, 2,200 in Hartford, Connecticut, 200 in Florida, and 500 at the company's software subsidiary in India. Business Services handles three functional areas: worldwide consumer services, worldwide corporate banking, and middle office services that cross departmental boundaries, such as real estate, human resources, credit exposure by country, and trading rooms across the company. Most technical professionals in Business Services have a Master's degree, and an average of five years of experience. In GCIB experience ranges from zero to twenty-five years, with a Bachelor's degree the average level of education. The career path includes Programmer, Programmer Analyst, Systems Analyst, Project Manager, Area Manager/Technical Consultant, Department Manager/Senior Technical Consultant, Division Manager, and CIO.

Citigroup hired 600 technical professionals for GCIB and 100 for its Business Services Group in the past year. Top schools for GCIB recruiting include Rutgers, Stevens, Stonybrooke, and New York University (NYU). Says Peggy Corrigan, Vice President, and Manger of Technical Staffing, for GCIB, "We look for college recruits who are eager not arrogant. Our managers are incentivized to help people grow; our career mobility program is a differentiator in the industry."

Business Services rarely hires entry-level candidates. Turnover ranges from 12 to 16 percent. In addition to relevant technical skills, experience in the financial industry is valued. Says Halpin, "People usually have dual backgrounds. It helps to understand the language." Adds Taub, "We look for team players who can show a record of accomplishment." Continues Taub, "We are all tied to everyone's success. We encourage people to communicate openly and help others. Problems don't age well." Candidates are found through employee referrals (29 percent), internal transfers (15 percent), and a combination of open houses, advertising, college recruiting, and online recruiting.

Recent Job Listings

Job Title	Education	Experience	Skills	Location
Programmer/ Analyst	BS CS	5+ years	DB2, CICS, Xerox PUNT, SDFII, VB, C, Intertest	Chicago, IL (Citibank)
Group Manager, e-Commerce Product Support	BS CS, CE, MS a plus	10 years	UNIX, Solaris, Java, JDBC, RMI, JSP, C++, Oracle	Jacksonville, FL (Citibank)
Sr. Systems Engineer			LDAP, SQL, Perl, Java, C	New York, NY (Salomon Smith Barney)
Analyst Developer			Sybase 11/12, C, C++, Uniface, Crystal Reports	New York, NY (Citigroup)
Sr. Oracle DBA	BA/BS	7+ years	Oracle Financials, Enterprise Data Warehouse, Portal, Kintana, Constellar, BMC SqlBacktrack	Tampa, FL (Citigroup)
Information Engineer		8+ years	VB, Visual C++, SQL Server, .NET, insurance experience	Hartford, CT (Travelers)
Information Systems Developer		3–5 years	Java 1.x, Swing, multi-threading	Hartford, CT (Travelers)
IT Business Requirements Specialist		3 years	COBOL, DB2, IMS, Endevor, Viasoft, StarTool, Lotus Notes	Hartford, CT (Travelers)

Contact

Web: www.citigroup.com
Email: david.halpin@citicorp.com
Phone: (813) 604-2090 (David Halpin)
Include "Source: Covin's Guide" on your resume and cover letter.

FIRST TENNESSEE NATIONAL CORPORATION

"Because we strive to bring a people approach to systems, you have the opportunity to develop creative solutions with a variety of technology. We are small enough that technical professionals have an opportunity to be involved in many different types of technology."

– Pat Ruckh
– Executive Vice President and Chief Technology Officer

• IBM mainframes, Sun Solaris •
• Visual Basic, COBOL, DB2, Oracle, IIS, Java •
• Financial services • Large shop •

Banking with a family-friendly corporation. First Tennessee National Corporation, one of the fifty largest bank holding companies in the United States, operates chiefly through its subsidiaries, First Tennessee Bank National Association and First Horizon.

First Tennessee budgets one to two percent of its pre-tax income for community investment. Projects include:

- Building for the Future, a program that teaches carpentry to minimum-security inmates to construct houses for community development
- Lesson Line, a free home-to-school messaging service available to teachers and principals to keep parents informed about homework assignments and upcoming tests. Nearly 700 schools receive around four million calls a year in this program.
- 30,000 volunteer hours from employees in community programs
- First Tennessee Housing Corporation which has renovated a long-vacant property and converted it to apartment buildings and converted a closed school into elderly housing with a daycare center.

The First Tennessee Foundation is giving $250,000 to relief efforts in the wake of the September 11, 2001 tragedies. Said Jim Hughes, First Tennessee Capital Markets CEO, "We lost many friends on Wall Street, people who shared their tremendous expertise with us, and this is one small way we can celebrate the lives they shared with us."

Surprise benefit: 93% of employees work on flexible schedules.

Fast Facts	Revenues: $2.426B (2000)
	Employees: 9,445 (2000)
	Founded: mid-1800s
	Financial services; banking
	Public: FTN (NYSE)
Awards	Fortune: 100 Best Companies to Work For in America #40 (2001, fourth year in a row)
	Forbes: Best of the Web (2001)

CIO: CIO 100 (1999)
Forbes: Most Profitable Banking Co. (fourth year in a
    row)
Working Mother: 100 Best Companies for Working
    Mothers (2001, sixth year in a row)
Business Week: Top 30 Family-Friendly Companies
    (1997)
Headquarters   165 Madison Ave.
Memphis, TN 38103
(901) 523-4444
http://www.ftb.com

Business

First Tennessee provides an array of financial services, including:

- Retail and commercial banking through 400 facilities in Tennessee, Arkansas, and Mississippi
- Insurance, investments, and consumer finance, including managing assets for high net worth individuals and investment and trusts for employee benefit plans
- Credit cards, including consumer and business cards, travel and purchasing cards
- Underwriting for government securities
- Transaction processing for automated teller machines in nine states
- Mortgage banking in 32 states, helping to provide homeownership for more than 460,000 customers.

First Tennessee has one of the highest customer retention rates in the country. They are the largest Tennessee-based credit card issuer. They lead the industry in credit card transaction processing for stores.

First Tennessee has almost 10,000 employees, with 3,000 at corporate headquarters in Memphis.

Technology

First Tennessee's hardware environment is based on IBM mainframes and Sun Solaris platforms. Languages used include C, C++, Visual Basic and Java, as well as COBOL II and Assembler. Additional software on the mainframe includes CICS, DB2, Focus, Easytrieve, VSAM, and Fileaid. In addition, the bank uses software ranging from Hogan and Bravo to ARGO, Oracle, ASP, Java Server Pages, EJBs, COM, DCOM, Linux, and IIS.

Among its online banking initiatives, First Tennessee recently allied with eScout.com, a web-based marketplace for independent businesses and banks. Designed to reduce procurement costs by making the economies of large-scale transactions available to small businesses in pooled purchases, eScout.com also streamlines the procurement process. First Tennessee was named one of Forbes' Best of the Web banking sites, noted for its easy user interface and sixteen months of transaction history. The company uses speech recognition on its corporate telephone system so that callers can say the name of the person they want to speak with and be directed to that person's phone or request the balance in their account or a record of their most recent transactions.

Culture

First Tennessee's headquarters are in a moderate size office building in downtown Memphis. Its Irving, Texas location is in a suburban campus setting outside of Dallas. Employees work in cubicles.

Vacation starts at two weeks after one year and increases to three weeks after five years and four weeks after fifteen years. Medical, dental, short- and long-term disability, and life insurance options are available. First Tennessee provides life insurance and, after one year, matches half of an employee's contribution to their 401(k) plan. Employees are eligible for discounts on installment and mortgage loans. All employees are eligible for stock options. Says Ruckh, "Our biggest recruiting draw is that the company is very employee-focused and we have a family-oriented culture. Our size gives candidates visibility so there is great opportunity for reward and recognition."

Dress is business casual, with khaki pants and polo shirts the most common. Average commuting time in Memphis is 20 minutes; in Irving 30–45 minutes. First Tennessee has positioned itself as an employer of choice with its flexible work schedules, including compressed work weeks, work-from-home, reduced time, and part time with full benefits options. Telecommuting is not common, but is allowed as an option on some projects, with management approval.

Hours are from 8 AM to 5 PM. While most people do not travel as part of their jobs, managers may travel up to 20 to 30 percent of the time. The company makes marginal adjustments to employee levels, laying off fewer than one percent of its staff a year, and offers healthy severance benefits when positions are eliminated.

Candidates

First Tennessee has 400 technical professionals. Half are in Memphis, the corporate headquarters; half at First Horizon in Irving, Texas. Job titles range from Trainee and Systems Engineer to Team Lead, Department Manager, Division Manager, and Chief Information Officer. There are both technical and management tracks, with Systems Engineers 1–6, where a Senior Systems Engineer is at the sixth level. The current technical staff, on average, have Bachelor's degrees in a technical discipline and 10 years of experience.

Technical candidates are found through online recruiting sites (monster.com, dice.com) and employee referrals. Candidates should have at least a Bachelor's degree in a technical field. Currently, candidates should have a minimum of two years of experience. Says Kristin Sidaway, Staffing Specialist, "We will be developing a new program for entry-level folks. They will have to have a Bachelor's degree and a 3.0 GPA." Continues Sidaway, "We are working on an internship program now, which will start in the Spring (2002)."

Intangible qualities important for candidates include a customer focus, a team orientation, the ability to juggle several projects, and the flexibility to handle change. Says Sidaway, "Our culture is to go above and beyond, so we look for candidates that can help our business partners think through things. These are people with good technical ability who can also understand the needs of non-technical folks."

Pre-employment screening at First Tennessee includes drug and background checks, with fingerprints.

Recent Job Listings

Job Title	Education	Experience	Skills	Location
Systems Engineer I	BA	2–3 years	Second level support for production systems	Dallas/Irving, TX
Systems Engineer II	Some college	3–5 years	Point-of-sale, DOS, SQL, database structures	Dallas/Irving, TX
Systems Engineer III	BA	4–7 years	SQL RDMS, MD tools	Dallas/Irving, TX
Systems Engineer IV	BA	3 years	Novell Groupwise Netwand NDS tree design	Dallas/Irving, TX
Information Technology Auditor III	BA	3–5 years	UNIX, Novell, computer security, disaster recovery	Memphis, TN
Senior Systems Administrator	BA, FileNet FCP Technician certification	3 years	FileNet, UNIX, NT	Dallas/Irving, TX
Network Systems Engineer	High School/GED, Novell Administrator, Engineer, Microsoft Engineer certification	5 years	NetWare 4.11 and 5.X and Windows NT 4.0, TCP/IP, IPX/SPX	Dallas/Irving, TX
Senior Information Security Engineer	BA, CISSP, MSCE	5 years	UNIX, NT administration, security response, policy, audits	Dallas/Irving, TX

Contact

Web: www.ftb.com
Email: Resumes@ftb.com
Include "Source: Covin's Guide" on your resume and cover letter.

FREDDIE MAC

"New software is constantly being evaluated. We have an advanced technologies group that looks for new uses of technology."

– Jennifer Garrett
– Director of Employment Services

• 350+ Sun servers, IBM 3090 •
• C, C++, Perl, COBOL, SAP, Oracle •
• Financial services • Large shop •

Putting people in homes. Freddie Mac is a Fortune 100, shareholder-owned company with a mission to increase homeownership in the United States. The company frees up more money for home loans and reduces the cost of financing a home. Freddie Mac buys mortgages from the original lenders, such as banks, thrifts, credit unions, and savings and loans. The company then packages these loans into securities, and resells them to institutional investors, such as insurance companies and pension funds. It bought 1.5 million single-family mortgages in 2000, representing a value of $207 billion. It has financed mortgages for more than 28 million families since it was founded in 1970.

Recent technical initiatives include:

- Setting up Internet-ready computers at McDonald's that link customers to a plain-English information site explaining the home loan and mortgage-application process.
- Setting up an Internet-based system that connects mortgage brokers and wholesale lenders.
- Working with industry groups to develop open guidelines for electronic mortgages.
- Moving Dutch auction financial transactions to the Internet.
- Developing a web-based client management tool to help non-profit organizations streamline the process for facilitating home ownership in the Latino community.

Surprise benefit: Beepers for expectant parents.

Fast Facts	Revenues: $29.969B (2000)
	Employees: 3,600 (2000)
	Founded: 1970
	Secondary mortgage market
	Public: FRE (NYSE)
Awards	Computerworld: 100 Best Places to Work in IT (2001)
	Washingtonian: Great Places to Work (2001)
	Fortune: Best Places for Minorities (2001)
Headquarters	8200 Jones Branch Dr.
	McLean, VA 22102-3110
	(703) 903-2000
	http://www.freddiemac.com

Business

Some interesting facts, according to Freddie Mac research:

- The lowest mortgage rate ever was 6.49 percent, the week of October 10, 1998.
- The highest was 18.63 percent, the week of October 8, 1981.
- Freddie Mac buys a mortgage every five seconds.

The secondary mortgage market was designed to reduce regional differences in loan rates. In 1970, when Freddie Mac was chartered, mortgage rates differed by up to 1.7 percent across the country. Now, they vary by only 0.1 percent. This stability helps reduce mortgage loan rates to homeowners.

Freddie Mac's business activity increases access to mortgages, by allowing lending institutions to re-capture their capital and loan it out to additional homeowners. Competitors include Fannie Mae, also a government-chartered organization with a mission to improve the secondary mortgage market.

Some notable technology achievements:

- Freddie Mac purchased the first electronic mortgage available under new federal guidelines published in the Electronic Signatures in Global and National Commerce Act (E-SIGN).
- Freddie Mac was the first corporation to market bonds over the Internet.

Freddie Mac is one of the largest corporate funders in the Washington, DC region. Among the organizations supported by Freddie Mac's giving and employee volunteerism are Habitat for Humanity, Healthy Families America (a child abuse prevention program), and Wednesday's Child (finding homes for children in foster care).

Technology

Freddie Mac has an IBM 3090 mainframe, more than 350 Sun Solaris servers, 125 NT servers, and 90 Novell servers. Languages used include C, C++, COBOL, Java, Perl, AWK (an interpretive language used with UNIX), Visual Basic, PeopleSoft, SAS, Stata, XML, Focus, and Shell. Additional software used includes Crystal Reports, SAP, Sybase, Oracle, Paradox, MS-Access, and Lotus Notes. Additional software tools used include Harvest, Rational Rose, Web Gain Studio, Sapient Framework, Patrol, and Autosys.

Communications gear and software used at Freddie Mac includes Cisco routers, MQ Series, Network File System, Domain Name System, Token Ring and Ethernet protocols, Dynamic Host Configuration Protocol and SCSI buses. Other hardware and software includes hand scanners, wireless technology, and speech recognition.

An example of Freddie Mac's technology projects was the development of an Internet-based version of its automated underwriting system, Loan Prospector. Loan Prospector uses statistical computer modeling of traditional underwriting factors and a link to credit agencies to determine a mortgage score. Lenders can determine, in a few minutes, whether a loan application should be approved quickly, or if more information is needed to approve the borrower, simplifying a process that used to take several days.

Culture

Freddie Mac observes 10 holidays and offers employees 8 sick days. Employees earn 10 standard days of vacation and may take up to 25 days, buying days they need or selling unused days. Medical insurance options include preferred provider organizations (PPOS) and health maintenance organizations (HMOs). Dental and vision care are available, as is domestic partner health care coverage. Additional insurance plans available include short-term and long-term disability, life, business travel, and accidental death and dismemberment.

A 401(k) plan includes a company-matching contribution. Employees may purchase company stock at a 15 percent discount. Subsidized childcare is available at nearby childcare centers, as well as emergency back up care. Adoption expenses are reimbursed. The Educational Assistance Program reimburses employees for completing college or professional certification courses.

Headquarters has an onsite fitness center, a convenience store where evening meals can be ordered in advance for pick up, dry cleaning services, a library, mail services, film drop-off, and a cafeteria serving two meals a day. Free coffee and sodas are available. Parking is free. Wellness credits, earned through not smoking and having blood pressure and cholesterol rates monitored, can be converted to cash or other benefits, such as extra vacation. There is a bonus for employee referrals.

Dress is business casual. Headquarters is a three-building suburban campus. Employee work sites range from cubicles to private offices. Hours are flexible, with core hours. Travel represents less than five percent of an employee's time. Telecommuting options are available and commuting vans are common. There have been no layoffs, but hiring has slowed somewhat this year.

Candidates

There are 1,009 technical professionals at Freddie Mac. Most work at the McLean, Virginia headquarters or Reston, Virginia office, with a few technical positions in regional offices. Technical professionals work in the Information Systems Services (ISS) and Technology Infrastructure & Operations (TIO) departments, as well as in all the company's major divisions. TIO is responsible for network operations, data architecture, and strategy engineering and integration. Careers include both technical and management positions. A background in business or finance is extremely valuable.

Freddie Mac hired 200 technical professionals in 2000. Turnover is 4.4%. Freddie Mac has an active college recruiting program and is maintaining its recruiting schedule this year for technical candidates at the University of Virginia, James Madison University, George Mason, the University of Maryland, Howard University, Virginia Tech, and Morgan State. The company has an 11-week training program for Liberal Arts graduates and a strong internship program. Candidates are found through Internet postings (36%), employee referrals (34%), college recruiting (6%), job fairs (2%), and advertisements (1%).

Freddie Mac looks for candidates who excel in a fast-paced environment, who are flexible and can work on multiple projects, and who are customer-focused. Entry-level candidates are given a programming aptitude test. They should have good analytical and problem-solving skills and excellent communication skills. A Bachelor's degree is preferred, with majors in Computer Science, Liberal Arts, or Business Administration.

Recent Job Listings

Job Title	Education	Experience	Skills	Location
Technical Project Manager III	BA CS/IS, Bus. Admin, Finance or equiv. exper.	10 years	Harvest 4.1.2, Rational Rose, Visual Cafe, Credit and criminal background check	VA
Tech Analyst Lead	BA CS or equiv. exper.	5 years	J2EE, Java Scripts, Oracle SQL, Perl, SAS	McLean, VA
Data Base Admin.	BA CS or equiv. exper.	3 years	Sybase, MS SQL, credit and criminal background check	McLean, VA
Business Technical Analyst Sr.	BA CS or equiv. exper.	5 years	Weblogic, J2EE, Oracle, XML, mortgage business process	McLean, VA
Data Base Administration Manager	BA IS/CS or equivalent experience	5 years	Client server and mainframe, credit and criminal background check	Reston, VA
Enterprise Network Services Director	BA CS, Business Admin.	10 years	Vendor negotiations, Web operations, data/voice communications, credit and criminal background check	Reston, VA
Business Applications Analyst Sr.	BA Bus. Admin., CS or equivalent experience	5 years	SAS/Intranet, JCL, MS Access, data modeling, data conversion	McLean, VA

Contact

Web: http://www.freddiemac.com
Include "Source: Covin's Guide" on your resume and cover letter.

HANNAFORD BROS. Co.

"We are the only retailer in the world to have a fully-implemented ATM network."

– Bill Homa
– Vice President, Chief Information Officer

- IBM ES9000, RS/6000 SP -
- COBOL, Java, AIX, DB2 -
- Grocery stores - Large shop -

Voice and data over the same line to their grocery stores. Video conferencing with their distribution centers. Hannaford Brothers is leveraging its ATM network to help track costs and coordinate inventory across stores, distribution centers, and its fleet of trucks, while combining retail and wholesale grocery delivery. And they train their own people on new technologies. All their Cisco people were trained internally.

Active in the communities in which its stores are located, Hannaford's community service contributions include Children's Charity Days, in which a portion of sales once a week for a month are donated to organizations such as the Children's Cancer Program, Children's Miracle Network, and the Ronald McDonald House; a contribution to a playground designed specifically for accessibility by physically-challenged elementary school students; and a new police dog for the Falmouth Police Department.

Surprise award: Harry B. McLean, a driver for Hannaford for 33 years, with more than 3 million safe driving miles, earned the State of Maine's Driver of the Month award for his driving record, courteousness, and knowledge.

Fast Facts	Revenues: $3.46B (1999)
	Employees: 24,600 (1999)
	Founded: 1883
	Retailer; grocery stores
	Public: DZA (NYSE)
	Subsidiary of Delhaize America, Inc.
Awards	Fortune 500 (#445) 1999
	PC Week: Fast-Track 500 (1998)
	Information Week: Top 500 Technology Innovators (1998)
Headquarters	145 Pleasant Hill Rd.
	Scarborough, ME 04074
	(297(883-2911
	www.hannaford.com

Business

Arthur Hannaford started Hannaford Brothers. He sold fresh produce from his family's farm from the back of a cart, and soon brought on his brother, Howard. The company expanded into the warehousing business, then into retail groceries. In 1971, the company hit $1M in revenues and went public on the New York Stock Exchange (HRD). In 1987, they reached $1B in sales.

They were delisted when Delhaize America acquired them. The acquisition was completed in July, 2000, making Hannaford, which retains its corporate headquarters in Maine, part of the fifth-largest U.S. grocery store chain. Delhaize America also includes Food Lion, with 1,144 stores, Kash and Karry, with 123 stores, and Save 'n Pack, with 18 stores in the Southeast and Mid-Atlantic. Delhaize is a Belgian food company. Hannaford's 150 Hannaford Brothers and Shop and Save stores are concentrated in New England, from New York to Maine. The company closed or sold its Southern and Mid-Atlantic stores during the acquisition, as required by the Federal Trade Commission. Nine hundred employees, called associates, work at corporate headquarters.

The company continues its aggressive use of technology to expand its services. While its foray into a web-based grocery-delivery service, HomeRuns.com, ended in the sale of that unit, they continue to act as the wholesale supplier to the business. More recently, they have signed on as a supplier through Priceline.com

Competitors include A&P, Shaw's and Wal-Mart, but none of these has the concentrated presence in New England that Hannaford has, nor offers the same combination of high-end merchandise for reasonable prices.

Technology

Hannaford has an IBM ES9000 and an IBM RS/6000 SP, which run the administrative systems and data warehouse, and several NT servers. Operating systems-level software includes CICS, AIX, and UNIX. Programming is primarily in COBOL and Java. The company is migrating from IDMS to a DB2 database management system. Applications software includes Lawson's Human Resources and Payroll modules, PeopleSoft's financials component, and IBM's Tivoli for network and systems management.

There are 2,500 PCs across the company, including 800 at corporate headquarters. The company's communications equipment is Cisco and Nortel-based, with an ATM infrastructure.

Typical projects last 12 to 18 months. Staff members recently implemented a company-wide labor cost management system at all stores that includes activity-based costing to manage actual against planned labor costs. This was developed in Java, under the Netscape Navigator browser, in a client-server environment, using the ATM network.

Another recent project was the development and rollout to all stores of SIP, the Strategic Information Process. This is a decision support system based on sales data collected at the check-out scanner and matched with an Average Cost Inventory System (ACIS), which pinpoints the inventory levels needed at specific stores, so that Hannaford can regionalize product offerings, tailored to local interests.

Culture

Corporate headquarters is an office building in a campus setting in a rural area. Staff members work in private cubicles. Official hours are from 8:00 AM to 5:00 PM, with a flextime schedule. The average workweek is 40 hours. Staff members travel less than 5 percent of the time. A couple of staff members telecommute for between one and four days a week. The average commute is ten minutes. Says Homa, "I used to commute across the Tappan Zee Bridge, which took about an hour against traffic in New Jersey. Now I have a five-minute drive along the ocean." Dress is business casual.

Benefits include a flexible program for medical and dental coverage and prescription drugs. The company pays 70 percent of the cost of medical, dental, and vision insurance. The company pays for life insurance for employees and short-term disability. Long-term disability, and dependent life insurance plans are available. After one year of service, employees over 21 years of age become members of the company-paid defined benefit pension plan. Retirement programs include a cash balance plan and 401(k) savings and investment programs. The company matches up to four percent of an employee's contribution to a 401(k) plan. The company provides tuition reimbursement and awards up to 50 scholarships annually to employees and their dependents.

The company observes eight to ten and a half holidays, depending on location. Employees earn two weeks of vacation to start, increasing to three weeks after three years, four weeks after twelve years, and five weeks after twenty years. Employees are entitled to discounts at many area stores, such as for tires. There is free coffee in the company cafeteria and free parking. Social activities include an annual picnic lunch. In 1992, there was a company downsizing when the Wellby Pharmacy chain was sold, because of the supporting staff for this subsidiary in the corporate office. A voluntary severance program and early retirement took care of most affected employees. Says Shirley Bloom, Director of Benefits, "We work hard, but are close to a large playground, with mountain climbing, canoeing, kayaking, and fishing nearby."

Candidates

There are 150 technical professionals at Hannaford Brothers, all working at corporate headquarters. Job titles range from Trainee to Senior Analyst.

The average level of education is between a Bachelor's and a Master's degree for Hannaford's current technical staff. The average level of experience is eight to ten years. Says Homa, "Twenty-five percent of our staff have worked at one of the company's stores sometime during their lives. We almost always take bright people from the stores who want to move into IT because they already have retail experience." The company looks not only for technical aptitude, but also for a cultural fit when hiring. Continues Homa, "We train people internally for technical skills. We look for candidates who will work hard and dig in to do what needs to be done." The quality of life in Maine is a big draw for candidates. Homa expands on this theme, "People work hard here so they can enjoy a balance of work and life. That's why they don't leave."

Recent Job Listings

Job Title	Education	Experience	Skills	Location
Decision Support Systems (DSS) Analyst	BA	4–6 years	Microstrategy DSS Agent, Architect, Web and Admin. experience, version 7	Scarborough, ME
Communications Specialist		2–5 years	AIX, NT, Cisco, Korn Shell, Perl	

| Information Security Specialist | BA/BS | RACF, CICS, IDMS, TSO |
| System Services Specialist—NOS/ Messaging | BA/BS | NOS Messaging Server, NT installation |

Contact

Web: www.hannaford.com
Email: working@hannaford.com
            bhoma@hannaford.com (Bill Homa)
Phone: (207) 885-2343 (Human Resources)
Mail: Hannaford Bros. Co., Employment Dept.
            P.O. Box 1000
            Portland, ME 04104
Include "Source: Covin's Guide" on your resume and cover letter.

INGERSOLL-RAND Co.

"You can have multiple careers in our organization. Our Senior Technology Specialists, for example, are available as a worldwide resource for the company. If they are in Kentucky and there is a problem in Mumbai, they get the call."

– Paul Fitterer
– Director, Information Technology

• HPs, N and L class, IBM RS/6000 SPs •
• COBOL, Oracle, MfGPRO, Haushahn •
• Manufacturing • Large shop •

Dig the hole for the building, build the assembly line, and the doors and the locks that go into the building, and develop the carts that carry you around the building. Bobcat. Steelcraft. Schlage. Club Car. Ingersoll-Rand (IR) began in 1871, with the invention of the steam-powered rock drill, used in construction and mining. Its four business units reflect the company's areas of focus: Security and Safety, Climate Control, Infrastructure Development, and Industrial Productivity. Its brands include such well-known names as Bobcat (small construction vehicles), Schlage (locks), Club Car (golf carts), Thermo-King (refrigerated trucks), and Torrington (precision bearings).

Company vision: customers respond to excellence. Company passion: make possible the impossible. Guiding principles: cultivate an atmosphere of trust; value swift action; set goals beyond reach but within stretch.

Surprise benefit: SOS, an international travel assistance program for employees living or traveling overseas.

Fast Facts	Revenues: $8.798B (2000)
	Employees: 51,000 (2000)
	Founded: 1871
	Manufacturer
	Public: IR (NYSE)
Awards	Fortune 500 (#199) 2000
	Information Week: Top 500 Technology Innovators (1999, 2000 #41)
	Fortune: Most Admired Companies (1998)
	Industry Week: 100 Best-Managed Companies (2000)
Headquarters	200 Chestnut Ridge Road
	Woodcliff Lake, NJ 07675
	(201) 573-0123
	www.ingersoll-rand.com

Business

Ingersoll-Rand, known informally, and now formally, as IR, has assembled independently-operated manufacturing facilities, which are well-known companies in their own right, along four broad business lines. The Climate Control unit includes recently-acquired Hussman, known for making the freezer equipment Birdseye first used, but also inventor of the first self-service frozen food case, the first patented meat display case, and the first multi-deck dairy merchandiser. This division also includes Thermo-King, which invented the refrigerated truck business in 1938, during a hot Minneapolis summer. The Industrial Productivity unit includes IR's drilling equipment and ARO, founded in 1930 to make lubrication equipment; Torrington, which makes precision bearings; Zimmerman; and Club Car, the golf car manufacturer. The Infrastructure Development unit includes Bobcat, the makers of small loaders and excavators, Blaw-Knox, which makes paving equipment, and IR's own road machinery, drilling solutions, and portable compressor divisions. The Security and Safety unit includes Dor-o-Matic, LCN, Locknetics, Schlage, Steelcraft, and Von Duprin. Steelcraft makes doors and frames. LCN makes the devices that slow the closing of heavy doors. Schlage invented the doorknob with the central push-button lock. More than 40 percent of the company's revenue comes from outside the United States.

IR's mission is to be the market leader in its business segments.

Technology

IR is standardizing on Oracle, under UNIX, at six regional data centers, on HP N and L series machines, and IBM RS/6000 SPs (Symmetrical Processors, that gang the RS/6000s). Facilities worldwide that are currently running legacy applications in a mixed hardware environment will be migrating to Oracle's ERP system. IR's distribution centers use Haushahn's automated warehouse systems. This is a Radio-Frequency (RF)-based system in which a pick list is transmitted to a warehouse employee when an order is entered. The transaction includes the location, order number, and quantity of the part being ordered; the part is then put onto a conveyor belt so it can be packed and shipped.

IR has also standardized on Oracle's project development methodology, Application Implementation Methodology (AIM). Legacy systems are a mix of purchased application software and homegrown COBOL systems. CrossWorlds Software's middleware, Enterprise Application Integration (EAI) package, is being used to develop the connectivity between legacy applications and the Oracle 11i ERP environments. PTC's (Parametric Technologies Corporation) mechanical engineering and manufacturing engineering application systems, which run on HP, Sun, and NT workstations, are the company's standard and are used throughout the organization.

The company has approximately 25,000 PCs worldwide, and has recently established a global Common Office Environment, with IBM as the standard PC platform. IR's Virtual Private Network (VPN) is supported by AT&T in the United States and Equant internationally. Switches and routers are from Cisco. IR communications are integrated worldwide.

The company is currently in the process of implementing Oracle financials, human resources, and e-procurement systems at their new Global Business Services center in Huntersville, North Carolina. Dedicated application teams convert the company's decentralized operations into a consistent systems environment at the Global Business Services Center. Teams include local IT and functional team members, Oracle SWAT team members for application and business process conversion, and database and technical support team members managing the hardware and software. Each local project lasts approximately four months, but the corporate-wide effort will take about two years to complete. This project will enable IR to share information across its business units, with a unified human resources and financial reporting function, while retaining local manufacturing systems for efficiency and product differentiation purposes.

Culture

IR's Corporate Center is located in Northern New Jersey with sales, distribution, and manufacturing facilities worldwide. Benefits include a range of medical insurance programs, dental insurance, a prescription drug plan, and flexible spending accounts. The company pays for life insurance, funds a pension plan, and contributes to a savings and stock investment program. Tuition for degree programs is reimbursable. There is a savings bonds program and the company matches contributions to colleges. There is a stock purchase program.

Employees are entitled to various discounts on the company's products. The company encourages active participation in professional organizations. There are a number of company-sponsored sports teams, including softball, bowling, and golf.

The dress code is business casual. Working hours vary by location, but are generally flexible between 6:00 AM and 6:00 PM. An average workweek is 40 hours. Telecommuting is acceptable in some situations. Travel requirements represent approximately five percent of a staff member's time.

Candidates

There is a small IT team supporting IR's Corporate Center. The rest of the IT staff are in IT departments supporting the company's business units and regional centers, for a total of 800 worldwide. The average level of education is a Bachelor's degree and 10 to 15 years of experience. Job titles include Core Title C, B, A, Senior, and Lead; IT Manager 1,2,3,4; Senior Technology Specialist; and Vice President. Core Titles represent a specialty area, such as database administration, technical support, or application developer. Fitterer looks for technical competence in Oracle and UNIX, but also, "the ability to work with ambiguity in a dynamic environment."

IR typically hires 30 entry-level professionals a year. The IT Leadership Development Program is one of the chief opportunities for entry-level candidates. It is a 30-month program with rotational assignments, beginning with a two-day assessment of candidates. Candidates are evaluated by a number of IT managers from various business units who have been brought together for this purpose, through a series of interviews and workshops on the first day. Then they are given a case study to prepare. For example, a recent case study asked candidates to write a business plan that would show how to integrate a disparate hardware environment into a single network. Candidates for this program typically have a Bachelor's degree in MIS or CS, a minimum of a 3.0 GPA, summer or co-op job experience, a well-defined career objective that includes a plan for increasing their technical expertise, and the ability to communicate technical objectives to a business audience.

Entry-level and experienced candidates are typically found through a combination of campus job fairs, employment agencies, advertisements, and online recruiting. Turnover is low. Top schools for recruiting include Purdue, Clemson, Virginia Tech, Penn State, Lehigh, and the University of Minnesota.

Recent Job Listings

Job Title	Education	Experience	Skills	Location
VP, IT and Business Solutions	Master's, advanced certifications in IT		Migrate business to a common platform, reduce costs through consolidation, streamlining, and leverage	Indianapolis, IN
Application Developer, Level C	BS Computer Programming, CIS, MIS	5 years	UNIX, SQL, VB, mainframe and client/server business systems	Gwinner, ND
VP, IT	BA/BS Technical or Business	10–12 years	Accelerate development of supporting technologies for e-business, CRM, supply chain management	Torrington, CT
e-Business Consultant	BA/BS	2 years	Lead new e-Business initiatives	Huntersville, NC
e-Business Program Manager	MBA preferred, PTC or Big 5 supplier certification	5–10 years	Siebel, Oracle, Crossworlds Tools, Actuate Reporting, C++, VB	Huntersville, NC
HRMS Analyst	BA/BS HR Mgt, IS	3 years	Oracle, IR HR mgt processes	Huntersville, NC

Contact

Web: www.irco.com
Include "Source: Covin's Guide" on your resume and cover letter.

LANDS' END Inc.

"On most plane trips I take, I meet someone new who tells me a great customer service story about the company as soon as they learn that I work at Lands' End. It's very gratifying."

– John Loranger
– Vice President, Information Services

• IBM ES 9000s, UNIX/AIX •
• COBOL, SQL, DB2, Perl, Java, Visual Basic •
• Direct mail retailer • Large shop •

Business casual made possible. Starting with writing advertisements, then catalogs for sailboat hardware, Gary Comer, a champion racing sailor and 10-year veteran copy-writer with Young and Rubicam in Chicago started a new business. Comer noticed that customers of a sailmaker also needed fittings, so he started providing them, launching the business in 1963. Canvas raincoats and duffel bags, made from the same material as the sails, soon followed. The first catalog was mailed in 1964. It was called the Lands' End Yachtsman's Equipment Guide. A typography error misplaced the apostrophe in that initial catalog and it was too expensive to reprint. The misplaced apostrophe remains today. By the time hardware was supplied with sailboats in the mid-1970s, the apparel business was well underway.

Leveraging technology at its best. E-Commerce and customer service. Land's End is the third largest mail order clothing retailer and the largest seller of apparel online. Taking its custom logo business to its natural extension, Lands' End sets up private Internet sites where companies like Saturn, CISCO, and Radio Shack sell corporate-customized clothes geared to employees. A feature of its own Web site, Oxford Express™, lets customers select the fabric, collar and cuffs, and size they want in a men's dress shirt. Lands' End is one of the largest online retailers of men's dress shirts.

Surprise benefit: a tollfree line for employees' children for help with their homework.

Fast Facts	Revenues: $1.462B (2001)
	Employees: 9,800 (2001)
	Rises by an additional 2,000 during the holiday season
	Founded: 1963
	Direct merchant—Catalog-e-Commerce
	Public: LE (NYSE)
Awards	Fortune: 100 Best Companies to Work For (1998—2000)
	Computerworld: 100 Best Companies to Work For in IT (1997, 1999, 2000)
Headquarters	Lands' End Lane
	Dodgeville, WI 53595
	(608) 935-9341
	www.landsend.com

Business

Comer's business philosophy was simple—sell quality products, guarantee them, and ship everything as quickly as possible. Shipments still go out the day after an order arrives, to arrive within two business days, anywhere in the United States. The company's eight business principles reflect the company's commitment to quality and the customer. Make the product better, price it fairly, accept any return for any reason, ship faster than anyone in the business, believe that what is best for the customer is best for the company, eliminate the middleman and deal directly with factories and mills, operate efficiently, and sell through cost-effective channels.

The apparel Lands' End sells is classically inspired. Nearly 90 percent of its customers have a college education and they are twice as likely as the average consumer to have Internet access. Most are between 35 and 54 years old. The company focuses its apparel line on a classic, casual style. Product lines include the traditional blazers, slacks, and polo shirts that have been the company's staple since the 1970s. They also now include tailored suits for men (Lands'End for Men®), tailored suits for women (First Person™), linens and accessories for the home (Coming Home®), private company-branded clothing (Corporate Sales), casual and school clothes and uniforms for children (Kids and School Uniforms), and online sales (landsend.com). The company has 16 outlet and inlet stores in four states.

In 1978, a new fulfillment and distribution center was opened in a 40-acre cornfield in Dodgeville, Wisconsin. Comer liked the people for their hard work (milk the cows before coming into work) and the area for its culture (friendly). In 1990, Dodgeville was established as the company's new headquarters.

Some statistics help show the scope of the business. In 1999, 236 million catalogs were distributed. Catalog printing and mailing represent more than forty percent of the company's operating costs. Lands' End customer service operations handled 15 million calls in 1999, averaging 40,000 to 50,000 a day, and peaking at 100,000 a day a few weeks before Christmas. On a single day, they shipped 146,000 orders. The company receives 500 e-mails a day and answers each one personally.

Trousers are hemmed for free; fabric swatches are provided for free; and a lost mitten from a pair will be replaced at half the cost of the pair—no shipping charge, during the same season it was purchased.

Technology

There are two IBM ES 9000s, an IBM 9672 running under VM, and an IBMAS/400. The company has 45 UNIX and 110 Intel-based servers. COBOL is the most often-used language, with Perl, Visual Basic, and Java common as well. Additional software includes SQL, DB2, SAS, Business Objects, JBuilder, Visual Studio, Claris, and Genesys. There are 2,500 PCs and 200 Macintoshes in Dodgeville, and an additional 200 PCs at other locations. Telxon RF scanners, with accompanying software, are used in warehouse operations.

Typical projects last from three to six months. Some major projects, such as the call center software replacement effort, span years, but are divided into smaller deliverables. A number of the company's efforts are now aimed at tying systems together, such as integrating Web-based applications to the back-office backbone. Lands' End has initiated a number of e-commerce projects recently, building private corporate marketplaces, participating in public marketplaces, and using technology to simplify the customer experience on its own Web site. LogoSnapShot™ shows how corporate logos would appear on various items in a private online store. The company teamed with Commerce One and Ariba through their online portals and is working with WebMethods for systems integration.

A Specialty Shopper keeps size and preference information for customers. Your Personal Model™ builds a 3-D model of a customer. Staff members have installed Cisco's Collaboration Server to connect the company Web site to a call center. Customers click through from an icon to a personal shopper to be contacted back by text chat or a phone call. Either way, the customer is contacted within 20 seconds. Shop with a Friend™ connects shoppers with a friend or family member by Internet chat or phone and synchronizes the Web pages they are looking at. Sales at the online site more than tripled from $18 million to $61 million in 1998 and by the end of 1999 exceeded a total of $138 million.

Lands' End competes on the quality of its clothing for a fair price, its unmatched guarantee, and its one-on-one customer service. Competitors include L.L. Bean, Eddie Bauer, The Gap, and Nordstrom.

Culture

Corporate headquarters is in a rural, campus setting. Staff members have private cubicles; most managers have private offices. For most positions, there is less than five percent travel. For those supporting overseas offices in England, Germany, and Japan, there may be annual three-to-four week trips. While there is no formal telecommuting program, most staff members have access from home. The average commute is less than 20 minutes.

Benefits include medical and dental insurance. Employees are 100 percent vested in the retirement program, which includes a 401(k) to which the company contributes and a profit-sharing plan funded by the company. The company pays for life insurance and offers disability insurance. Employees are eligible for substantial discounts of catalog merchandise. There are seven holidays, and two half-day holidays. Vacation starts at one week during the first year, two weeks after the first year, then increases to three weeks after five years, and four weeks after ten years. Employees receive a personal day off each year as well. There has been one salaried staff layoff in the company's history, in 1998, after new management consolidated business functions. An attractive severance package was provided to affected employees.

Employees may use the free activity center, which has an Olympic-sized swimming pool, indoor track, exercise equipment, and racquetball courts. The company offers tuition reimbursement, adoption assistance, and childcare reimbursement for off-site travel. Coffee and apples are available for free. Social activities include the annual summer picnic, discounted tickets to an outdoor Shakespeare theatre, and a number of company-sponsored sports teams. Garrison Keilor, of Prairie Home Companion fame, was featured at an annual Lands' End show. Dress is casual, with shorts on some occasions. Most employees wear Lands' End clothing.

Candidates

There are 245 technical professionals at Lands' End, supplemented with between 75 and 100 contractors. Except for those supporting international operations, all work at corporate headquarters. Job titles include Entry-level Programmer, Programmer Analyst, Senior Programmer Analyst, Technical Specialist, Business Systems Specialist, Manager, Senior Manager, Director, and Vice President. There is a dual technical/management career track, starting at the Senior Programmer Analyst level. Current staff members have an average of an associate's or bachelor's degree and an average of six to seven years of experience.

The company hired 50 technical staff members in the past year, including five at the entry-level position. The company recruits entry-level professionals at the University of Wisconsin at Eau Claire, the University of Wisconsin at Whitewater, and Madison Area Technical College. Technical staff is found through advertising (35 percent), online recruiting (25 percent), employee referrals (25 percent; there is a substantial referral bonus and sometimes a raffle for Green Bay Packer tickets), college recruiting (10 percent) and unsolicited resumes (5 percent). Turnover is five percent.

Says Loranger, "We look for people who are a good fit for the Lands' End culture. They are non-political, down-to-earth, team players, friendly, highly motivated, and looking for exciting new challenges. Currently, we are hiring people with a lot of the hot new skills in networking and infrastructure." Entry-level professionals should be able to demonstrate situations in which they have exercised leadership. Continues Loranger, "We don't look for an exact match necessarily, as in Basic or COBOL classes. Rather, we want go-getters with potential."

Recent Job Listings

Job Title	Education	Experience	Skills	Location
Web Designer	BFA, BA Design, Graphic Design, Art Direction, Industrial Design	2–3 years	PhotoShop, Dreamweaver, Macromedia Flash, QuarkXpress, JavaScript	Dodgeville, WI
Project Manager for Enterprise Data Warehouse			MVS, data modeling, data warehouse	Dodgeville, WI
Project Manager for Technical Services	BA/BS		Web enterprise servers, Java, JavaScript, Perl, Netscape server, Oracle	Dodgeville, WI
DB2 Database Administrator			DB2/UDB, SQL, DDL	Dodgeville, WI
Intel Administrator	BA/BS		Ethernet, TCP/IP, VBScript	Dodgeville, WI

Contact

Web: www.landsend.com
Email: elmacke@landsend.com
        Erin Mackesey, Sr. Recruitment and Development Specialist
Phone: (608) 935-4589 (Erin Mackesey)
Include "Source: Covin's Guide" on your resume and cover letter.

MELLON FINANCIAL Corporation

"We still deal with typical, single platform development. But, more interesting are our cross-platform projects, combining web, client-server, and mainframe [technologies] for a solution."

– Kevin Shearan
– Senior Vice President, Software Engineering

• **Multi-data centers, redundant processor, disk and networks** •
• **IBM 9672s, 2064s, RS/600s, Sun servers** •
• **COBOL, Visual Basic, Java, SAS, Tivoli** •
• **Financial services** • **Large shop** •

Mellon. Financing twentieth century industrial development. Bequeathing the nation a wealth of cultural treasures. That was then. This is now. One of America's top ten bank holding companies in terms of market capitalization. Global operations in wealth management, investment management, investment services, and cash management. And Mellon uses technology to drive its financial operations.

Consider just two examples :

- client fund managers buy and sell foreign currencies electronically, with the results linked to a client's internal information system;
- portfolio advisors and asset managers are provided with Internet delivery channels that include transparent linkages between Web-based client server software and mainframe-based legacy applications.

Mellon's recent corporate focus is on its asset management and processing and corporate services segments. It is the parent organization for Dreyfuss Corporation, a leading mutual fund company. Mellon has operations in Pittsburgh, New York, Boston, Denver, Los Angeles, San Francisco, and London, and joint ventures and other business operations that give it a global presence.

Mellon continues its aggressive approach to technology development and deployment. Applications range from on-line security auctions and electronic invoice presentment and payment to providing Web portals for clients whose investment management operations are outsourced to Mellon. Some of the newest technologies Mellon is investigating, according to Shearan, include "data mining and IVR (Interactive Voice Response) technologies that will significantly enhance our ability to provide services that involve extensive amounts of data storage and retrieval."

Surprise fact: The four buildings in Mellon's downtown campus are linked by more than 3,000 miles of fiber optic network, the largest fiber network in the country.

Fast Facts	
	Revenues: $5.979B (2000)
	Employees: 25,800 (2000)
	Founded: 1869
	Financial services provider
	Public: MEL (NYSE)

Awards	Computerworld: 100 Best Places to Work in IT (2001)
	Information Week: Top 500 (#18)
	Computerworld: Premier 100 IT Leaders (2001)
	Morgan Stanley Dean Witter: Tech Edge 26 Group of
	stocks
	MM Level 2 certified software engineering practices
	in place across multiple lines of business
	SO-9001: 2000, Registered electronic payment
	provider
Headquarters	One Mellon Bank Center
	Pittsburgh, PA 15258-0001
	(412) 234-5000
	www.mellon.com

Business

Mellon's history is one of focused growth and strategic acquisitions. As a result, the company is now responsible for approximately $2.8 trillion in assets under management, administration, or custody, including more than $585 billion under management. It provides wealth and asset management and investment and cash management services, including trust and custody, securities lending, employee benefit solutions, foreign exchange, and transfer agent services.

Founded in 1869 by retired Judge Thomas Mellon and his sons, Andrew and Richard, Mellon has always been deeply rooted in Pittsburgh, aggressive about applying new technology, and selective in acquiring other financial institutions. Andrew Mellon went on to become U.S. Secretary of the Treasury. Mellon became one of the first banks to acquire its own computer. One of its acquisitions, Girard Bank, made a name for itself in the early days of automated teller machines with its extensive network. A branch of another acquisition, Commonwealth National Bank, in York, Pennsylvania, stands where the first Continental Treasury, precursor to the U.S. Treasury, was once based. Philadelphia Savings Fund Society, now known as Mellon PSFS, was America's first savings bank, patterned after a similar system in Scotland for workers to deposit and earn interest on small amounts of money.

Technology

Three IBM 9672s and two IBM 2064 mainframes, 75 RS/6000s in Pittsburgh and 19 more in New York, 170 Sun servers, 10 HPs, 7 AS/400s, and 9 DECs represent the majority of hardware in Mellon's computing environment. Applications are developed on the legacy systems in COBOL, Focus, and SAS, and in the client-server environment in Visual Basic, Java, and C++. Additional software used includes PeopleSoft, IBM's Tivoli, HP's OpenView, and IBM's MQ Series middleware connecting legacy systems to the Web. The communications environment includes Shiva, Citrix Winframe, Network Data Mover (NDM), PCDatamover, Direct NDM, TCS, and Cisco routers and switches. The company is investigating the use of biometrics to take the place of passwords.

Mellon has more than 18,000 PCs. Typical projects span the mainframe, web, and client-server worlds. In addition, Mellon actively works with 3rd party vendors to test new technologies, such as its partnership with SEI to produce a Web-enabled front-office client server environment for processing trust management applications. Another project creates a lock box environment in which exception reports are transmitted on CD-ROMs, including check images and bank statements. Mellon routinely works with companies like Microsoft, Cisco, EMC, and IBM to evaluate the latest technologies and jointly develop new technology solutions.

Culture

Mellon's downtown Pittsburgh campus includes one of the city's most architecturally distinguished high-rises, the company's 54-story headquarters building, a new $150 million client services center, and Mellon Green, a 1.8-acre park of rolling lawns and promenades. Technical staff members, including some managers, work in cubicles. The company offers a smoke and drug-free environment. Key components of the company's menu-style benefits program include contributory major medical, dental and vision plans, as well as pre-tax funds for expenses like health care, dependent care, and transportation. Life and accidental death insurance, and short- and long-term disability insurance are fully company paid. The company offers tuition reimbursement, contributes to a 401(k) plan, and funds a retirement savings plan. Employees are eligible for stock options and an incentive bonus program. The company observes six core holidays and offers six more that are determined at local sites. Vacations range from three weeks to start to five weeks after 25 years. Additional activities may include holiday parties and discounted tickets to local events like plays and the racetrack or to the corporate-sponsored Pittsburgh Penguins.

When there is a layoff, Mellon first places as many people as possible through internal transfers with a formal displacement program. Remaining employees receive out-placement services and severance packages that generally include two weeks' salary for each year of service.

Dress is business casual for all employees, with employees expected to respect the business etiquette appropriate to particular work assignments. Hours are 8:30 AM to 5:00 PM, with an hour for lunch. The data center, telecommunications, and LAN support are shift-work positions. More than 25 percent of the Information Systems staff take advantage of the Alternate Work Arrangement program which offers telecommuting, flextime, flexday, compressed work week and part-time options. Software engineers officially work a 37 1/2-hour week. As Shearan says, "We don't drop our pencils at 5." Unpaid overtime averages three to four hours a week. Travel is dependent on the position; a core of supervisory and specialist technicians travel occasionally to support other geographic locations.

Candidates

Mellon has 2,200 technical staff members and 200 contractors. One thousand of these are in data center operations and technical and network support; the balance in software engineering and business analysis. Sixty percent work at corporate headquarters in Pittsburgh; the rest are scattered between Boston, New York, and England. A variety of career paths are available in the network, PC, UNIX, and mainframe systems programming and engineering areas, starting with introductory positions and extending to senior engineering roles. The career path for software engineers starts at Associate Programmer, then moves to Senior Programmer Analyst 1,2,3, and Software Engineer. Systems engineers have a similar career path. The management track moves from Associate Systems Coordinator, to Senior Systems Coordinator 1,2,3; Section Manager 1,2;

Project Manager 1,2,3; Division Manager 1,2; Division Head 1,2; Business Unit Manager, and CIO.

Mellon hired 300 technical staff members in 2000, of which 73 were for entry-level positions. Current staff members generally have a Bachelor's degree and an average of 15 years of experience, although this ranges from zero to 25 years. Mellon finds candidates through employment agencies (39 percent), employee referrals (32 percent), college recruiting (9 percent) , the Internet (9 percent), and other sources (11 percent). Top schools for recruiting include Carnegie-Mellon University, and the University of Pittsburgh, Penn State University, Rochester Institute of Technology, Massachusetts Institute of Technology, and Case Western Reserve University.

Mellon focuses on specific technical support skills for system engineering positions. For example, Microsoft and Cisco-certified engineers are preferred candidates for many of the computer infrastructure positions.While Mellon looks for relevant technical experience in appication development, the real differentiator among candidates is business experience in the financial industry, such as familiarity with mutual funds, or the trust and custody business. Additional prized skills are the ability to communicate well and work on a team. Shearan describes the ideal entry-level candidate as someone with, "an aptitude for creative problem-solving and analytical skills, a Bachelor's degree with a Grade Point Average of 3.0 or higher, planning and self-organization skills, and the ability to get along with colleagues."

Recent Job Listings

Job Title	Education	Experience	Skills	Location
Sr. Programmer Analyst	BA/BS MIS, CS	5+ years	SWIFT, mainframe and PCs	Pittsburgh, PA
Sr. Business Systems Consultant	BA/BS	5+ years	SEI, CMM, securities processing, trust, or investment experience	Pittsburgh, PA
Programmer Analyst	BA/BS IS, CS	3 years	Windows NT, VB, Microsoft SQL	Pittsburgh, PA
Implementation Specialist	BA/BS, CCP certification	3–5 years	Sybase, Oracle, SQL Server	Houston, TX

Contact

Include "Source: Covin's Guide" on your resume and cover letter.
Web: www.mellon.com/jobs
             www.buckconsultants.com (NJ)
             www.dreyfus.com (NY)
Email: recruiting@mellon.com

MILLENNIUM PHARMACEUTICALS, Inc.

"We are working to improve the quality of life for people worldwide."

– Sandra DiCesare
– Vice President, Information Systems

- Sun Ultra enterprise-class servers, Mac, NT •
- Web-Centric, Java, Perl, SAS, Oracle •
- BioPharmaceuticals • Large shop •

Computational biology. Informatics. Mining DNA. Applying the power of computers to the complexity of human genes and proteins. Sorting out the environmental factors from the genetic factors that affect an individual's ability to be and stay healthy. Addressing the cause of the disease and not just the symptoms. Industrializing drug discovery. Finding out how to identify the one to two percent of the population that may have a toxic reaction to a drug. This is the promise Millennium Pharmaceuticals holds out. A challenge with an ethical underpinning.

Says DiCesare, "We are not just focused on one area of biotechnology, like data, or genes, or drugs. Our strategy is to go from gene to patient. We want to get the right drug to the right person at the right time." As a result, the company uses not only an Information Technology (IT) group to provide the infrastructure for rapid technical deployment, but also a substantial Informatics group. This group consists mainly of scientists and software engineers who use computers for rapid analysis and correlation of the massive amounts of data thrown off by the company's research and the efforts of public organizations, like the Human Genome Project.

Surprise company team: rock climbing.

Fast Facts	Revenues: $196.3M (2000)
	Employees: 1,330 (2000)
	Founded: 1993
	BioPharmaceuticals
	Public: MLNM (Nasdaq)
Awards	Red Herring: Top 100 (1999, 2000)
	Fast 50 Biotech Companies in Massachusetts
Headquarters	75 Sidney Street
	Cambridge, MA 02139
	(617) 679-7000
	www.mlnm.com

Business

Millennium Pharmaceuticals, Inc. was founded in 1993 by venture capitalist Mark Levin. He had taken it upon himself to start companies in bio-technology for his employer, Mayfield Fund, when he thought there was a business opportunity. With Millennium, Levin stayed on as Chief Executive Officer. Positioning the company to work on the entire drug discovery and development process, he has developed a pipeline of products, a stable of partnerships, and a portfolio of patents. Millennium's innovative drug discovery platform is applied across the entire healthcare sector, from gene identification through patient management. The company is focused on revolutionizing the process to tackle the most critical issue facing the pharmaceutical industry today, productivity.

Millennium licenses its technology platform to pharmaceutical companies, but in an approach that differentiates it from competitors like Incyte Pharmaceuticals and Human Genome Sciences, has developed a method for screening target genes for their reaction to drugs. Finding genes that respond to drugs, then determining which diseases they are related to, shortens the time it takes to develop a drug and yields a higher probability that the drug developed for that specific gene-disease combination will be successful. Mark Levin says on the company's web site "We believe that nothing is impossible," but the company's strategy is designed to increase the odds that the impossible will be accomplished in our lifetimes.

Technology

According to DiCesare, "We are aggressive adopters of technology and we plan to leverage cluster and domain technology to meet critical high-availability needs." This explains the more than 100 Sun and Compaq servers, connecting 1,500 Macintoshes and PCs. Continues DiCesare, "Our databases have both OLTP and OLAP requirements. Indeed, access to Millennium's multi-terabytes of data is just a few keystrokes away. What makes this environment so challenging is that on any given day, scientists may discover that yesterday's unimportant gene plays a critical role in a disease process. All this data must be online and easily accessible." IT is also working to facilitate communication within the company by implementing web-based collaboration tools and streaming audio and video.

Languages used include both object-oriented and Internet development languages from Java, to Perl, C++, Smalltalk, SQL, and JavaScript. All network communications equipment is standardized on Cisco. Millennium is a member of the Customer Advisory Board for the Veritas-Oracle-Sun (VOS) initiative. Much of the software developed in-house is based on CORBA standards and the company is represented on the OMG board. Millennium is investigating wireless and Internet business strategies to their growing Internet strategy. They recently signed a partnership agreement with Caliper Technologies to develop lab-on-a-chip technologies, the first in genomics.

Culture

Millennium is headquartered with six sites in Cambridge, Massachusetts and is at the center of a triangle bounded by Harvard University, MIT, and Boston University. The company has also expanded globally, with recent office openings in Japan and Israel, and a merger with CDC of Cambridge, England. The office environment is a mix of private and shared offices and private cubicles. The company spells out its core values: hire the best, create an environment where people can excel, search for breakthrough products, listen and learn, integrity with all, create focused teams, act ethically, and nothing is impossible.

The company offers employees a choice of HMO or point-of-service medical plans, dental, life, and accident insurance. The company matches a portion of employee contributions to a 401(k) plan. Employees are eligible for a discounted stock purchase plan and all employees have stock options. Vacations start at three weeks a year; there are 10 company holidays. Tuition is reimbursed. There is financial assistance for parking and transportation. Coffee, tea, and hot cocoa are free.

Social activities include weekly gatherings where employees enjoy food and drink, exchange ideas, and get to know each other. The company emphasizes working hard, having fun, and taking risks. John Sanchez, Human Resources Manager, says, "We have a dedicated Fun Team that organizes social events, such as afternoon teas and evening parties." Other events include Halloween parties, summer outings, and occasional company-wide scavenger hunts. The company sponsors teams or clubs for recreational activities, such as softball. "The IT department has both a foosball and a ping pong table," says Sanchez. Other events have included name-the-t-shirt-theme parties, ski trips, a paint ball outing, and a winter holiday party with "Lisa Lisa" and "Kool and the Gang" to entertain.

Standard dress is very casual, including shorts and t-shirts. Official hours are from 8:30 AM to 5:30 PM. Travel is optional for many positions.

Candidates

Technical staff members are divided between those that work in applications development and other information technology infrastructure projects (more than 40 employees) and those that work on computation-intensive Informatics projects (more than 80 employees). IT staff members may work in the Technical Services, Systems Engineering, Business Information Technology, or Technical Planning departments. Those in Informatics may work in Informatics Management, Technology Management, Information Science, Process Technology, Informatics Applications, Informatics Infrastructure, or Technology Transfer departments. The IT technical career path leads from Systems Technician through Principal Engineer/Architect. There are dual management and technical tracks.

Millennium hired 25 technical professionals in the last year. In general, two to three of their new hires are entry-level. The company expects to hire 30 technical staff members in the next year. They have five percent turnover. Top college recruiting spots are Harvard, MIT, and the University of California at Berkeley. New candidates are generally found through employee referrals (36 percent), the Internet (18 percent), employment agencies (18 percent), advertising (11 percent), college recruiting (7 percent), unsolicited resumes (5 percent), and other means (5 percent).

In the IT department, staff members generally have a Bachelor's degree and five to ten years of experience. On the Informatics side, staff members, on average, hold advanced Computer Science, Biology, or Chemistry degrees. Demonstrated technical skills are required as the price of entry, but a cultural fit with the organization is also important. The company is addressing complex business and science problems, and, says DiCesare, "this requires great technical skills, great communication skills, and the ability to prioritize many highly visible projects." Entry-level candidates should have a genuine interest in the biotechnology industry. DeCesare explains, "We are working to improve the quality of life for people worldwide. That gets you out of bed in the morning."

Recent Job Listings

Job Title	Education	Experience	Skills	Location
Lead Software Engineer	MS/Phd CS, Medicinal Chemistry		Software analysis, design, implementation, process and productivity improvements in medicinal chemistry	Cambridge, MA
Bioinformaticsw Computer Scientist	MS Biology, Biochemistry, Math, CS, Statistics		Perl, Java, biological database, microarray analysis	Cambridge, MA
Sr. Software Engineer	MA/MS Software Engineering	3 years	Oracle, UNIX, Apache, mod_perl, Mason	Cambridge, MA
Bioinformatics Scientist—Protein Annotation	PhD Biological Science, training in programming		Computational biology, Perl scripting	Cambridge, MA

Contact

Web: www.mlnm.com
Include "Source: Covin's Guide" on your resume.

NEW YORK LIFE INSURANCE COMPANY

"We continue proving that this Fortune 100 company provides an engaging environment for IT professionals. Our new state-of-the-art Internet facility is only one of the many benefits of being part of this team."

— Judy Campbell
— Chief Information Officer

• Microsoft IIS, IBM WebSphere, Vignette StoryServer •
• COBOL, Oracle, CA-IDMS, DB2, C++, Java •
• Insurance • Large shop •

"The most personalized insurance experience on the web," says eMarketer magazine in their 1999 survey, ranking New York Life #2 in top insurance sites. "[New York Life] seems to have genuinely considered the matter from the customer's point of view."

Web-based customer service and internal communication with a series of coordinated Intranets for employees and agents give New York Life its edge in corporate Internet design and development. Computing horsepower in the form of IBM mainframe systems providing daily support to millions of policyholders, are the backbone of the company's operations, and form the core repositories of critical customer data, much of which is now accessible to customers on the Web.

Surprise benefit: employees may volunteer in the community through company-facilitated programs.

Fast Facts	Revenues: $21.996B (2000)
	Employees: 11,800 (2000)
	Founded: 1845
	Financial services; life insurance
	Mutual company
Awards	Information Week: Top 500 Technology Innovators
	Business 2.0: Top 100 Net Economy Companies (1999)
	Dalbar: #2 web site in life insurance (2000)
	Financial Technology Expo: Java Cup (1998)
	Financial NetNews: Best Insurance Site (1998)
	About.com: Best Insurance Site of the Net
	Business Marketing: Netmarketing 200
Headquarters	51 Madison Avenue
	New York, NY 10010
	(212) 576-7000
	www.newyorklife.com

Business

New York Life was founded as Nautilus Insurance Company in 1845, changing to its current name four years later. As a mutual company, rather than a publicly-traded stock company, its members are its owners. They vote for the Board of Directors, and receive dividends from the distribution of excess profits. Their slogan, "The Company You Keep," is founded on their belief in financial strength, integrity, and humanity for customers, agents, and employees. Five thousand of the company's more than 6,000 employees work at corporate headquarters.

Some milestones in the company's history serve to show how they became one of the top-rated insurance companies in the country. In 1845, they paid the first cash dividend ever paid to policy owners in America. In 1899, they became the first American insurance company to publish a detailed financial report for policy holders. In 1894, they became the first company to issue insurance policies to women, at equal rates as those for men, and two years later, the first to issue policies to the disabled and those working in hazardous jobs. More recent initiatives revolve around the Internet. In 1998, they became the first insurer to offer a full range of customer services on the Web, since reflected in the many awards their site has won in the industry.

New York Life Insurance's products include a range of life insurance options. Through its subsidiary, New York Life Investment Management LLC, the company offers investment management and trust services to individual, institutional, and corporate clients. Through another subsidiary, New York Life International, Inc., the company extends its insurance and investment services to emerging markets in Asia and Latin America. The company's philanthropic arm, the New York Life Foundation, has focused on support of less fortunate children in the United States. Additional corporate awards include *Working Mother's* Top 100 Employers for Working Mothers and *Computerworld's* Best Places to Work in IS.

New York Life's headquarters building is a landmark in the New York city skyline, noted for its distinctive cone top, lead-covered copper finished in gold gilt. The company's consistent financial performance and credit ratings such as AA1 from Moody's, AA+ from Standard & Poor's, and A++ from A.M. Best set it apart from competitors like MetLife and Prudential. That, and a well-trained network of 9,000 agents that have kept the company an industry leader in number of agents qualifying for the Million Dollar Round Table sales award for 45 years in a row.

Technology

New York Life uses Cisco routers, switches, and other network equipment and Cabletron hubs. EMC is their primary storage vendor; STK supplies their tape systems, and IBM their high-volume printer systems. Nortel, Octel, and Mitel are used for voice communication systems.

Languages used include C, C++, Visual Basic, and Java for the client-server environment, as well as COBOL, Assembler, and PL/I with CICS on the mainframe side. Software for Web servers and related processing includes Netscape Server, Microsoft IIS, WebSphere, and Vignette StoryServer. Databases include CA-IDMS, DB2, Sybase, and Oracle. Tools used include Candle's mainframe monitoring tools, CA products for mainframe security and scheduling, SAP on UNIX and NT systems, Tivoli for software monitoring and distribution, and Entrust for web-based authentication.

Culture

Most staff members work in midtown Manhattan. The data center, in Clinton, New Jersey, is an office complex set on a scenic rural campus. Additional supporting technology units are based in Reno, Nevada; Tampa, Florida; and Austin, Texas. The Internet development team works in a dedicated facility, which includes a kitchen that offers complimentary coffee and tea.

Dress is business formal during the week and business casual on Fridays for the Manhattan home office. Technology sites outside the home office, including the Internet development team, observe a year-round business casual policy. Travel is limited to five percent of a staff member's time. Sixty telecommuters work from home for three to five days a week.

Benefits include a flexible plan in which employees choose benefits from a menu of options for medical and dental coverage, long-term disability and life insurance, and legal services. There are pre-tax spending accounts for health care and dependent care expenses, and a 401(k) plan after one year of service. Additional benefits include tuition reimbursement, a child care and elder care referral service and emergency backup child care center, as well as a Mother's center and adoption assistance. There are also fitness and medical centers onsite, and a subsidized cafeteria. The company observes 10 holidays. Alex LoBiondo, Director, Human Resources Technical Recruiting, says that candidates are "attracted by the fact that, as a Fortune 100 company, it is incumbent upon us to continue applying emerging applications—both hardware and software—in order to remain competitive. As a result, our IT staff gets to work with some of the most current technology in the industry." LoBiondo adds that the company also offers "skill bonus, performance awards, and multiple reward and recognition programs" as incentives.

The company supports a number of charitable and civic activities, such as a holiday toy food, and blood donation drives. Through its service program, Volunteers for LIFE, the company helps employees get involved in the community by offering a range of volunteer programs.

Candidates

New York Life has more than 1,100 technical professionals. On average, they have Bachelor's degrees and eight years of experience. Job titles range from Entry Level, to Programmer, Programmer Analyst, Specialist, Senior Specialist, Engineer, Assistant Vice President, Corporate Vice President, Vice President, Senior Vice President/CIO.

The company hired 60 technical professionals in 2000; approximately 10 percent of these were for entry-level positions. Employment agencies are used for more than half of the company's hiring needs, with employee referrals the second most used source for candidates (15 to 20 percent), as well as unsolicited resumes (15 to 20 percent). They expect to hire 50 to 100 technical professionals in the next year. Turnover is just over 5.7 percent.

When evaluating candidates, New York Life looks for a Bachelor's degree or equivalent experience, a strong technical background across disciplines, excellent interpersonal skills, and some business skills. "Also, project management experience is helpful," according to Barbara Scaturro, Corporate Vice President of the Resource Management team for the technology department. Adds Scaturro, "We appreciate candidates with qualities such as financial services experience, an understanding of customer service, and creativity." LoBiondo indicates that entry-level candidates should have a "Computer Science degree, with related applied experience, work-related experience outside the classroom, and a good GPA."

Recent Job Listings

Job Title	Education	Experience	Skills
No IT jobs currently posted. Sample job listings are shown below.			
Sr. Data Specialist	BA/BS	7 years	DB2
Programmer Analyst	BA/BS	5 years	BAL, COBOL II, JCL; IBM mainframe
Systems Programming Engineer	BA/BS	5 years	LAN/WAN network infrastructure; Cisco router & switch IOS configuration, maintenance management, and tuning; TCP/IP
Web developer	BA/BS	1 year	HTML, Java, JSP, Lotus Notes, Oracle, UNIX, Vignette StoryServer

Contact

Web: www.newyorklife.com
Email: barbara_scaturro@newyorklife.com
        Barbara Scaturro, Corporate Vice President
Email: recruit@newyorklife.com
Fax: (212) 447-4213
Mail: New York Life Insurance Company
        Corporate Information Dept., Recruiting Group
        51 Madison Avenue, Room 301
        New York, NY 10010
Include "Source: Covin's Guide" on your resume and cover letter.

NIELSEN MEDIA RESEARCH

"Our business is information processing, so a technical professional here is involved directly in the main business."

– Kim Ross
– Chief Information Officer

---

* IBM ES9000s, Sun E10000s *
* PL/I, SAS, C++, Sybase, Red Brick, WebLogic *
* Media research * Large shop *

Which programs stay on the air? When will they air? How much does a one-minute commercial cost? Television industry executives turn to Nielsen Media Research to help answer these questions. First comes measurement, then comes delivery. How to deliver the volumes of information needed for these decisions, in the fast-paced world of television, is Nielsen's Media's challenge and opportunity.

For more than 50 years, Nielsen Media Research has been the premier provider of audience information to the television industry. Television has evolved in that time from just three commercial broadcast networks and public television in the 1950s to nine commercial broadcast networks, more than 100 cable networks, more than 1,000 local television stations, and more than 100 nationally syndicated programs today.

More than 30,000 homes currently have electronic meters installed to capture television usage data for Nielsen Media Research. In 5,000 of these homes, additional demographic viewer information is collected and updated daily. At least four times a year, paper diaries, more than one million a year, are used to develop local ratings reports. The entire business is a massive data crunching, data warehousing, data mining exercise. And Nielsen Media Research invented it.

Surprise time off option: Employees may donate time to volunteer at local schools.

Fast Facts	Revenues: $506.5M (2000)
	Employees: 2,800 (2000)
	Founded: 1923
	Media Market Research
	Public: VNU (Dutch exchange)
	Subsidiary of VNU, a Dutch publishing company
Awards	PC Week: Fast Track 500 (1998)
Headquarters	375 Patricia Avenue
	Dunedin, FL 34698
	(727) 738-3280
	www.nielsenmedia.com

Business

Arthur C. Nielsen, an engineer who tested products for manufacturers to be sure they met specifications, realized his customers had no way of knowing how well their products were selling in comparison to their competitors. He started visiting stores in various locations to compare how different brands were selling, creating the new industry of market research. In 1936, Nielsen saw an MIT demonstration of a mechanical device that monitored radio listening, recording when a radio was on and what station it was set to. He bought the device and by 1942 was ready to launch the Nielsen Radio Index, using a national sample of 800 homes. Television ratings followed later, and finally, web ratings.

Nielsen Media Research provides an objective audience measurement service that allows advertisers and media to negotiate their rates. By delivering independent research on viewers' habits, advertisers and television broadcasters can determine a fair market value for a minute of airtime. In addition, which shows remain on the air, where they are scheduled, and when tune-in promotions appear are all partially determined by Nielsen Media Research data.

Corporate headquarters for Nielsen Media Research is on Park Avenue, in New York City, near the advertising agencies and networks that make up the company's primary customer base. Operations, however, moved to Florida, just north of Clearwater, in 1972. Approximately 300 employees work at corporate headquarters and more than 2,000 at the Florida site. In 1996, Dun & Bradstreet, then the parent of Nielsen Media Research, spun off the unit, and separated Nielsen Media Research from ACNielsen, a separate company that does consumer product market research. In 1999, VNU, a Dutch publisher of consumer and business magazines, textbooks, and directories, bought Nielsen Media Research. Also in 1999, the company started a joint venture with Net Ratings called Nielsen/Net Ratings, to focus on, what else, advertising on the Internet.

Technology

Two IBM ES9000s and 130 Sun servers form the core of Nielsen Media Research's hardware, along with 2,000 PCs. Eighty percent of development work is now on the Suns, primarily in C++ and PowerBuilder, but, more and more in Java. Sybase is the primary database management system, and Red Brick the Informix data warehouse engine. Lawson provides Enterprise Resource Planning (ERP). BEA Systems' WebLogic is used as an application server, a middleware product that holds the business application logic independent of web browsers and the database server. On the legacy side of the house, development is in PL/I, Assembler, and SAS, under VM, MVS, and CMS. Model 204 and DB2 are the databases supporting these applications. Additional tools used include HP/OpenView; BMC Patrol, a systems management tool; and Remedy, a help desk tool for recording customer calls.

Nortel Bay Networks' network routers form the backbone of an extensive nationwide network which connects 30,000 set-top boxes to the company's central computers, transmitting survey data up until 7:00 AM. It is processed, loaded into databases, and accessible through Internet browsers for customers by noon.

A typical project runs for 18 months, but the average varies between four months and four years, with 5 to 20 people on a team. One long-term project involved development of multi-media image handling, using pattern matching and digital signal processing (DSP) technology to determine which commercials have run, tagging them, and recording them so customers can review competitors' advertising. Video databasing, distribution, and tagging algorithms were developed in C++. Another sample project involved preparing an historical analysis of five years of summarized national viewing data, a 60gigabyte database in Sybase. This project initially took 18 months to complete and has had three major version releases since its first release. It was developed in PowerBuilder and has been delivered to customers on a private TCP/IP network. A third project incorporated an application server between the database and browser and involved building a national TV ratings database with daily ratings data held in a two-terabyte Red Brick data warehouse. It took two years to complete.

The newest technology Nielsen Media Research is investigating is extraction, loading, and transformation (ELT) for decision analysis, in which data is extracted from a database and loaded directly into a data warehouse. As Ross says, "Because we are in the electronic media business, a highly volatile industry which now spans TV and satellite distribution and the convergence of cable and the Internet, we are early adopters of solid technology."

Culture

Employees in Florida work in a campus setting. The company is located on a peninsula within a few miles of the fresh water of Tampa Bay and the salt water of the Gulf of Mexico. Nearby Lake Tarpon was home to the state's record bass. Outdoor sports like golf, tennis, and the Iron Man Triathlon (running, swimming, biking) are popular. Orlando, home of Disney World, is two hours away.

Benefits include medical, dental, and long-term disability insurance. Vacation starts with two weeks and increases to four weeks after 15 years. Nielsen Media Research observes 12 holidays and offers 10 sick days. They offer tuition reimbursement, an optional vision insurance program, and pension and 401(k) retirement programs. The company matches employees' charitable donations. They offer free coffee and a subsidized cafeteria, and sponsor golf, bowling, running, and softball teams. The engineering department has ping-pong and pool tables. There have been occasional spot job eliminations; no large-scale layoffs, and none of these has affected technical positions. Employees are given an overview of severance benefits as part of their initiation package. Turnover is 4.27 percent.

Dress in Florida is very casual; shorts are fine. In New York, dress is business formal during the week and business casual on Fridays. Standard hours are from 8:30 AM to 5:00 PM. Flexible work hours, including a 9-day alternate work schedule, are available to technical staff members. Typically, technical staff members work just over 40 hours a week, but occasional 50-hour weeks may be expected when a new system is going live or there is a production crisis that requires immediate resolution. There is little need for travel. And, as Betsy Williams, Vice President of Human Resources says, "Most employees in Florida live within 15 or 20 minutes of the company's offices."

Candidates

Four hundred technical staff members work in the Florida office; 20 in the New York office. Staff members are split among three departments—supporting national services and local TV stations, and data collection. Electrical engineers make up a portion of the technical jobs, but most technical jobs are data processing oriented. Jobs range from application development to network administration, database administration, and firmware and DSP development. On average, current staff members have a Bachelor's degree and three to five years of experience. Job titles range from Programmer/Analyst to Senior Software Engineer and Architect, including specialist positions in database technology, process assurance, and software quality assurance. On the management track, titles start at Project Manager, then continue through Senior Project Manager, Director, and Vice President.

Candidates should have the specific skills that match the company's technical environment. Ross explains, "We are not big on degrees, but we look for skills proven by experience, like Java or Sybase, not just experience with a related technology." Nielsen Media Research has dual management and technology tracks. "On the technical track," says Ross, "we look for creative, innovative people who are also willing to sit down and complete the job." For managers and lead developers, continues Ross, "Communication is vitally important. This is a fast-paced environment where our employees need to work in close coordination and learn from each other." Further, managers are expected to mentor team members and coordinate with marketing and senior management on project requirements.

Nielsen Media Research finds candidates primarily through online listings (monster. com) and employment agencies.

Recent Job Listings

Job Title	Education	Experience	Skills	Location
Sr. Programmer Analyst			C, PowerBuilder, XML, Java, wireless	Dunedin, FL
Software Engineer	BS/MS CS, EE	5+ years	C, C++, Java, sockets, TCP/IP, DHTML, JavaTV, Liberate, OpenTV SQL, ATSC, DVB, MPEG, AC-3	Tampa, FL
Sybase Database Administrator	BA/BS CS	5 years	Sybase Adaptive Server 11, Replication, IQ, PowerDesigner, ERWIN, Red Brick Data Warehouse, Rational Rose, SQL AnyWhere	Dunedin, FL

Contact

Web: www.nielsenmedia.com
Include "Source: Covin's Guide" on your resume and cover letter.

STATE FARM INSURANCE COMPANIES

"We have one of the largest privately-owned computer networks in the country."

– Dave Temby
– Superintendent, Corporate Employment

- Varied hardware environment -
- COBOL, PL/I, DB2, Visual Basic, C++ -
- Insurance and financial services - Large shop -

Pushing the limits of connectedness. State Farm has 185,900 workstations, connected through 20,000 servers, with 25 IBM S/390 class mainframes and 370 HP 3000s. Their communications environment looks like a top vendor's list from the industry – Cisco, Lucent, 3Com, Wall Data, WRQ, and Sterling Software, to start. Average commuting time – 15 to 20 minutes. Or, you could live in the country, in the farm-belt area halfway between Chicago and St. Louis.

Interviews are respectful, because, as Temby puts it, "With one-fourth of the country's car owners insured by State Farm, the person you are interviewing could be a policyholder." Increase those odds when you consider that the company is also the largest homeowner's insurance policyholder, the largest in recreational boats insurance, a significant player in life and health insurance, and has recently entered the financial services arena.

Surprise technology being investigated: hands-free wearable computers with a wireless networking interface.

Fast Facts	Revenue: $47.863B (2000)
	Employees: 81,516 (2001)
	Independent, contractor agents: 15,223
	Founded: 1922
	Insurance and financial services
	Mutual (owned by policyholders)
Awards	Computerworld: Best Places to Work in IT (2001)
	Information Week: Top 500 Innovators (2001)
	LATINA Style Magazine: 50 Best Companies for Latinas to work for in the U.S. (2001)
	The Black Collegian: Top 100 Employers (2001)
	Hispanic Magazine: Hispanic Corporate 100 (2001)
Headquarters	State Farm Insurance – Corporate South
	3 State Farm Plaza South
	Bloomington, IL 61791-0001
	(309) 766-2311
	http://www.statefarm.com

Business

State Farm's founder, George Mecherle, retired after twenty years as a farmer, when his wife's health started to fail. He worked as a successful insurance salesman, then decided that farmers, who drove much less often than their city counterparts, on streets much less congested and accident-prone, ought to get a better rate for this disparity in claims. His employers laughed at the idea, so he started his own company—owned by the farmers who bought the policies.

Within 20 years, State Farm had become the largest automobile insurer in the country, and remains so to this day. State Farm Mutual Automobile Insurance Company, known informally as the State Farm Insurance Companies, includes affiliates and subsidiaries that also offer insurance for property, renters, and high-risk motorists. Their network includes 25 regional offices and more than 1,000 claims service centers, servicing 66.2 million policies.

State Farm continues to emphasize its belief in shared values of quality service, mutual trust and integrity, and financial strength, to distinguish itself from its competitors. Its commitment to being its customers' first choice may explain why it boasts a 96 percent renewal rate for its auto policies, against an industry average of 92.5 percent.

Technology

IBM mainframes and Hewlett Packard 3000s form the backbone of State Farm's processing environment. Add to this more than 900 Netware servers, 18,000 Windows NT servers, and 925 UNIX servers, and almost 186,000 workstations. The company uses Lucent's PBX, remote access hub and telephone equipment. Cisco provides LAN and WAN switches and routers. 3Com supplies PCMCIA modems and LAN cards. Wall Data offers IBM host emulation with Rumba, and WRQ provides HP host emulation with Reflections. Sterling Software's TCP/IP runs on the IBM mainframe. The environment also includes Novell's Netware and NDS, and NetScape's Web Server and LDAP. HP's Open View software provides network management. Best/1 is used for configuration management of the workstations, Net/Op for troubleshooting, and CD-Lan for off-site connections.

Software development on the mainframe is in COBOL and PL/I, with Rexx and ISPF/DSM, and IMS and DB2 databases. On the HP 3000s, development is in HP COBOL. At the workstation level, software is developed in Visual Basic, C++, and WISE, primarily, with some Java and ASP scripting on the integration server. Additional database software includes Informix, Lotus Notes, Visio, and Flowcharter. There is some software in use specifically designed for the visually impaired.

Projects typically last six months and span efforts in support of a business initiative, infrastructure needs, or requirements for legislative changes. The Systems Department is divided into seven major areas:

- Systems Project Development
- Business and Information Systems
- Policyholder and Agency Systems
- Systems Technology/Department Services
- Systems Department Services
- Systems Enterprise Resource Planning
- Systems Enterprise Customer Care.

Culture

State Farm's headquarters is a nine-building complex in a suburban campus setting, sharing space with a lake, ducks and geese, and prairie land. Technical professionals work in cubicles that adjoin open areas to facilitate communications. Managers have offices. Dress is business casual – no jeans.

Official hours are from 8:00 AM to 4:15 PM, Central Standard Time. Technical professionals typically work from 40 to 60 hours a week. Overtime is not paid for exempt professionals; however, the company offers a number of flexible work schedules. One to two percent of systems employees telecommute. Seventy-five to eighty percent of the systems staff does not travel. The remainder travel from 20 to 50 percent of the time.

State Farm pays a portion of employees' group health or HMO, dental, and life insurance. In addition, the company offers optional accidental death, long-term care, and disability insurance. The company fully funds an employee retirement plan, contributes to employees' 401(k) and thrift plans, and offers tuition reimbursement. There are seven fixed holidays and three personal days. Employees earn two weeks of vacation to start, increasing to six weeks after 30 years.

Employees are encouraged to take one day off a year to support education activities at local schools. Managers continue a birthday tradition begun by the company's founder by remembering employees with a card and/or a rose.

State Farm Park includes 88 acres of facilities such as swimming pools; all-weather tennis courts; volleyball, badminton, and shuffleboard courts; a miniature golf course; softball fields; beach house; and fishing. The company sponsors leagues for baseball, racquetball, golf, billiards, and bowling. Company clubs include chess, camping, theatre, shooting, scuba, and gardening

Candidates

There are more than 5,506 Systems employees at State Farm. The Bloomington headquarters has the largest number of these (5,411). On average, technical/professional employees have Bachelor's degrees and 12 years of experience. There are three traditional career paths—for technical professionals, project managers, and managers. On the technical track, positions range from Data Processing Specialist to Analyst, Senior Analyst, and Systems Specialist. Project management positions include Project Manager, Program Director, and Technical/Business Director. The management track includes Manager/Supervisor, Function/Staff Director, Area Head (AVP), and Systems Vice President.

State Farm hired 325 technical professionals in the first half of 2001. Nearly half were entry-level positions. State Farm also recruits for IT positions from non-IT professional positions. Some of its current IT staff were formerly doctors, lawyers, and teachers. Turnover is 4.3 percent. Candidates are found through a combination of internal job postings, employee referrals, the Internet, and advertising. The company uses Hotjobs.com, Monster.com and a variety of other sites specifically aimed at attracting a diverse population.

State Farm's recruits from Michigan to Louisiana. Its top schools for entry-level professionals include Illinois State University, Illinois Wesleyan University, and University of Illinois—Urbana/Champaign. Candidates for the company's intern program should have a B+ Grade Point Average (GPA), strong communication and interpersonal skills and a major or minor in Computer Science or a related field.

State Farm looks for candidates with technical experience matching the position being filled. Because of its emphasis on customer focus, the company looks for candidates with above average communication skills, enthusiasm, a strong work ethic, and respect for others.

Recent Job Listings

Job Title	Education	Experience	Skills	Location
Systems Analyst Intern	Majoring in CS	B+ GPA	3 hours C, C++, COBOL, Java, PL/I, Pascal, Smalltalk, Visual Basic	Bloomington, IL
Business Analyst Intern	Majoring in Accounting, Insurance, Finance, MIS/CIS	6–9 hours in alternate discipline (i.e. Accounting major should have CS courses)	B+ GPA	Bloomington, IL
Directory Services/Security Analysts	High School, or equivalent work experience		HPUX, NOS, X. 500, GDS, Perl, LDAP	Bloomington, IL
PeopleSoft Security Analyst	High School or equiv.	1–2 years	PeopleSoft	Bloomington, IL
Electronic Funds Transfer (EFT) Systems Analyst	BA or equiv.	Experienced	COBOL, JCL, DB2, IMS	Bloomington, IL
Human Factors Specialist	Ph.D or MS in Human Factors Psychology	Experienced	GUI, WUI, creating metrics, HCI	Bloomington, IL

Contact

Candidates should submit their credentials to the following. Include CODE 99AD73 on all correspondence.

By mail: State Farm Human Resources
           CODE 99AD73
           3 State Farm Plaza South, K-1
           Bloomington, IL 61791-0001
By fax: (309) 763-2831
By email: jobopps.corpsouth@statefarm.com
By website: http://www.statefarm.com

A.G. Edwards, Inc.

Fast Facts   Revenues: $2.839B (2001) Employees: 17,000 (2001) Founded: 1887
Financial services; retail brokerage Public: AGE (NYSE)

Awards   Fortune: 100 Best Companies to Work For in America
Information Week: 500 Top Technology Innovators

Headquarters   1 N. Jefferson Avenue
St. Louis, MO 63103
(314) 955-3000
http://www.agedwards.com

Job Title	Education	Experience	Skills	Location

Technology Overview: Bull, Himalaya, HP-UNIX, Sun servers
No IT positions listed.

Ace Hardware Corporation

Fast Facts   Revenues: $2.945B (2000) Employees: 5,513 (2000) Founded: 1924
Retail; consumer hardware products for the home Cooperative

Awards   Information Week: Top 500 Technology Innovators
Computerworld: 100 Best Places to Work in IT

Headquarters   2200 Kensington Court
Oak Brook, IL 60523
(630) 990-6600
http://www.acehardware.com

Job Title	Education	Experience	Skills	Location
Network Analyst—SMS			MSI, Microsoft SMS, Novell	Oak Brook, IL
Associate Support Technician			Receiving equipment for the build room	Downers Grove, IL
Lead Computer Operator			Console, tape mounts	Oak Brook, IL

Aetna, Inc.

Fast Facts   Revenues: $26.819B (2000) Employees: 40,700 (2000)
Founded: 1853 Insurance; health care Public: AET (NYSE)

Awards   Computerworld: 100 Best Places to Work in IT
Information Week: Top 500 Technology Innovators

Headquarters   151 Farmington Avenue
Hartford, CT 06156
(860) 273-0123
http://www.aetna.com

Job Title	Education	Experience	Skills	Location
Architecture Manager		Experienced	RUP, OOAD, UML, SDLC	Middletown, CT
Web Designer		Experienced	HTML, VISIO	Middletown, CT
Project Manager, Billing Systems		5–10 years	TSO, COBOL, VSAM, IDMS, MQ Series	Middletown, CT
Lead Programmer Analyst		5+ years	CICS, DB2, IDMS, Endevor, COBOL II	Fort Washington, PA
Senior Application Developer	BS CS	5+ years	IBM Visual Age for Java, UML, UDB, DB2	Blue Bell, PA

Alcoa, Inc.

Fast Facts Revenues: $22.936B (2000) Employees: 142,000 (2000)
Founded: 1888 Manufacturer; aluminum Public: AA (NYSE)
Awards Industry Week: 100 Best Managed Companies
Fortune: Most Admired Companies
Headquarters 201 Isabella St. at 7th Street Bridge
Pittsburgh, PA 15212-5858
(412) 553-4545
http://www.alcoa.com

Job Title	Education	Experience	Skills	Location
EBS Data Warehouse Architect	BA/BS IT	8 years	OLAP, Oracle, Alcoa businesses	Pittsburgh, PA
Sr. Analyst—PeopleSoft HRMS		1–3 years	COBOL, SQR, PeopleCode, Oracle	Pittsburgh, PA
Sr. Project Leader—PeopleSoft HRMS	BA/BS IT	10 years	PeopleCode, Oracle, SQR, COBOL, Unix	Pittsburgh, PA
EBS Program Manager	BS or equivalent experience	10 years	EBS, Oracle, ERP	Pittsburgh, PA
Technical Writer	BA Technical Writing, English	1–3 years	PageMaker, HTML, Illustrator	Spartanburg, SC

Alcon Laboratories, Inc.

Fast Facts Revenues: $2.1B est. (1998) Employees: 9,500 (1998)
Founded: 1945 Manufacturer; vision products Subsidiary: Nestlé
Awards Fortune: 100 Best Companies to Work for in America
PC Week: Fast-Track 500

Headquarters	6201 South Freeway Fort Worth, TX 76134 (817) 293-0450 www.alconlabs.com			

Job Title	Education	Experience	Skills	Location
IT Manager, e-Commerce	BS CS, MS MIS or MBA preferred	11 years	EDI, e-Commerce	
Sr. Info Specialist—Oracle DBA	BA/BS IS, CS	9 years	Oracle 8i, PL/SQL, RMAN, AIX	
VPN with Remote Access Expert	BS Math, CS or MS	6 years	VPN	Ft. Worth, TX

The Allstate Corporation

Fast Facts	Revenues: $29.134B (2000) Employees: 41,800 (2000) Founded: 1930 Insurance; auto, home owners Public: ALL (NYSE)
Awards	Computerworld: 100 Best Places to Work in IT Fortune: Most Admired Companies
Headquarters	Allstate Plaza, 2775 Sanders Rd. Northbrook, IL 60062 (847) 402-5000 http://www.allstate.com

Job Title	Education	Experience	Skills	Location
Consultant		3 years	ASP, VB COM, Oracle, DB2, MQ Series, CICS	Arlington Heights, IL
Sr. Financial Analyst	BA/BS preferred		ASP, Java Script, SQL Server	Northbrook, IL
System Staff Programmer	BS preferred		Oracle, MS Excel, TenFold	Chicago, IL
Tech Consultant	BA/BS preferred	2 years	Brio, Essbase, BSS, Monarch	Atlanta, GA
Asc Systems Consultant	BS CS		Oracle, Precise TKPROF, C, Perl	Chicago, IL

Alston & Bird LLP

Fast Facts	Revenues: $160M (1998) Employees: 1,000 est. (1998) Founded: 1893 Legal services Partnership
Awards	Fortune: 100 Best Companies to Work for in America
Headquarters	1 Atlantic Center, 1201 W. Peachtree Street Atlanta, GA 30309-3424 (404) 881-7000 http://www.alston.com

Job Title	Education	Experience	Skills	Location

Technology Overview: Netware 4.1, Windows NT, Unix, Counsel Connect, Westlaw, Lexis/Nexis

No job openings posted.

American Cast Iron Pipe Co. (ACIPCO)

Fast Facts	Revenues: $600M (2000) Employees: 2,800 (2000) Founded: 1905
	Manufacturer; iron and steel pipes Private
Awards	PC Week: Fast-Track 500
	Fortune: 100 Best Companies to Work for in America
Headquarters	1501 N. 31st Avenue
	Birmingham, AL 35207
	(205) 325-7701
	http://www.acipco.com

Job Title	Education	Experience	Skills	Location

No job listings posted.

American Century Investments, Inc.

Fast Facts	Revenues: $772M (1999) Employees: 2,924 (1999) Founded: 1958
	Financial services; mutual funds Private
Awards	Fortune: 100 Best Companies to Work for in America
Headquarters	4500 Main Street, Suite 1500
	Kansas City, MO 64111
	(816) 531-5575
	http://www.americancentury.com

Job Title	Education	Experience	Skills	Location

No jobs posted.

American Electric Power Company, Inc.

Fast Facts	Revenues: $13.694B (2000) Employees: 26,376 (2000)
	Founded: 1920s Utility; electricity Public: AEP (NYSE)
Awards	Computerworld: 100 Best Places to Work in IT
Headquarters	1 Riverside Plaza
	Columbus, OH 43215-2373
	(614) 223-1000
	http://www.aep.com

Job Title	Education	Experience	Skills	Location
IT Business Administrator	BA/BS	8 years	Enterprise Risk Profile	Columbus, OH
Security Systems Administrator	BA/BS CS	4 years	Tripwire, BindView, OS390/ RACF, Oracle	Columbus, OH
IT Security Architect	BA/BS CS	6 years	Lotus Notes, DB2 Security, Systor SAM	Columbus, OH
IT System Administrator	BA/BS, MCSE, MCP + I, Sun OS certification	4 years	NT, 2000 Server, TCP/IP, FTP	Columbus, OH
IT Co-Op	Pursuing degree	N/A	C, Java, Powerbuilder, Lotus Notes	

American Express Company

Fast Facts	Revenues: $23.675B (2000) Employees: 89,000 (2000) Founded: 1850 Financial services; credit card, travelers' checks Public: AXP (NYSE)
Awards	Fortune: 100 Best Companies to Work for in America PC Week: Fast-Track 500
Headquarters	World Financial Center, 200 Vesey St. New York, NY 10285 (212) 640-2000 http://www.americanexpress.com

Job Title	Education	Experience	Skills	Location
Sr. Manager, Technology Services		3 years	LANs, telecommunications	US
Business Systems Analyst		2 years	Risk management, merchant fraud	Arizona
MIS Analyst II			SQL, trend analysis	US
Business Analyst I	BS Finance/ Marketing a plus		Performance trends	US

American Family Insurance Group

Fast Facts	Revenues: $4.388B (2000) Employees: 7,300 (2000) Founded: 1927 Insurance; personal (auto, property-casualty) Mutual company
Awards	Computerworld: 100 Best Places to Work in IT

Headquarters 6000 American Parkway
Madison, WI 53783-0001
(608) 249-2111
http://www.amfam.com

Job Title	Education	Experience	Skills	Location
I/S AT Sr. Application Engineer			COBOL, CICS, Adabas, DB2, VB, ASP, Java, Webspher	Madison, WI
Information Services Intern	Transcript, aptitude test	Summer 2002	Web, database administration, network security	Madison, WI
Computer Services Technician 1	AA/AS Electronics, Computer Technology or equivalent experience, A+ certification		Installation, maintenance microcomputers, terminals, printers, data communications equipment	Madison, WI

American Skandia

Fast Facts Revenues: $10B (1999) Employees: 1,387 (1999) Founded: 1987
Insurance Subsidiary: Skandia Insurance Company, Ltd. (Sweden)
Awards Fortune: 100 Best Companies to Work for in America
Headquarters 3 Corporate Drive
Shelton, CT 06484
(203) 926-1888
http://www.americanskandia.com

Job Title	Education	Experience	Skills	Location
Web Instructional Designer			Intranet site, web	Shelton, CT

Amgen Inc.

Fast Facts Revenues: $3.448B (2000) Employees: 7,300 (2000) Founded: 1981
Manufacturer; drugs Public: AMGN (Nasdaq)
Awards Computerworld: 100 Best Places to Work in IT
Fortune: 100 Best Companies to Work for in America
Headquarters 1 Amgen Center Drive
Thousand Oaks, CA 91320-1799
(805) 447-1000
http://www.amgen.com

Job Title	Education	Experience	Skills	Location
Sr. Programmer/ Systems Analyst	BA/BS MBA preferred, Siebel certification a plus	8+ years	Orion	Thousand Oaks, CA
Sr. Network/ Systems Engineer	CCNA, CCNP	5–8+ years	Spectrum, Concord, Cisco Works2000	Thousand Oaks, CA
Sr. Database Administrator	BA/BS	4–7 years	Cshell, Cognos, Java, Kshell, Oracle, Siebel, E rwin, Source Safe, Microstrategy	Thousand Oaks, CA
Sr. Data Warehouse Archhitect	BA/BS or equivalent	5 years	Oracle 8i, Data Mart, Cognos	Thousand Oaks, CA
Technologist	BS CS, MCSE, MCP, CNE	3 years	Norton Ghost, Altiris PC Transplant Pro	Longmont, CO

Anheuser-Busch Companies, Inc.

Fast Facts	Revenues: $12.262B (2000) Employees: 23,725 (2000) Founded: 1852 Manufacturer; beverages (beer) Public: BUD (NYSE)
Awards	Industry Week: 100 Best Managed Companies Information Week: Top 500 Technology Innovators
Headquarters	1 Busch Place St. Louis, MO 63118 (314) 577-2000 http://www.anheuser-busch.com

Job Title	Education	Experience	Skills	Location

No IT positions posted.

Avon Products, Inc.

Fast Facts	Revenues: $5.715B (2000) Employees: 43,000 (2000) Founded: 1886 Manufacturer; cosmetics Public: AVP (NYSE)
Awards	Industry Week: 100 Best Managed Companies Computerworld: 100 Best Places to Work in IT
Headquarters	1345 Avenue of the Americas New York, NY 10105-0196 (212) 282-5000 http://www.avon.com

Job Title	Education	Experience	Skills	Location
Web Architect/ Sr. Web Architect		1–3 years	Oracle 8x, AS400, OS/390, Java, ASP, XML	Rye, NY
PeopleSoft Developer	BS CS	5+ years	Crystal, SQR, Cognos Powerplay, Impromptu	Rye, NY
Lead IT Analyst	BS CS	5 years	Manugistics, Mercator, Java, C++, Maestro, QAD MRP	Rye, NY
Sr. IT Analyst	BS CS or equivalent	2–5 years	VB 6.0, Oracle 8i, 3-tier	Rye, NY
Lead IT Analyst/ Sr. IT Analyst	BS CS or equivalent	2–5 years	Microstrategy, Oracle, Spanish language a plus	Rye, NY

AXA Financial, Inc.

Fast Facts	Revenues: $6.125B (2000) Employees: 17,400 (2000)
	Founded: 1890s Financial services Subsidiary: AXA (France)
Awards	Computerworld: 100 Best Places to Work in IT
Headquarters	1290 Avenue of the Americas
	New York, NY 10104
	(212) 554-1234
	http://www.axa-financial.com

Job Title	Education	Experience	Skills	Location

No jobs posted. Submit resume online for openings.

Barton Protective Services Inc.

Fast Facts	Revenues: $165M (1999) Employees: 9,446 (2000) Founded: 1977
	Services; security (guards) Private
Awards	Fortune: 100 Best Companies to Work for in America
Headquarters	11 Piedmont Center, Suite 410
	Atlanta, GA 30305
	(404) 266-1038
	http://www.bartonsolutions.com

Job Title	Education	Experience	Skills	Location

No IT positions posted.

Battelle Memorial Institute

Fast Facts	Revenues: $950M (2000) Employees: 7,100 (2000) Founded: 1923 Contract research Not-for-profit
Awards	Computerworld: 100 Best Places to Work in IT
Headquarters	505 King Avenue Columbus, OH 43201-2693 (614) 424-6424 http://www.battelle.org

Job Title	Education	Experience	Skills	Location
Sr. Programmer			C++, statistical data, LINUX, clearance	St. Robert, MO
Application Analyst I or II	BS CS, IS		Windows NT/ 2000, Microsoft SQL Server, VB	Columbus, OH
Help Desk Specialists 1 or 2	BS CS, IS	1–2 years	Directories, security software	Columbus, OH

Baxter International Inc.

Fast Facts	Revenues: $6.896B (2000) Employees: 43,000 (2000) Founded: 1931 Manufacturer; medical products Public: BAX (NYSE)
Awards	Industry Week: 100 Best Managed Companies Information Week: Top 500 Technology Innovators
Headquarters	1 Baxter Parkway Deerfield, IL 60015 (847) 948-2000 http://www.baxter.com

Job Title	Education	Experience	Skills	Location
Systems Analyst	BA/BS CS	4 years	RPG, AS/400, JDEdwards	Deerfield, IL
Lead Software Engineer		10 years	EDI, FDA, embedded systems programming	Deerfield, IL
ERP Program Manager		10 years	ERP for 3+ locations, 30 people, $1.5M budget	Glendale, CA
Principal Systems Engineer	BS Engineering, SQE certification		Medical device, V&V, software testing	Round Lake, IL
Sr. Principal Software Engineer R&D	BS EE, CS, MS preferred		Rational Rose, C, C++, circuit emulators,UML	Largo, FL

The Beck Group

Fast Facts	Revenues: $950M (2000) Employees: 687 (2000) Founded: 1912 Construction; commercial Private
Awards	Fortune: 100 Best Companies to Work for in America
Headquarters	1700 Pacific Avenue, Suite 3800 Dallas, TX 75201-4619 (214) 965-1100 http://www.beckgroup.com

Job Title	Education	Experience	Skills	Location

No IT jobs posted.

Becton, Dickinson and Company

Fast Facts	Revenues: $3.618B (2000) Employees: 25,000 (2000) Founded: 1897 Manufacturer; medical devices Public: BDX (NYSE)
Awards	Industry Week: 100 Best Managed Companies Computerworld: 100 Best Places to Work in IT
Headquarters	1 Becton Drive Franklin Lakes, NJ 07417-1880 (201) 847-6800 http://www.bd.com

Job Title	Education	Experience	Skills	Location
Junior Software Engineer	AS/BS CS	4+ years	Software development	San Jose, CA
Oracle DBA/ SAP Basis & UNIX Administrator	BA/BS IT	2 years	AIX, SAP, Oracle	San Jose, CA
Software Quality Engineer	BS/MS CS, EE, Math	3 years	Java, UML, SilkTest, FDA	San Jose, CA
Sr. Mac Software Engineer	BS CS	6 years	C++, MacApp, medical devices	San Jose, CA

Best Buy Co., Inc.

Fast Facts	Revenues: $15.327B (2001) Employees: 75,000 (2001) Founded: 1966 Retailer; consumer electronics Public: BBY (NYSE)
Awards	Fortune: Most Admired Companies Computerworld: 100 Best Places to Work in IT
Headquarters	7075 Flying Cloud Dr. Eden Prairie, MN 55344 (952) 947-2000 http://www.bestbuy.com

Job Title	Education	Experience	Skills	Location
Consultant 2, Technical		6 years	Retek, HP UX, Oracle, PL/SQL	Eden Prairie, MN
Consultant 2, Technical	BA Marketing or equivalent	12+ years	Infrastructure, integration	Eden Prairie, MN
Consultant 4, Technical	BS CS or related	8+ years	Java, J2EE, MQ Integrator, Oracle, Retek, i2, Clarify	Eden Prairie, MN
Consultant 4, Technical	BS Computer Engineering or equivalent experience	10+ years	Consumer technologies, life cycle, business modeling	Eden Prairie, MN
Mgr 2, Product/ Capability		5+ years	Retail, registers, kiosks	Eden Prairie, MN

BorgWarner Inc.

Fast Facts   Revenues: $2.646B (2000) Employees: 14,000 (2000) Founded: 1928
Manufacturer; auto powertrains Public: BWA (NYSE)

Awards   Industry Week: 100 Best Managed Companies

Headquarters   200 S. Michigan Avenue
Chicago, IL 60604
(312) 322-8500
http://www.bwauto.com

Job Title	Education	Experience	Skills	Location

No job listings at corporate site. Job listings decentralized at subsidiaries.

Bowater Incorporated

Fast Facts   Revenues: $2.5B (2000) Employees: 6,400 (2000) Founded: 1950s
Manufacturer; paper and pulp Public: BOW (NYSE)

Awards   Industry Week: 100 Best Managed Companies

Headquarters   55 E. Camperdown Way
Greenville, SC 29602
(864) 271-7733
http://www.bowater.com

Job Title	Education	Experience	Skills	Location

No job listings posted.

Bright Horizons Family Solutions, Inc.

Fast Facts   Revenues: $291.1M (2000) Employees: 11,800 (2000)
Founded: 1986 Services; day care center Public: BFAM (Nasdaq)

Awards   Fortune: 100 Best Companies to Work for in America

Headquarters   200 Talcott Avenue South
                    Watertown, MA 02472
                    (617) 673-8000
                    http://www.brighthorizons.com

Job Title	Education	Experience	Skills	Location

No IT job listings posted.

Brinker International, Inc.

Fast Facts   Revenues: $2.474B (2001) Employees: 78,500 (2001) Founded: 1975
                  Restaurant chains Public: EAT (NYSE)
Awards   Computerworld: 100 Best Places to Work in IT
                  Information Week: Top 500 Technology Innovators
Headquarters 6820 LBJ Freeway
                  Dallas, TX 75240
                  (972) 980-9917
                  http://www.brinker.com

Job Title	Education	Experience	Skills	Location
Front Line Support Analyst	BA/BS	1 year	LAN, WAN, Routers, NT Server, Access, SQL, Btrieve	Dallas, TX
Corporate Help Desk Analyst	BA/BS, Comp TIA certifications, A+, Net+, MCP, MCSE a plus	1 year	Microsoft networking, RAS, VPN, restaurant experience	Dallas, TX

Bristol-Myers Squibb Company

Fast Facts   Revenues: $18.216B (2000) Employees: 44,000 (2000)
                  Founded: 1887 Manufacturer; pharmaceuticals Public: BMY (NYSE)
Awards   Industry Week: 100 Best Managed Companies
                  Fortune: Most Admired Companies
Headquarters 345 Park Avenue
                  New York, NY 10154-0037
                  (212) 546-4000
                  http://www.bms.com

Job Title	Education	Experience	Skills	Location
Analyst Senior Advisor	BA/BS IT, Business, CS	5–6 years	Data Mart, Oracle PLSQL, Impromptu, PowerBuilder, Crystal, C, pharmaceutical experience	Plainsboro, NJ

Job Title	Education	Experience	Skills	Location
Sr. Advisor Architect			Data Modeling, ER Gap Analysis, Star schema	Plainsboro, NJ
Client/Server Developer	BS CS or equivalent	2–3 years	SAP DM FSS COTC, VB C++, Oracle, Wonderware, InTouch, Visual SourceSafe	Evansville, IN
AR Team Lead Project Manager	BS, MBA or MS desirable		COBOL, SAS, CARRS, SAP OTC	Evansville, IN
Principal Analyst	BA/BS, MA/MS CS	3–6 years	JavaScript, DreamWeaver	Skillman, NJ

Brobeck, Phleger & Harrison LLP

Fast Facts Revenues: $476M (2000) Employees: 1,514 (1999) Founded: 1926
Professional services; legal Partnership
Awards Fortune: 100 Best Companies to Work for in America
Headquarters 1 Market, Spear Street Tower
San Francisco, CA 94105
(415) 442-0900
http://www.brobeck.com

Job Title	Education	Experience	Skills	Location
Database Developer	BA/BS	7–10 years	Database design, law firm experience	San Francisco, CA

Burlington Coat Factory Warehouse Corporation

Fast Facts Revenues: $2.4B (2001) Employees: 22,000 (2001) Founded: 1972
Retailer; clothing Public: BCF (NYSE)
Awards Computerworld: 100 Best Places to Work in IT
Information Week: Top 500 Technology Innovators
Headquarters 1830 Route 130
Burlington, NJ 08016
(609) 387-7800
http://www.coat.com

Job Title	Education	Experience	Skills	Location
Oracle Applications DBA/Project Leader		2+ years	Oracle Rel 11i, SQLNet, PL/SQL, Form 4.5, Financials	Burlington, NJ
Entry-Level Printer Operator			MS Excel, price tickets	Burlington, NJ

Cabot Corporation

Fast Facts	Revenues: $1.523B (2000) Employees: 4,500 (2000) Founded: 1882 Manufacturer; carbon black Public: CBT (NYSE)
Awards	Computerworld: 100 Best Places to Work in IT Information Week: Top 500 Technology Innovators
Headquarters	75 State Street Boston, MA 02109-1806 (617) 345-0100 http://www.cabot-corp.com

Job Title	Education	Experience	Skills	Location
No IT jobs posted.				

Capital One Financial Corporation

Fast Facts	Revenues: $5.424B (2000) Employees: 19,247 (2000) Founded: 1995 Financial services; credit cards Public: COF (NYSE)
Awards	Fortune: 100 Best Companies to Work for in America Computerworld: 100 Best Places to Work in IT
Headquarters	2980 Fairview Park Drive, Suite 1300 Falls Church, VA 22042-4525 (703) 205-1000 http://www.capitalone.com

Job Title	Education	Experience	Skills	Location
IT Director of Integrated Testing	BA/BS, graduate degree preferred	10–15 years	Load/capacity testing, UNIX, NT, OS/390, Unisys, Tandem	Falls Church, VA
SQL DBA	BA/BS CS, IS, Business	3–5 years	Oracle 8i, 500Gb with 2000- 3000 users, DTS, BCP scripts	Plano, TX
Senior Desktop Architect	BS CS, CNE, MCSE, CAN, MVP, CCNA certification	10+ years	Managing dll's, Windows NT and 2000 servers	Richmond, VA
Datawarehouse Development Associate	BA/BS	1+ years	Oracle, HP-UX, SQL Plus, UNIX korne shell, ETL tools	Boise, ID
Business Information Officer— Telephony	BA/BS, Postgraduate degree preferred	16+ years, executive level	Primary Business IT advocate	Falls Church, VA

Caterpillar Inc.

Fast Facts	Revenues: $20.175B (2000) Employees: 68,440 (2000)
	Founded: 1890s Manufacturer; heavy equipment Public: CAT (NYSE)
Awards	Information Week: Top 500 Technology Innovators
	Computerworld: 100 Best Places to Work in IT
Headquarters	100 NE Adams Street
	Peoria, IL 61629
	(309) 675-1000
	http://www.cat.com

Job Title	Education	Experience	Skills	Location
Principal Computer Systems Specialist	MS CS, minor in Linguistics preferred		Arbortext, Softquad, Transit, Trados, Java, Perl	San Diego, CA
AS/400 Programmer Analyst	BA/BS CS	3 years	AS/400, RPG III	Peoria, IL
Business System Analyst	BA/BS technical		Solar Turbine, data integrity, CADDS	San Diego, CA
Systems Analyst	BA/BS or GED	2 years	SDLC, Caterpillar Financial Services Corporation (CFSC)	Nashville, TN

CIGNA Corporation

Fast Facts	Revenues: $19.994B (2000) Employees: 43,200 (2000)
	Founded: 1792 Insurance; group plans Public: CI (NYSE)
Awards	Information Week: Top 500 Technology Innovators
	Computerworld: 100 Best Places to Work in IT
Headquarters	1 Liberty Place
	Philadelphia, PA 19192-1550
	(215) 761-1000
	http://www.cigna.com

Job Title	Education	Experience	Skills	Location
DB2/UDB System Administrator	BA/BS CS	5–7 years	Oracle, AIX	Hartford, CT
Information Protection Engineering Specialist			SSO/Smartcards, PKI, LDAP, SIRT, LOBs	Bloomfield, CT

Sr. Analyst, Information Architecture and Mgt.	BA Business, Finance, Healthcare Administration	3–5 years	Medicom, RedBrick, Phoenix, Cognos Powerplay, Impromptu, SAS, QMF	Bloomfield, CT
e-Commerce Senior Developer	BA/BS CS	3+ years	IBM Visual Age, EJB, WebSphere, AIX, UDB/DB2, MQ Series	Bloomfield, CT
AVP, Technology/ Process Improvement	BA/BS	10 years	CPAY, CES II, Hyperion, Oracle A/P	Philadelphia, PA

Cincinnati Financial Corporation

Fast Facts	Revenues: $2.331B (2000) Employees: 3,106 (2000) Founded: 1950 Financial services; insurance Public: CINF (Nasdaq)
Awards	Computerworld: 100 Best Places to Work in IT Information Week: Top 500 Technology Innovators
Headquarters	6200 S. Gilmore Road Fairfield, OH 45014-5141 (513) 870-2000 http://www.cinfin.com

Job Title	Education	Experience	Skills	Location

Technology overview: Mainframe, networked, and PC-based systems. Current projects center around the development of client-server or Web-based systems.

No IT jobs posted online. Submit resume.

Colgate-Palmolive Company

Fast Facts	Revenues: $9.358B (2000) Employees: 38,300 (2000) Founded: 1806 Manufacturer; consumer products (personal care) Public: CL (NYSE)
Awards	Industry Week: 100 Best Managed Companies Information Week: Top 500 Technology Innovators
Headquarters	300 Park Avenue New York, NY 10022 (212) 310-2000 http://www.colgate.com

Job Title	Education	Experience	Skills	Location

No job listings posted. Submit resume.

Comerica Incorporated

Fast Facts	Revenues: $4.088B (2000) Employees: 10,3610 (2000)
	Founded: 1849 Financial services; banking Public: CMA (NYSE)
Awards	Computerworld: 100 Best Places to Work in IT
	PC Week: Fast-Track 500
Headquarters	Comerica Tower at Detroit Center
	500 Woodward Avenue, MC 3391
	Detroit, MI 48226
	(313) 222-4000
	http://www.comerica.com

Job Title	Education	Experience	Skills	Location

No IT jobs posted online. Submit resume.

The Container Store

Fast Facts	Revenues: $260M (2001) Employees: 1,500 (2001) Founded: 1978
	Retailer; specialty (consumer storage products) Private
Awards	Fortune: 100 Best Companies to Work for in America
	PC Week: Fast-Track 500
Headquarters	2000 Valwood Parkway
	Dallas, TX 75234-8800
	(214) 654-2000
	http://www.containerstore.com

Job Title	Education	Experience	Skills	Location

No IT jobs posted.

Continental Airlines, Inc.

Fast Facts	Revenues: $9.899B (2000) Employees: 54,300 (2000) Founded: 1934
	Transportation; airline Public: CAL (NYSE)
Awards	Fortune: 100 Best Companies to Work for in America
Headquarters	1600 Smith Street
	Houston, TX 77002
	(713) 324-5000
	http://www.continental.com

Job Title	Education	Experience	Skills	Location

In light of recent events, Continental is temporarily suspending all hiring activity.

Adolph Coors Company

Fast Facts	Revenues: $2.414B (2000) Employees: 5,850 (2000) Founded: 1873
	Manufacturer; beverages (beer) Public: RKY (NYSE)
Awards	Industry Week: 100 Best Managed Companies
	Fortune: Most Admired Companies
Headquarters	311 10th Street
	Golden, CO 80401-0030
	(303) 279-6565
	http://www.coors.com

Job Title	Education	Experience	Skills	Location
IT Manager—SAP			FI/CO SAP v. 4.6, VSAP	Golden, CO
IT Group Manager Level II		7 years	PMI ISO9000, SAP, SD, manage 50–100	Golden, CO
Sr. Business Analyst		3–5 years	SAP, Business Objects, IDS, Q+E, Oracle, Process Book	Elkton, VA
IT Manager II		5–10 years	SAP R/3, PP-PI, APO-PP/DS	Golden, CO
Business Team Lead		5–10 years	SAP R/3, MM	Golden, CO

Corning Incorporated

Fast Facts	Revenues: $7.127B (2000) Employees: 40,300 (2000) Founded: 1851
	Manufacturer; fiber optic cable Public: GLW (NYSE)
Awards	Computerworld: 100 Best Places to Work in IT
	Fortune: 100 Best Companies to Work for in America
Headquarters	1 Riverfront Plaza
	Corning, NY 14831-0001
	(607) 974-9000
	http://www.corning.com

Job Title	Education	Experience	Skills	Location
Corporate Staff Infrastructure Leader	BA/BS		NT Server, WAN, 1,500 users, $1.5 million budget	Corning, NY
Database/ Datawarehouse Analyst	BA/BS		Database performance, recovery	Painted Post, NY
Finance—Information Delivery Analyst	BA/BS		PeopleSoft, financials	Horseheads, NY

Lead Developer, Supervisor	BA/BS		Erwin, IDM, SCC	Painted Post, NY
Voice/Video Team Leader	BA/BS		Wireless, video conferencing, PBX, ACD	Corning, NY

Dana Corporation

Fast Facts	Revenues: $12.46B (2000) Employees: 79,300 (2000) Founded: 1904 Manufacturer; auto parts (axles, engines) Public: DCN (NYSE)
Awards	Industry Week: 100 Best Managed Companies Fortune: Most Admired Companies
Headquarters	4500 Dorr Street Toledo, OH 43697 (419) 535-4500 http://www.dana.com

Job Title	Education	Experience	Skills	Location
Engineering Systems Information Technologies	BS CS, UNIX certification		Unigraphics, Pro-E, Abaqus, Gambit, Tgrid, Visual C, VB, Fortan, Lotus Notes, Domino	Lisle, IL

David Weekly Homes

Fast Facts	Revenues: $828M (2000) Employees: 1,010 (2000) Founded: 1976 Construction; private homes Private
Awards	Fortune: 100 Best Companies to Work For in America
Headquarters	1111 N. Post Oak Road Houston, TX 77055 (713) 963-0500 http://www.davidweeklyhomes.com

Job Title	Education	Experience	Skills	Location

No IT jobs posted.

Deere & Company

Fast Facts	Revenues: $12.964B (2000) Employees: 43,700 (2000) Founded: 1837 Manufacturer; heavy equipment Public: DE (NYSE)
Awards	Computerworld: 100 Best Places to Work in IT Information Week: Top 500 Technology Innovators

Headquarters   1 John Deere Place
Moline, IL 61265-8098
(309) 765-8000
http://www.deere.com

Job Title	Education	Experience	Skills	Location
Business System Analyst			Systems development, health care	Moline, IL
Infrastructure Analyst	MCSE, CNA certification desirable		Linux, Apache, Microsoft SQL Server	Des Moines, IA
Database Analyst	BA/BS MIS, CS or equivalent experience		SQL, data modeling, data warehouse	Des Moines, IA
Information Technology Analyst	BA/BS MIS, CS or equivalent experience	2+ years	Java, ASP, XML, Javascript, MQSeries, e-Commerce	Des Moines, IA
Information Technology Analyst	BA/BS MIS, CS or equivalent experience	1–2 years	Quality assurance, authentication technologies	Des Moines, IA

DPR Construction, Inc.

Fast Facts   Revenues: $1.2B (2000) Employees: 2,000 (2000) Founded: 1990
Construction; large-scale commercial Private
Awards   Computerworld: 100 Best Places to Work in IT
Headquarters   1450 Veterans Boulevard
Redwood City, CA 94063
(650) 474-1450
http://www.dprinc.com

Job Title	Education	Experience	Skills	Location

No IT jobs posted.

Duncan Aviation

Fast Facts   Revenues: $225M (2000) Employees: 1,850 (2000) Founded: 1956
Services; aircraft maintenance Private
Awards   Fortune: 100 Best Companies to Work for in America
Headquarters   Lincoln Airport
Lincoln, NE 68524
(402) 475-2611
www.duncanaviation.com

Job Title	Education	Experience	Skills	Location
No IT jobs posted.				

E.I. du Pont de Nemours and Company (DuPont)

Fast Facts   Revenues: $28.268B (2000) Employees: 93,000 (2000)
Founded: 1802 Manufacturer; chemical products Public: DD (NYSE)

Awards   Industry Week: 100 Best Managed Companies
Fortune: Most Admired Companies

Headquarters   1007 Market Street
Wilmington, DE 19898
(302) 774-1000
http://www.dupont.com

Job Title	Education	Experience	Skills	Location
Manufacturing Site IT Leader	BS CS, MIS or equivalent experience	5–10 years	Lotus Notes, Domino.doc, DCS, PMS	LaPorte, TX
Information Systems Specialist	BS/MS IS, CS		SAP/HR, fluency in English	Asturias, Spain
Information Systems Specialist	AS/BS IS, CS		SAP/HR, Lotus Notes, Domino, fluency in English	Asturias, Spain
Database Administration/ Programmer Analyst	BS CS, MIS, Math, Engineering, Liberal Arts with relevant course work	5 years	Oracle, MS SQL, DEC/VAX, C++, VB, Cognos, Impromptu, Crystal Reports	Wilmington, DE
Programmer Analyst	BS CS, MIS, Math, Engineering, Liberal Arts with relevant course work	5 years	Cognos, D atastage, V BA-Excel, PL/SQL	Wilmington, DE

East Alabama Medical Center

Fast Facts   Revenues: $221.1M (2000) Employees: 1,829 (2000) Founded: 1952
Medical services; hospital Government-owned

Awards   Fortune: 100 Best Companies to Work for in America

Headquarters   2000 Pepperell Parkway
Opelika, AL 36801
(334) 749-3411
http://www.eamc.org

Job Title	Education	Experience	Skills	Location
No IT jobs posted.				

Eastman Chemical Company

Fast Facts	Revenues: $5.292B (2000) Employees: 14,600 (2000) Founded: 1920 Manufacturer; specialty chemicals Public: EMN (NYSE)
Awards	Computerworld: 100 Best Places to Work in IT Interactive Week: The Internet 500
Headquarters	100 N. Eastman Road Kingsport, TN 37660 (423) 229-2000 http://www.eastman.com

Job Title	Education	Experience	Skills	Location

No IT jobs posted.

Eaton Corporation

Fast Facts	Revenues: $8.309B (2000) Employees: 59,000 (2000) Founded: 1911 Manufacturer; heavy equipment parts (axles,) Public: ETN (NYSE)
Awards	Industry Week: 100 Best Managed Companies
Headquarters	Eaton Center, 1111 Superior Avenue Cleveland, OH 44114-2584 (216) 523-5000 http://www.eaton.com

Job Title	Education	Experience	Skills	Location
Division IT Manager		7–10 years	Execute critical IT initiatives	Milwaukee, WI
Infrastructure Supervisor/Lead Analyst		7–10 years	Network, telephone, help desk services	Auburn, IN
Programmer/ Analyst	AS CS or equivalent experience	3–5 years	AS/400	Fayetteville, NC
Software Engineer	BS CS or related discipline	1–3 years	C, C++, Pascal, Ada, PLC's, UART drivers, DSP's	Milwaukee, WI
Information Technology Development Program	Pursuing undergraduate degree in technology or recent graduate	Entry-level and summer intern	B2B applications, Oracle, portal strategies	Various locations

Ecolab Inc.

Fast Facts	Revenues: $2.264B (2000) Employees: 14,250 (2000) Founded: 1923 Services; commercial cleaning and maintenance Public: ECL (NYSE)
Awards	Industry Week: 100 Best Managed Companies
Headquarters	370 N. Wabasha Street St. Paul, MN 55102 (651) 293-2233 http://www.ecolab.com

Job Title	Education	Experience	Skills	Location
Systems Manager	BS CS	8 years	AS/400, RPG IV	Grand Forks, ND
Sr. Systems Auditor	BS, CISA certification	4 years	IT risk assessment, Spanish or Asian languages a plus	St. Paul, MN

Edison International

Fast Facts	Revenues: $11.717B (2000) Employees: 18,530 (2000) Founded: 1886 Utility; electricity Public: EIX (NYSE)
Awards	Computerworld: 100 Best Places to Work in IT Information Week: Top 500 Technology Innovators
Headquarters	2244 Walnut Grove Avenue Rosemead, CA 91770 (626) 302-1212 http://www.edison.com

Job Title	Education	Experience	Skills	Location
Internet Support Specialist	BA/BS		Perl, Javascript, ASP, Lotus Notes, Domino, Java, INET	So. California Edison
Technical Lead			OS/390, HAGEO, SMP/E, RS/6000	So. California Edison
Supply Chain Analyst	BA/BS Business, CPM certificate	5 years	Supply chain methodology, activity-based costing	Rosemead, CA
Information Security Technical Specialist	BS CS, IS, Engineering, CISSP, MS preferred	3 years	Authentication, forensics, PKI, digital certificates	So. California Edison

Edward Jones

Fast Facts	Revenues: $2.212B (2000) Employees: 23,432 (2000) Founded: 1871 Financial services; brokerage Private
Awards	Fortune: 100 Best Companies to Work for in America
Headquarters	12555 Manchester Road
	Des Peres, MO 63131
	(314) 515-2000
	http://www.edwardjones.com

Job Title	Education	Experience	Skills	Location
Technical Consultant, Development Environment	BA/BS or equivalent experience	5+ years	COBOL, C, or Java, MF, IDMS, DB2	St. Louis, MO
Sr. Technical Consultant— Architecture Technology Advisor		7+ years	N-tiered architectures	St. Louis, MO
Team Leader CICS MQ Series	BA/BS or equivalent experience	10 years	CICS, MQSeries, IDMS, DB2	St. Louis, MO
Systems Programmer II— Data Center Operations	BA/BS	3–5 years	OS/390, SMP	St. Louis, MO
Sr. Programmer Analyst— Trades	Bachelor's	5+ years	COBOL, IDMS, DB2, JCL, CICS	St. Louis, MO

Eli Lilly and Company

Fast Facts	Revenues: $10.862B (2000) Employees: 35,700 (2000)
	Founded: 1876 Manufacturer; pharmaceuticals Public: LLY (NYSE)
Awards	Fortune: 100 Best Companies to Work for in America
	Industry Week: 100 Best Managed Companies
Headquarters	Lilly Corporate Center
	Indianapolis, IN 46285
	(317) 276-2000
	http://www.lilly.com

Job Title	Education	Experience	Skills	Location
Systems Analyst	BA/BS		SAP, Catalyst WMS	Indianapolis, IN
Web/Java Developer	BA/BS CS, IS or equivalent experience		Java, Cold Fusion, RUP	Indianapolis, IN

Job Title	Education	Experience		Skills	Location
Java/Oracle Developer	BS CS	2 years		JDBC, EJB, Oracle, Korn, Cold Fusion	Indianapolis, IN
Systems Analyst (GBIP Security)	BA/BS			SAP BASIS, R/3, BW, APO, Oracle, KRA 2	Indianapolis, IN
Scientific Systems Analyst				Solaris, IRIX, Oracle, C++, Perl, Shell	Indianapolis, IN

Emerson

Fast Facts	Revenues: $15.545B (2000) Employees: 123,400 (2000) Founded: 1890 Manufacturer; electrical control Public: EMR (NYSE)
Awards	Industry Week: 100 Best Managed Companies Information Week: Top 500 Technology Innovators
Headquarters	8000 W. Florissant Avenue St. Louis, MO 63136 (314) 553-2000 http://www.gotoemerson.com

Job Title	Education	Experience	Skills	Location
System Administrator— AS/400	BS CS	5 years	JDE, Pentasafe, Pegerine Trusted Link	St. Louis, MO

Engelhard Corporation

Fast Facts	Revenues: $5.543B (2000) Employees: 6,420 (2000) Founded: 1902 Manufacturer; specialty chemicals Public: EC (NYSE)
Awards	Industry Week: 100 Best Managed Companies Information Week: Top 500 Technology Innovators
Headquarters	101 Wood Avenue Iselin, NJ 08830 (732) 205-5000 http://www.engelhard.com

Job Title	Education	Experience	Skills	Location

No jobs posted.

Equifax Inc.

Fast Facts	Revenues: $1.966B (2000) Employees: 12,200 (2000) Founded: 1899 Financial services; credit card processing Public: EFX (NYSE)
Awards	Computerworld: 100 Best Places to Work in IT Information Week: Top 500 Technology Innovators

Headquarters	1550 Peachtree Street N.W. Atlanta, GA 30309 (404) 885-8000 http://www.equifax.com			

Job Title	Education	Experience	Skills	Location
Lead DBA	BA/BS CS	3–4+ years	Oracle, SQL*Loader, C, C++	Lombard, IL

Fannie Mae

Fast Facts	Revenues: $44.089B (2000) Employees: 4,100 (2000) Founded: 1938 Financial services; secondary mortgages Public: FNM (NYSE)
Awards	Fortune: 100 Best Companies to Work for in America Computerworld: 100 Best Places to Work in IT
Headquarters	3900 Wisconsin Avenue N.W. Washington, DC 20016-2892 (202) 752-7000 http://www.fanniemae.com

Job Title	Education	Experience	Skills	Location
Sr. Developer	BA/BS	6–8 years	WebLogic, Objective C, Web Objects	Herndon, VA
Engineer	BS CS, Engineering or equivalent experience		Perl, C, DNS, SMTP, WebLogic, iPlanet, J2EE	Washington, DC
Developer	BS CS	3–5 years	C++, UML, Rational Rose	Herndon, VA
Technical Project Manager	BS, MS CS desirable	7+ years	WebLogic, J2EE, XML	Herndon, VA
Sr. IT Analyst	BA/BS Math, Statistics	5 years	Remedy, Crystal Reports, Sybase	Washington, DC

FedEx Corporation

Fast Facts	Revenues: $19.629B (2001) Employees: 215,000 (2001) Founded: 1971 Services; package delivery Public: FDX (NYSE)
Awards	Fortune: 100 Best Companies to Work for in America Computerworld: 100 Best Places to Work in IT
Headquarters	942 South Shady Grove Road Memphis, TN 38120 (901) 818-7500 http://www.fedex.com

Job Title	Education	Experience	Skills	Location
Sr. Technical Analyst	BA/BS Business, Math	3–5 years	JavaScript, EJB, Oracle 8x, WebLogic, ETL	Memphis, TN
Sr. Technical Analyst	BA/BS Business, Math	5 years	Java, EJB, Shell Scripting, Oracle 8x, WebLogic	Tennessee
Sr. Technical Advisor	BA/BS	6–8 years	Oracle, data modeling, COBOL, ETL	Memphis, TN

Fenwick & West LLP

Fast Facts	Revenues: $148M (2000) Employees: 627 (2000) Founded: 1972
	Professional services; legal Partnership
Awards	Fortune: 100 Best Companies to Work for in America
Headquarters	Two Palo Alto Square
	Palo Alto, CA 94306
	(650) 494-0600
	http://www.fenwick.com

Job Title	Education	Experience	Skills	Location

No IT jobs posted.

Fifth Third Bancorp

Fast Facts	Revenues: $4.276B (2000) Employees: 12,246 (2000) Founded: 1863
	Financial services; banking Public: FITB (Nasdaq)
Awards	Computerworld: 100 Best Places to Work in IT
	Information Week: Top 500 Technology Innovators
Headquarters	38 Fountain Square Plaza
	Cincinnati, OH 45263
	(513) 579-5300
	http://www.53.com

Job Title	Education	Experience	Skills	Location
Business Analyst	BA/BS		UDS, CDs, IRAs, deposit experience	Cincinnati, OH
Business Analyst II	BA/BS		LOMAS, mortgage experience	Cincinnati, OH
Lead Business Analyst	BA Business, MIS, Finance or equivalent experience, MA preferred		LOMAS, banking experience	Cincinnati, OH

Systems Analyst II	BS CS, IS		VB, ASP, SQL Server	Cincinnati, OH
Telecommunications Analyst III	BA/BS	2 years	Wiring closets, cabling runs, telephony	Cincinnati, OH

FleetBoston Financial Corporation

Fast Facts	Revenues: $22.608B (2000) Employees: 53,000 (2000) Founded: 1791 Financial services; banking Public: FBF (NYSE)
Awards	Computerworld: 100 Best Places to Work in IT Fortune: Most Admired Companies
Headquarters	100 Federal Street Boston, MA 02110 (617) 434-2200 http://www.fleetboston.com

Job Title	Education	Experience	Skills	Location
Lead Tech Analyst			IDS, OPC, CA7, TSO, MVS JCL, banking experience	Waltham, MA
Tech Group Manager II			IIS, iPlanet	Ridgefield Park, NJ
Tech Business Partner I			SLAs, .net enterprise server	Ridgefield Park, NJ
Sr. Tech Analyst	AAS Telecommunications	3–5 years	MVS JCL, OPC, CA7, LAN, WAN	Albany, NY
Tech Analyst II			CA7, ACF2 Security, OS/390, Stratus, AS/400, Tandem	Johnston, RI

FPL Group, Inc.

Fast Facts	Revenues: $7.082B (2000) Employees: 9,838 (2000) Founded: 1925 Utility; electricity Public: FPL (NYSE)
Awards	Computerworld: 100 Best Places to Work in IT
Headquarters	700 Universe Boulevard Juno Beach, FL 33408-0420 (561) 694-4000 http://www.fplgroup.com

Job Title	Education	Experience	Skills	Location
Programmer Analyst	BS CS or equivalent experience	5–7 years	ABAP/4, R/3, 3-tier	N. Palm Beach, FL

Project Manager	BA technical discipline, PMI certification	5–10 years	TCMS2	Juno Beach, FL
Business Systems Analyst	BA/BS MIS, Business	5+ years	IM, developing user requirements	Juno Beach, FL
Technology Consultant		7+ years	SAP 4.5x, AIX, FI/CO, HR, BW, EBP	Juno Beach, FL
Computer Systems Analyst	BS technical discipline	7+ years	SAP FI/CO, HR, R/3, MM 4.5x, HR 4.6x	Juno Beach, FL

Frank Russell Company

Fast Facts	Revenues: $500M (2000) Employees: 1,300 (2000) Founded: 1936 Financial services; investment management. Subsidiary: Northwestern Mutual
Awards	Fortune: 100 Best Companies to Work for in America
Headquarters	909 A Street Tacoma, WA 98402 (253) 572-9500 http://www.russell.com

Job Title	Education	Experience	Skills	Location
No IT jobs posted. Previous sample jobs include:				
Sr. Technical Analyst	BA	5–7 years	VM/VSE, NCP, TCP/IP	Tacoma, WA
Sr. Engineer— Internet Infrastructure and Security	BA/BS CS	10–15 years	Best practices	Tacoma, WA
Rollout Analyst	BA/BS CS	5–7 years	EDM packaging, Install Shield	Tacoma, WA
Account Manager	BA/BS CS, Business, Finance, Master's a plus	10+ years	Financial industry, multiple platforms	Tacoma, WA

GATX Corporation

Fast Facts	Revenues: $1.312B (2000) Employees: 5,500 (2000) Founded: 1898 Financial services; leasing rail cars Public: GMT (NYSE)
Awards	Computerworld: 100 Best Places to Work in IT Information Week: Top 500 Technology Innovators
Headquarters	500 W. Monroe Street Chicago, IL 60661-3676 (312) 621-6200 http://www.gatx.com

Job Title	Education	Experience	Skills	Location

No IT jobs posted.

Genentech, Inc.

Fast Facts	Revenues: $1.646 (2000) Employees: 4,459 (2000) Founded: 1976
	Manufacturer; drugs Public: DNA (NYSE)
Awards	Fortune: 100 Best Companies to Work for in America
Headquarters	1 DNA Way
	S. San Francisco, CA 94080-4990
	(650) 225-1000
	http://www.gene.com

Job Title	Education	Experience	Skills	Location
Operations Specialist I	NT MCSE certification	2–3 years	ARCUS, ESO, UNIX, NT	
Systems Administrator II	BS CS	3–5 years	Legato, SAN StorageTek	
Sr. Statistical Programmer Analyst	BS Statistics, Math, CS or equivalent experience	4 years	SAS, Lifetest GLM, Mixed, Oracle Clinical	
Sr. Program Manager— Information Delivery	BS CS, MS or MBA preferred	7 years	CRM, Web portal, EIS	
Business Systems Analyst II	BA/BS Finance, Accounting, MBA a plus	3 years	Hyperion Essbase, Cognos PowerPlay, Lawson	

General Dynamics Corporation

Fast Facts	Revenues: $10.356B (2000) Employees: 43,300 (2000)
	Founded: 1952 Manufacturer; systems integrator Public: GD (NYSE)
Awards	Industry Week: 100 Best Managed
	Fortune: Most Admired Companies
Headquarters	3190 Fairview Park Drive
	Falls Church, VA 22042-4523
	(703) 876-3000
	http://www.gendyn.com

Job Title	Education	Experience	Skills	Location
Systems Engineer/ Architect	BS EE, CS		Visual C++, Java, Sybase, Threading, clearance	Chantilly, VA
Sr. Realtime Software Engineer	BS/MS CS, EE	7+ years	C, C++, SEI, VxWorks, PowerPC	Houston, TX

Manager Systems Engineering	BS CS, EE	10 years	SE, CMM, air traffic control	Columbia, MD
Senior Software Engineer	BS Engineering, Math, CS	8–12 years	C, C++, real-time embedded OS, encryption, COMPUSEC, clearance	Scottsdale, AZ
Sr. Principal MTS	BS EE, CS	20 years	RF-based tactical communication systems, waveform design	Taunton, MA

General Electric Company

Fast Facts Revenues: $129.417B (2000) Employees: 313,000 (2000)
Founded: 1879 Manufacturer; light industrial Public: GE (NYSE)

Awards Industry Week: 100 Best Managed Companies
Information Week: Top 500 Technology Innovators

Headquarters 3135 Easton Turnpike
Fairfield, CT 06431-0001
(203) 373-2211
http://www.ge.com

Job Title	Education	Experience	Skills	Location
Black Belt—ERP Process	BA/BS technical, MBA, Six Sigma, GB certification		Minitab, DMAIC, DFSS, Workout!	Atlanta, GA
Software Engineer	BA/BS Business, CS, Math, IMLP/ISLC	3 years	Six Sigma, UNIX, NT	Cincinnati, OH; Louisville, KY; Parkersburg, WV; Schenectady, NY
e-Engineer	BS, Engineering, CS, MS preferred		C, C++, VB/VBA, MFC, XML, EJB, JINI, J2EE	Niskayuna, NY
TPS Client Integration Manager	DMAIC training	5–7 years	Oracle, SAP, JD Edwards AP, IMLP	Bergen op Zoom
Infrastructure Site Leader—Global Signaling	BA/BS CS, Business, Master's a plus, GE Leadership program	3 years	Six Sigma, network, voice, video, server and desktop	Kansas City, MO

General Mills, Inc.

Fast Facts	Revenues: $7.078B (2001) Employees: 11,001 (2001) Founded: 1866
	Manufacturer; cereals Public: GIS (NYSE)
Awards	Computerworld: 100 Best Places to Work in IT
	Industry Week: 100 Best Managed Companies
Headquarters	1 General Mills Boulevard
	Minneapolis, MN 55426
	(763) 764-7600
	http://www.generalmills.com

Job Title	Education	Experience	Skills	Location
Technology overview: Oracle, SQL, VB, Visual InterDev, IIS, SAP, HP-UX, MVS				
Sr. Research Information Scientist	BA/BS Food Science, Biology, Chemistry, MA/MS Library Science, IS	3+ years	Dialog, STN, patents, patent process, technical surveillance	Minneapolis, MN

Georgia-Pacific Corporation

Fast Facts	Revenues: $22.218B (2000) Employees: 80,000 (2000)
	Founded: 1927 Manufacturer; paper products Holding co: Georgia-Pacific Group
Awards	Computerworld: 100 Best Places to Work in IT
Headquarters	Georgia-Pacific Center, 133 Peachtree St. N.E.
	Atlanta, GA 30303
	(404) 652-4000
	http://www.gp.com

Job Title	Education	Experience	Skills	Location
Technical Analyst	BA/BS, Cisco CCNA certification		LAN/WAN 650+ locations, PBX, frame relay, ATM, IP	Atlanta, GA
Systems Analyst	BA/BS	3–5 years	SAP WM	Atlanta, GA
Lead Analyst	BA/BS CS	7–10 years	EDI translator maps, SAP	Atlanta, GA
Sr. Systems Analyst	BA/BS	5–7 years	SAP SD Pricing	Atlanta, GA
Technical Lead	BA/BS	4+ years	MQSeries, Biztalk, WebMethods, VB/COM, Java	Atlanta, GA

The Goldman Sachs Group, Inc.

Fast Facts	Revenues: $33B (2000) Employees: 22,627 (2000) Founded: 1869
	Financial services; investment banking Public: GS (NYSE)
Awards	Fortune: 100 Best Companies to Work for in America
	Red Herring: 100 Top Companies of the Electronic Age
Headquarters	85 Broad Street
	New York, NY 10004
	(212) 902-1000
	http://www.gs.com

Job Title	Education	Experience	Skills	Location

Technology overview: C, C++, Sybase, VB, Java

No IT jobs listed. Submit resume online.

Granite Rock Company

Fast Facts	Employees: 716 (1999) Founded: 1900
	Manufacturer; construction materials, rock quarry, asphalt Private
Awards	Fortune: 100 Best Companies to Work for in America
Headquarters	411 Walker Street
	Watsonville, CA 95076
	(831) 768-2000
	http://www.graniterock.com

Job Title	Education	Experience	Skills	Location

No IT jobs posted.

Griffin Hospital

Fast Facts	Revenues: $63M (1999) Employees: 748 (1999) Founded: 1909
	Health care; hospital Non-profit
Awards	Fortune: 100 Best Companies to Work for in America
Headquarters	130 Division Street
	Derby, CT 06418
	(203) 735-7421
	http://www.griffinhospital.org

Job Title	Education	Experience	Skills	Location
Data Analyst/ Research Assistant II	Master's Public Health		SAS procedures and statistics	Derby, CT

Guidant Corporation

Fast Facts	Revenues: $2.549B (2000) Employees: 9,252 (2000) Founded: 1994 Manufacturer; medical equipment Public: GDT (NYSE)
Awards	Industry Week: 100 Best Managed Companies Fortune: 100 Best Companies to Work for in America
Headquarters	111 Monument Circle, 29th Floor Indianapolis, IN 46204 (317) 971-2000 http://www.guidant.com

Job Title	Education	Experience	Skills	Location
Software Engineer	MS EE, CS	7–15 years	Embedded systems development, C, C++, OO, microprocessor assembly languages	St. Paul, MN

Harley-Davidson, Inc.

Fast Facts	Revenues: $2.906B (2000) Employees: 7,700 (2000) Founded: 1903 Manufacturer; motor cycles Public: HDI (NYSE)
Awards	Fortune: 100 Best Companies to Work For in America Computerworld: 100 Best Places to Work in IT
Headquarters	3700 W. Juneau Avenue Milwaukee, WI 53201-0653 (414) 343-4680 http://www.harley-davidson.com

Job Title	Education	Experience	Skills	Location
Programmer Analyst	BA/BS CS, Math, Business	1–7 years	AS/400, RPG, COBOL, Hyperion Enterprise, Business Objects	Milwaukee, WI

Harleysville Group Inc.

Fast Facts	Revenues: $802.6M (2000) Employees: 2,533 (2000) Founded: 1917 Insurance; personal and commercial Public: HGIC (Nasdaq)
Awards	Computerworld: 100 Best Places to Work in IT
Headquarters	355 Maple Avenue Harleysville, PA 19438-2297 (215) 256-5000 http://www.harleysvillegroup.com

Job Title	Education	Experience	Skills	Location
Application Developer			Code, test, debug	Harleysville, PA
Client/Server Applications Analyst			Recommendations on packaged PC software	Harleysville, PA
Data Modeler			Design, audit databases	Harleysville, PA
IT Training/ Implementation			Implementation plans of new systems	Field offices

Harrah's Entertainment, Inc.

Fast Facts	Revenues: $3.471B (2000) Employees: 40,000 (2000) Founded: 1937 Entertainment; casinos Public: HET (NYSE)
Awards	Computerworld: 100 Best Places to Work in IT Fortune: Most Admired Companies
Headquarters	One Harrah's Court Las Vegas, NV 89119 (702) 407-6000 http://www.harrahs.com

Job Title	Education	Experience	Skills	Location
Director, IT Development		9 years	Marketing and branding units	Las Vegas, NV
Manager	BA/BS CS, MIS	3–5 years	Property support	Joliet, IL
SDS (Slot Data Systems) Administrator			ALLTS (Loss Limits Systems), Par systems, Bravo units, AS/400	Memphis, TN
Vice President, Enterprise Systems Providers	BA/BS Business, Engineering, IT, Master's preferred	18–20 years	UNIX, AS/400, $26–35M budget	Memphis, TN
Support Specialist I or II	BA/BS CS or equivalent technical training	1–3 years	AS/400, UNIX, NT server, SDS, Events, Pit Player tracking, Saflok, POS	Las Vegas, NV

HCA, Inc.
(Columbia Information Systems)

Fast Facts	Revenues: $16.67B (2000) Employees: 164,000 (2000) Founded: 1968 Health care; hospitals Public: HCA (NYSE)
Awards	Computerworld: 100 Best Places to Work in IT

Headquarters	1 Park Plaza		
	Nashville, TN 37203		
	(615) 344-9551		
	http://www.hcahealthcare.com		

Job Title	Education	Experience	Skills	Location
Web Application Developer		3+ years	VB, SQL Server 6.5 7/2K, COM, ASP, MTS	Nashville, TN
Consulting Application Engineer	BA/BS, Lawson Application Certification	1–3 years	OS/390, UNIX, COBOL, Java, DB2	
Internet Services Analyst	BA/BS	1–3 years	CWA, Intranet element design, structure and flow	
Sr. Systems Business Analyst	BA/BS	3–7 years	WMP, SDLC, QA testing, financial systems	
Business Analyst	MA/MS/MBA preferred	1–3 years	Supply chain data warehouse	

Herman Miller, Inc.

Fast Facts	Revenues: $2.236B (2001) Employees: 9,951 (2001) Founded: 1923
	Manufacturer; office furniture Public: MLHR (Nasdaq)
Awards	Fortune: 100 Best Companies to Work for in America
	Industry Week: 100 Best Managed Companies
Headquarters	855 E. Main Avenue
	Zeeland, MI 49464-0302
	(616) 654-3000
	www.hermanmiller.com

Job Title	Education	Experience	Skills	Location

No IT jobs posted.

Hershey Foods Corporation

Fast Facts	Revenues: $4.221B (2000) Employees: 15,700 (2000) Founded: 1894
	Manufacturer; chocolate-based candy Public: HSY (NYSE)
Awards	Industry Week: 100 Best Managed Companies
	Information Week: Top 500 Technology Innovators
Headquarters	100 Crystal A Drive
	Hershey, PA 17033-0810
	(717) 534-6799
	http://www.hersheys.com

Job Title	Education	Experience	Skills	Location
Applications Programming Intern	Pursuing a degree in CS, EE, or Applications Engineering	Intern	MS Access, MS VB, Java	Hershey, PA
Sales Information and Technology Intern	Pursuing a degree in CS, Business, Communications	Intern, one to three terms, Spring, Summer, Fall or longer	MS Office, Access. Will provide exposure to SAP	Hershey, PA

Hewitt Associates LLC

Fast Facts
Revenues: $1.275B (2000) Employees: 12,050 (2000) Founded: 1940
Professional services; human resources Private

Awards
Computerworld: 100 Best Places to Work in IT

Headquarters
100 Half Day Rd.
Lincolnshire, IL 60069-3342
(847) 295-5000
http://www.hewitt.com

Job Title	Education	Experience	Skills	Location
Senior Project Manager, Communication and Relationship Expert	BA/BS, Master's preferred, technical or project management certifications	5+ years	WinSDT, Server Desktop Cluster	Lincolnshire, IL
CRM System Architect	BS CS	10+ years	SAP, PeopleSoft, Siebel, Vantive	Lincolnshire, IL
DB Cool Developer				US
DB2/Informix Database Design Consultant	BA/BS or equivalent technical experience	5 years	DB2, Informix, ERWin	Lincolnshire, IL
MVS/Mainframe System Performance Specialist		8+ years	SAS, ZOS, ThroughPut Manager, IODF gens	Lincolnshire, IL

The Home Depot, Inc.

Fast Facts
Revenues: $45.738B (2001) Employees: 227,000 (2001)
Founded: 1978 Retailer; home repair supplies Public: HD (NYSE)

Awards
Computerworld: 100 Best Places to Work in IT
Information Week: Top 500 Technology Innovators

Headquarters   2455 Paces Ferry Road
Atlanta, GA 30339-4024
(770) 433-8211
http://www.homedepot.com

Job Title	Education	Experience	Skills	Location
No IT jobs posted.				

Home Shopping Network

Fast Facts   Revenues: $1.8B (2000) Employees: 4,500 (2000) Founded: 1977
Entertainment; television network Subsidiary: USA Networks, Inc.
Awards   Computerworld: 100 Best Places to Work in IT
Headquarters   1HSN Drive
St. Petersburg, FL 33729
(727) 872-1000
http://www.hsn.com

Job Title	Education	Experience	Skills	Location
Systems Analyst— IR		3–5 years	Oracle, UNIX, Data warehousing, Data stage, Data Mart, ETL	Tampa Bay, FL
Security Analyst	CISSP, CCSA		PKI, Digital Signatures, BS 7799, ESM, Bindview, ISS Suite, Axent, VPN	Tampa Bay, FL
Sr. Programmer Analyst—RETEK	BA preferred	1–2 years	Developer 2000, Oracle Form Design, PVCS, JAD	Tampa Bay, FL
Sr. Telecom Engineer—Voice— Call Center Support	BS or equivalent experience		Lucent, Edify, ACD, CTI, PBX, ACD, IVR	Tampa Bay, FL
Systems Analyst— Merchandise and Retail Systems	BS CS	4 years	VB, Pro C, SQL, Java, MQ Series, Developer/2000, Crystal Reports	Tampa Bay, FL

HON INDUSTRIES Inc.

Fast Facts   Revenues: $2.046B (2000) Employees: 11,500 (2000) Founded: 1944
Manufacturer; office furniture Public: HNI (NYSE)
Awards   Industry Week: 100 Best Managed Companies
Fortune: Most Admired Companies

Headquarters	414 E. 3rd. Street Muscatine, IA 52761-0071 (563) 264-7400 http://www.honi.com

Job Title	Education	Experience	Skills	Location
No jobs posted.				

Household International, Inc.

Fast Facts	Revenues: $11.961B (2000) Employees: 28,000 (2000) Founded: 1878 Financial services; personal loans Public: HI (NYSE)
Awards	Computerworld: 100 Best Places to Work in IT Fortune: Most Admired Companies
Headquarters	2700 Sanders Road Prospect Heights, IL 60070 (847) 564-5000 http://www.household.com

Job Title	Education	Experience	Skills	Location
Management Information Analyst	BA/BS	2 years	SAS, Web design	Pomona, CA
PowerBuilder Technical Lead	BS CS or equivalent experience		PowerBuilder, Cafe, global collections	Wood Dale, IL
Manager Business Systems	BA/BS technical, Master's preferred	3 years	Release delivery, BankCard operations, software factory model, Big 5 consulting experience	Salinas, CA
Business Information Developer	BA/BS or equivalent experience	2+ years	SAS, SQL	Prospect Heights, IL
Middleware Developer	BA/BS	5+ years	MQSeries, DB2Connect, IP Socket	Wood Dale, IL

Illinois Tool Works Inc.

Fast Facts	Revenues: $9.984B (2000) Employees: 55,300 (2000) Founded: 1912 Manufacturer; fasteners, adhesives Public: ITW (NYSE)
Awards	Industry Week: 100 Best Managed Companies Information Week: Top 500 Technology Innovators

Headquarters   3600 W. Lake Avenue
Glenview, IL 60025-5811
(847) 724-7500
http://www.itw.com

Job Title	Education	Experience	Skills	Location

No jobs posted.

Immunex Corporation

Fast Facts   Revenues: $861.8M (2000) Employees: 1,425 Founded: 1981
Manufacturer; drugs Public: IMNX (Nasdaq)

Awards   Fortune: 100 Best Companies to Work for in America
Red Herring: 100 Top Companies of the Electronic Age

Headquarters   51 University Street
Seattle, WA 98101
(206) 587-0430
http://www.immunex.com

Job Title	Education	Experience	Skills	Location
Help Desk Technician	BA/BS preferred, MCSE, A+ preferred		Lotus Notes, Internet Explorer, MS Office	Seattle, WA
Automation Engineer	BS Engineering (Chemical, Electrical, Mechanical), Registration in state of Rhode Island	5 years	PLCs, DCS, BAS, MCCs, 480 VAC, P&IDs	Warwick, RI
Automation Engineer	BS Engineering (Chemical, Electrical, Mechanical)	5 years	Allen-Bradley PLC, DCS, BAS, MCCs, VAC, P&Ids	Bothell CCF, WA

International Truck and Engine Corporation

Fast Facts   Revenues: $8.407B (2000) Employees: 17,000 (2000) Founded: 1831
Manufacturer; heavy-duty trucks Public: NAV (NYSE) Navistar

Awards   Computerworld: 100 Best Places to Work in IT

Headquarters   455 N. Cityfront Plaza Drive
Chicago, IL 60611
(312) 836-2000
http://www.navistar.com

Job Title	Education	Experience	Skills	Location

No IT jobs posted.

J. B. Hunt Transport Services, Inc.

Fast Facts	Revenues: $2.160B (2000) Employees: 15,980 (2001) Founded: 1969 Transportation; truck transport of goods Public: JBHT (Nasdaq)
Awards	Computerworld: 100 Best Places to Work in IT
Headquarters	615 J.B. Hunt Corporate Drive Lowell, AR 72745 (501) 820-0000 http://www.jbhunt.com

Job Title	Education	Experience	Skills	Location
Mid-Range Systems Programmer			OS/400, Java, MQSeries, Gemstone/J, WebFocus	Arkansas
Network Engineer		3 years	TCP/IP, SNA, MSSQL, DB2	Arkansas
IS Intern	Pursuing a college degree, at least one year before graduation	Intern, 20 hours a week	Hardware/PC repair, Windows NT	Arkansas

J. C. Penney Company, Inc.

Fast Facts	Revenues: $31.846B (2001) Employees: 267,000 (2001) Founded: 1902 Retailer; clothing Public: JCP (NYSE)
Awards	Computerworld: 100 Best Places to Work in IT Interactive Week: The Internet 500
Headquarters	6501 Legacy Drive Plano, TX 75024-3698 (972) 431-1000 http://www.jcpenney.net

Job Title	Education	Experience	Skills	Location
System Support Analyst			HP-UX, SCO, Solaris, RF networks, NT 4.0, Office 97 and 2000	Haslet, TX

JM Family Enterprises, Inc.

Fast Facts	Revenues: $6.6B (2000) Employees: 3,195 (2000) Founded: 1968 Retailer; auto dealerships Private
Awards	Fortune: 100 Best Companies to Work for in America

Headquarters   100 N.W. 12th Avenue
                     Deerfield Beach, FL 33442
                     (954) 429-2000
                     http://www.jmfamily.com

Job Title	Education	Experience	Skills	Location
Lead Business Analyst	BA/BS	5–7 years	PC Client/Server, Windows NT/2000	Deerfield Beach, FL
PC Support Specialist		2+ years	Windows NT 4.0, Compaq, Extra Terminal Emulation, Lotus Notes	Mobile, AL
Sr. PC Support Specialist	BA/BS or equivalent experience	3+ years	Windows NT 4.0/ 2000, 300+ nodes, Lucent G3R, Lotus Notes, MS Office, IE	Commerce, GA

The J. M. Smucker Company

Fast Facts	Revenues: $651.4M (2001) Employees: 2,250 (2001) Founded: 1897 Manufacturer; food, peanut butter and jelly Public: SJM (NYSE)
Awards	Fortune: 100 Best Companies to Work for in America
Headquarters	1 Strawberry Lane
	Orrville, OH 44667-0280
	(330) 682-3000
	http://www.smucker.com

Job Title	Education	Experience	Skills	Location

No jobs posted online.

John Hancock Financial Services, Inc.

Fast Facts	Revenues: $7.598B (2000) Employees: 8,503 (2000) Founded: 1862 Financial services; insurance (life) Public: JHF (NYSE)
Awards	Computerworld: 100 Best Places to Work in IT
Headquarters	John Hancock Place
	Boston, MA 02117
	(617) 572-6000
	http://www.johnhancock.com

Job Title	Education	Experience	Skills	Location
Sr. Security Engineer/Analyst	BA/BS preferred	5 years	Windows NT, 2000, OS/390, UNIX	Boston, MA

Job Title	Education	Experience	Skills	Location
Application Management	BA/BS	3 years	Microfocus COBOL, Oracle	Tampa, FL
Client/Server Technical Programmer		4 years	Sybase, CAST Workbench, Spy, ClearCase, Faxination, Business Objects, Informatica, insurance experience	Tampa, FL
Professional Development Manager	BA/BS	10 years	Microfocus COBOL, PowerBuilder, iplanet, J2EE, insurance experience	Tampa, FL
Vantage Sr. Technical Programmer	BA/BS	7 years	Vantage, COBOL, CICS, VSAM, JCL	Tampa, FL

Johnson & Johnson

Fast Facts	Revenues: $29.139B (2000) Employees: 98,500 (2000)
	Founded: 1886 Manufacturer; consumer products Public: JNJ (NYSE)
Awards	Industry Week: 100 Best Managed Companies
	Fortune: 100 Best Companies to Work for in America
Headquarters	1 Johnson & Johnson Plaza
	New Brunswick, NJ 08933
	(732) 524-0400
	http://www.jnj.com

Job Title	Education	Experience	Skills	Location
Sr. Analyst/ Consultant	BA/BS or equivalent experience	3–5 years	CIM, CEWS, QCS/TRG	New Brunswick, NJ
Sr. Web Designer/ Developer	BA/BS or equivalent experience	3–5 years	EPharma web site, color maps, traffic statistics analysis	Milltown, NJ
Sr. Consultant	BA/BS or equivalent experience	6–10 years	Documentum 4i, Domino, eRoom, IIS, MS Sharepoint, Conference Server, Instant Messaging	Raritan, NJ
Sr. Consultant	BA/BS or equivalent experience	3–5 years	Exchange 2000	Raritan, NJ
Sr. Analyst/ Consultant	BA/BS or equivalent experience	3–5 years	NT domains, LAN, 2nd level Help Desk	Jacksonville, FL

Johnson Controls, Inc.

Fast Facts	Revenues: $17.155B (2000) Employees: 105,000 (2000)
	Founded: 1885 Manufacturer; auto components Public: JCI (NYSE)
Awards	Industry Week: 100 Best Managed Companies
	Computerworld: 100 Best Places to Work in IT
Headquarters	5757 N. Green Bay Avenue
	Milwaukee, WI 53201
	(414) 524-1200
	http://www.johnsoncontrols.com

Job Title	Education	Experience	Skills	Location
IT Analyst	BA/BS MIS	3–6+ years	Oracle, Novell, ERP, QAD MfgPro	Northwood, OH

Kinko's, Inc.

Fast Facts	Revenues: $2B est. (2000) Employees: 26,000 est. (2000)
	Founded: 1970 Services; photocopying Private
Awards	Fortune: 100 Best Companies to Work for in America
Headquarters	255 W. Stanley Avenue
	Ventura, CA 93002-8000
	(805) 652-4000
	http://www.kinkos.com

Job Title	Education	Experience	Skills	Location

No IT jobs posted.

Lear Corporation

Fast Facts	Revenues: $14.073B (2000) Employees: 121,600 (2000)
	Founded: 1917 Manufacturer; car seats Public: LEA (NYSE)
Awards	Industry Week: 100 Best Managed Companies
	Information Week: Top 500 Technology Innovators
Headquarters	21557 Telegraph Road
	Southfield, MI 48086-5008
	(248) 447-1500
	http://www.lear.com

Job Title	Education	Experience	Skills	Location

No IT jobs posted.

LensCrafters, Inc.

Fast Facts	Revenues: $1.33B (2000) Employees: 17,000 (2000) Founded: 1983
	Retailer; eye glasses Subsidiary: Luxottica (Italy)
Awards	Fortune: 100 Best Companies to Work for in America
Headquarters	8650 Governor's Hill Drive
	Cincinnati, OH 45249
	(513) 583-6000
	http://www.lenscrafters.com

Job Title	Education	Experience	Skills	Location
Systems Developer	BA/BS		VBA, Oracle	Finance & Accounting Dept.
HRIS Specialist	BA/BS CS, IS, Business, HR or equivalent experience	1–3 years	HRIS	Human Resources Dept.
Systems Developer Analyst—JDA	AAS or BA/BS Business, CS	1–3 years	Design, code, test, implement	Information Systems Dept.
Database Administrator	BA/BS Business, CS	5+ years	RDBMS, retail experience	Information Systems Dept.
Systems Development Manager	BA/BS Business, CS	10–12 years	Project oversight, SDLC	Information Systems Dept.

Liz Claiborne, Inc.

Fast Facts	Revenues: $3.104B (2000) Employees: 8,300 (2000) Founded: 1976
	Retailer; women's clothes Public: LIZ (NYSE)
Awards	Industry Week: 100 Best Managed Companies
	Fortune: Most Admired Companies
Headquarters	1441 Broadway
	New York, NY 10018
	(212) 354-4900
	http://www.lizclaiborne.com

Job Title	Education	Experience	Skills	Location
Sr. Application Designer/ Developer	BS or equivalent experience	3–6 years	PL/SQL, Oracle Designer 2000, VB/Pro, C++	North Bergen, NJ
Sr. Internetwork Engineer		3 years	SNA LAN, WAN	North Bergen, NJ
Technical Specialist	BA/BS CS or equivalent experience	4+ years	Oracle Tools, VB/Pro, C/C++	North Bergen, NJ

Job Title	Education	Experience	Skills	Location
IT Systems Network Technician	AA/AS CS, Math, Engineering	5 years	PC systems, networks, protocols	Los Angeles, CA
Business Analyst	BS or equivalent experience		External design deliverables, apparel/retail experience	North Bergen, NJ

Lost Arrow Corporation

Fast Facts   Revenues: $200M est. (2000) Employees: 1,100 est. (2000)
                  Founded: 1957 Retailer; outdoor clothing, climbing equipment
                      Private
Awards   Fortune: 100 Best Companies to Work for in America
Headquarters 259 W. Santa Clara Street
                  Ventura, CA 93001
                  (805) 643-8616
                  http://www.patagonia.com

Job Title	Education	Experience	Skills	Location

No IT jobs posted.

Marriott International, Inc.

Fast Facts   Revenues: $10.017B (2000) Employees: 153,000 (2000)
                  Founded: 1927 Hotel services Public: MAR (NYSE)
Awards   Fortune: 100 Best Companies to Work for in America
                  CIO: Top 100
Headquarters 10400 Fernwood Rd.
                  Bethesda, MD 20817
                  (301) 380-3000
                  http://www.marriott.com

Job Title	Education	Experience	Skills	Location
No IT jobs currently posted. Previous job listings are shown below.				
Programmer/ Analyst—Web Development	BA/BS		DHTML, ASP, IIS, JavaScript, Oracle	Bethesda, MD
Sr. Systems Analyst		4 years	PowerBuilder, Oracle, MS Interdev, PL/SQL	Bethesda, MD
VM Systems Administrator			VM	Bethesda, MD
Network System/ 390 Programmer			System/390	Bethesda, MD

Maytag Corporation

Fast Facts	Revenues: $4.248B (2000) Employees: 24,657 (2000) Founded: 1893 Manufacturer; kitchen appliances Public: MYG (NYSE)
Awards	Industry Week: 100 Best Managed Companies Information Week: 500 Top Technology Innovators
Headquarters	403 W. Fourth Street North Newton, IA 50208 (641) 792-7000 http://www.maytagcorp.com

Job Title	Education	Experience	Skills	Location

No IT jobs posted.

MBNA Corporation

Fast Facts	Revenues: $7.869B (2000) Employees: 25,000 (2000) Founded: 1982 Financial services; credit cards, banking Public: KRB (NYSE)
Awards	Fortune: 100 Best Companies to Work For in America Fortune: Most Admired Companies
Headquarters	1100 N. King Street Wilmington, DE 19884-0131 (302) 453-9930 http://www.mbnainternational.com

Job Title	Education	Experience	Skills	Location

No IT jobs posted.

McCutchen, Doyle, Brown & Enersen, LLP

Fast Facts	Revenues: $120M est. (2000) Employees: 700 (2000) Founded: 1883 Professional services; legal Partnership
Awards	Fortune: 100 Best Companies to Work for in America
Headquarters	3 Embarcadero Center San Francisco, CA 94111 (415) 393-2000 http://www.mccutchen.com

Job Title	Education	Experience	Skills	Location
Attorney	Technical degree in CS, EE, Mechanical Engineering, or Physics, Member of the California Bar	2–4 years	IP patent prosecution	San Francisco, CA

Medtronic, Inc.

Fast Facts   Revenues: $5.552B (2001) Employees: 26,050 (2001) Founded: 1949
                      Manufacturer; medical devices (cardiac, vascular) Public: MDT
                      (NYSE)
Awards   Fortune: 100 Best Companies to Work for in America
                      Industry Week: 100 Best Managed Companies
Headquarters   710 Medtronic Parkway, NE
                      Minneapolis, MN 55432-5604
                      (763) 514-4000
                      http://www.medtronic.com

Job Title	Education	Experience	Skills	Location

No jobs posted online.

The Men's Wearhouse, Inc.

Fast Facts   Revenues: $1.334B (2001) Employees: 12,000 (2001) Founded: 1973
                      Retailer; men's clothing Public: MW (NYSE)
Awards   Fortune: 100 Best Companies to Work for in America
Headquarters   5803 Glenmont Drive
                      Houston, TX 77081-1701
                      (713) 592-7200
                      www.menswearhouse.com

Job Title	Education	Experience	Skills	Location
Java/eCommerce Application Developer	BA/BS CS	2+ years	Java, JHTML, Oracle, Blue Martini	Houston, TX
UNIX Administrator		4+ years	500+ users, Perl, BMC Patrol, PeopleSoft	Houston, TX

Merck & Co., Inc.

Fast Facts   Revenues: $40.363B (2000) Employees: 69,300 (2000)
                      Founded: 1891 Manufacturer; drugs Public: MRK (NYSE)
Awards   Computerworld: 100 Best Places to Work in IT
                      Fortune: 100 Best Companies to Work for in America
Headquarters   1 Merck Drive
                      Whitehouse Station, NJ 08889-0100
                      (908) 423-1000
                      http://www.merck.com

Job Title	Education	Experience	Skills	Location
Sr. Applications Architect		5–7 years	BroadVision, Plumtree, JavaScript, ASP, Oracle 8i	Franklin Lakes, NJ
Sr. Systems Programmer			MVS OS/390	Fair Lawn, NJ
Project Manager IT	BA/BS, MCSE	3 years	20+ Exchange servers, SMTP, MMMC, XP	Montvale, NJ
Applications Architect		4–9 years	C, C++, Javascript, HP-UX, Broadvision,	Franklin Lakes, NJ
Sr. Programmer Analyst		3–6 years	C, C++, SQL, Open VMS, Oracle	Blue Bell, PA

Merrill Lynch & Co., Inc.

Fast Facts   Revenues: $44.872B (2000) Employees: 72,000 (2000)
Founded: 1885 Financial services; brokerage Public: MER (NYSE)
Awards   Computerworld: 100 Best Places to Work in IT
Information Week: Top 500 Technology Innovators
Headquarters   World Financial Center, North Tower, 250 Vesey Street
New York City, NY 10281
(212) 449-1000
http://www.ml.com

Job Title	Education	Experience	Skills	Location

No jobs in the US at this time.

Metropolitan Life Insurance Company

Fast Facts   Revenues: $31.947B (2000) Employees: 46,700 (2000)
Founded: 1863 Financial services; insurance Public: MET (NYSE)
Awards   Computerworld: 100 Best Places to Work in IT
Information Week: 500 Top Technology Innovators
Headquarters   1 Madison Avenue
New York, NY 10010-3690
(212) 578-2211
http://www.metlife.com

Job Title	Education	Experience	Skills	Location
PeopleSoft Financials/Oracle DBA		5+ years	PeopleSoft Financials (no HR)	New York City, NY

Project Manager	PMP, PMO	3–5 years	Vantage, COBOL, CICS	Scranton, PA
Sr. Business Analyst			Vantage-One, JETS, Insurance experience	Los Angeles, CA
Sr. Mainframe Analyst		3+ years	COBOL, CICS, DB2, IDMS, insurance experience	Los Angeles, CA
UNIX Systems Administrator		2–5 years	UDB, Sybase, Oracle, SAN, AIX, Sun	Rensselear, NY

MFS Investment Management

Fast Facts	Revenues: $1.589B (2000) Employees: 2,500 (1999) Founded: 1924 Financial services; mutual funds Subsidiary: Sun Life of Canada
Awards	Fortune: 100 Best Companies to Work for in America
Headquarters	500 Boylston Street Boston, MA 02116 (617) 954-5000 http://www.mfs.com

Job Title	Education	Experience	Skills	Location

No jobs posted online. Email resume.

Minnesota Mining and Manufacturing Company (3M)

Fast Facts	Revenues: $16.724B (2000) Employees: 75,000 (2000) Founded: 1902 Manufacturing; industrial products, adhesives Public: MMM (NYSE)
Awards	Industry Week: 100 Best Managed Companies Fortune: 100 Best Companies to Work for in America
Headquarters	3M Center St. Paul, MN 55144 (651) 733-1110 http://www.mmm.com

Job Title	Education	Experience	Skills	Location
Analyst IT	BA/BS CS, Business or equivalent experience	4+ years	MS SQL, order processing, manufacturing experience	Maplewood, MN

Minnesota Mutual Companies, Inc.

Fast Facts Revenues: $2.5B (2000) Founded: 1880s est.
Financial services; insurance (life) Private
Awards Computerworld: 100 Best Places to Work in IT
Headquarters 400 Robert Street North
St. Paul, MN 55101
(651) 665-3500
http://www.minnesotamutual.com

Job Title	Education	Experience	Skills	Location
Network Services Analyst (Nos Infrastructure)			Frame relay, ISDN, Shiva, VPN, ATM, Sonet Ring services, SHNS	
Testing Technician			Testing through implementation	

Mohawk Industries, Inc.

Fast Facts Revenues: $3.256B (2000) Employees: 24,005 (2000) Founded: 1878
Manufacturer; carpet Public: MHK (NYSE)
Awards Industry Week: 100 Best Managed Companies
Fortune: Most Admired Companies
Headquarters 160 S. Industrial Boulevard
Calhoun, GA 30703
(706) 629-7721
http://www.mohawkind.com

Job Title	Education	Experience	Skills	Location
No job listings online. Submit resume.				

The MONY Group Inc.

Fast Facts Revenues: $1.252B (2000) Employees: 2,466 (2000) Founded: 1842
Financial services; insurance, mutual funds Public: MNY (NYSE)
Awards Computerworld: 100 Best Places to Work in IT
Headquarters 1740 Broadway
New York, NY 10019
(212) 708-2000
http://www.mony.com

Job Title	Education	Experience	Skills	Location
Help Desk Analyst	Criminal conviction check, credit history review		Level 2 technical assistance, LAN, WAN	New York City, NY
Help Desk Analyst	Criminal conviction check, credit history review		Level 1, 2, technical assistance, PC, mainframe, midrange	Syracuse, NY
Server Support Specialist	MCSE, criminal conviction check, credit history review		Lotus Notes, Kerberos, Secure ID, PGP, PPTP, VPN, DNS	Syracuse, NY

National City Corporation

Fast Facts	Revenues: $9.051B (2000) Employees: 36,097 (2000) Founded: 1845 Financial services; banking Public: NCC (NYSE)
Awards	Computerworld: 100 Best Places to Work in IT CIO: Web Business 50/50
Headquarters	1900 E. 9th Street Cleveland, OH 44114-3484 (216) 575-2000 http://www.national-city.com

Job Title	Education	Experience	Skills	Location

No IT jobs posted.

Nationwide Financial Services, Inc.

Fast Facts	Revenues: $3.17B (2000) Employees: 4,800 (2000) Founded: 1926 Financial services; life insurance, mutual funds Public: NFS (NYSE)
Awards	Computerworld: 100 Best Places to Work in IT Fortune: Most Admired Companies
Headquarters	1 Nationwide Plaza Columbus, OH 43215 (614) 249-7111 http://www.nationwide.com

Job Title	Education	Experience	Skills	Location
Software Specialist III	BA/BS CS	8 years	Oracle, PeopleSoft, Hyperion Enterprise, Essbase	OH

Unit Manager Systems/ Programming	BA/BS	8 years	3–15 direct reports	OH
GM Programmer/ Analyst	BA/BS	3 years	COBOL, C, Focus, C++	OH

Nordstrom, Inc.

Fast Facts Revenues: $5.528B (2001) Employees: 49,000 (2001) Founded: 1901
Retailer; women's clothing Public: JWN (NYSE)

Awards Fortune: 100 Best Companies to Work for in America
Computerworld: 100 Best Places to Work in IT

Headquarters 1617 Sixth Avenue
Seattle, WA 98101-1742
(206) 628-2111
http://www.nordstrom.com

Job Title	Education	Experience	Skills	Location
IT Enterprise Security Engineer		2+ years	OS/390, AS/400, DMZ, Proxy, SecurID, TACACS, PKI	Seattle, WA
Technical Consultant— Sales Audit		5+ years	Oracle, UNIX	Seattle, WA
Sr. Oracle DBA Financial		5+ years	PL/SQL, Data Mart/Warehouse, Microstrategy, Multi-terabyte databases	Seattle, WA
Sr. Software Test Analyst		5+ years	DB2, Retek, RMS, RSS	Seattle, WA

Office Depot, Inc.

Fast Facts Revenues: $11.57B (2000) Employees: 48,000 (2000) Founded: 1986
Retailer; home office supplies Public: ODP (NYSE)

Awards Computerworld: 100 Best Places to Work in IT
CIO: Web Business 50/50

Headquarters 2200 Old Germantown Road
Delray Beach, FL 33445
(561) 438-4800
http://www.officedepot.com

Job Title	Education	Experience	Skills	Location

No IT jobs posted. Submit resume online.

PACCAR Inc.

Fast Facts   Revenues: $7.919B (2000) Employees: 18,000 (2000) Founded: 1905
                    Manufacturer; large-scale trucks Public: PCAR (Nasdaq)
Awards   Industry Week: 100 Best Managed Companies
Headquarters   777 106th Avenue N.E.
                    Bellevue, WA 98004
                    (425) 468-7400
                    http://www.paccar.com

Job Title	Education	Experience	Skills	Location
Sr. SAP Programmer	BA/BS IT, CS	2 years	R/3 4.6c, HR/ Payroll, ALE	WA
Sr. Tech Support Analyst	BA/BS CS, ISM, Business	5 years	NT/UNIX server	TX
Systems Analyst	BS CS	3–5 years	MS Visual Studio, ASP, MTS, SQL	TX

Parker Hannafin Corporation

Fast Facts   Revenues: $5.98B (2001) Employees: 46,300 (2001) Founded: 1934
                    Manufacturer; industrial products, hydraulics Public: PH (NYSE)
Awards   Computerworld: 100 Best Places to Work in IT
                    Industry Week: 100 Best Managed Companies
Headquarters   6035 Parkland Boulevard
                    Cleveland, OH 44124-4141
                    (216) 896-3000
                    http://www.parker.com

Job Title	Education	Experience	Skills	Location

No IT jobs posted.

Pella Corporation

Fast Facts   Revenues: $900M est. (1999) Employees: 6,755 (1999)
                    Founded: 1925 Manufacturer; windows and doors Private
Awards   Fortune: 100 Best Companies to Work for in America
Headquarters   102 Main Street
                    Pella, IA 50219
                    (641) 628-1000
                    http://www.pella.com

Job Title	Education	Experience	Skills	Location
Systems Engineer	BA		Oracle Workflow, PL/SQL	Pella, IA

Peoples Energy Corporation

Fast Facts   Revenues: $1.418B (2000) Employees: 2,694 (2000) Founded: 1850s
Utility; natural gas Public: PGL (NYSE)

Awards   Computerworld: 100 Best Places to Work in IT
Information Week: 500 Top Technology Innovators

Headquarters   130 E. Randolph Dr., 24th Floor
Chicago, IL 60601-6207
(312) 240-4000
http://www.pecorp.com

Job Title	Education	Experience	Skills	Location
ABAP Programmer	BS CS or equivalent	3+ years	VB, C++, PowerBuilder, SQL Server, Oracle, R/3	
LAN Analyst		5 years	Windows 2000, RAS, Citrix, SMS, SQL Server, 250 nodes	
Programmer/ Programmer Analyst	BS CS (3.0/4.0 GPA)		COBOL II, DB2, JCL, SQL, Sybase	
Visual Basic Sr. Systems Analyst	BS CS	2+ years	ASP, Active X, Java, ADO, Visual Interdev, IIS	

Pfizer Inc.

Fast Facts   Revenues: $29.574B (2000) Employees: 90,000 (2000)
Founded: 1849 Manufacturer; drugs Public: PFE (NYSE)

Awards   Industry Week: 100 Best Managed Companies
Fortune: Most Admired Companies

Headquarters   235 E. 42nd Street
New York, NY 10017-5755
(212) 573-2323
http://www.pfizer.com

Job Title	Education	Experience	Skills	Location
Research Apps Developer		Experienced	Veterinary medicine informatics	Groton, CT
Sr. Clinical Systems Analyst	BA/BS CS, Statistics	Experienced	VNC, CCTR, PPG, PGRD, Sandwich, Ann Arbor, Tokyo, Pfizer customer experience	Groton, CT

Scientific Apps Developer	Experienced	Veterinary medicine, develop and maintain applications	Groton, CT
Research Apps Consultant	Experienced	Human Resources applications	Groton, CT; Ann Arbor, MI; La Jolla, CA
Coordinator Clinical Systems	Experienced	Clinical research Phase I applications	Groton, CT; Ann Arbor, MI; La Jolla, CA

Plante & Moran, LLP

Fast Facts   Revenues: $140M (1999) Employees: 1,226 (1999) Founded: 1924
Professional services; accounting Private
Awards   Fortune: 100 Best Companies to Work for in America
Headquarters 27400 Northwestern Highway
Southfield, MI 48034
(248) 352-2500
http://www.plante-moran.com

Job Title	Education	Experience	Skills	Location
Information Technology Manager	BA/BS		AS/400, LAN/ WAN, bar coding, EDI	Farmington Hills, MI; distribution company, a client of Plante-Moran's

The PNC Financial Services Group, Inc.

Fast Facts   Revenues: $7.623B (2000) Employees: 24,900 (2000) Founded: 1852
Financial services; banking Public: PNC (NYSE)
Awards   Computerworld: 100 Best Places to Work in IT
Information Week: 500 Top Technology Innovators
Headquarters 1 PNC Plaza, 249 5th Avenue
Pittsburgh, PA 15222-2707
(412) 762-2000
http://www.pnc.com

Job Title	Education	Experience	Skills	Location
Sr. Systems Project Manager	BS CS, EE, Computer Engineering, Master's preferred	7–10+ years	J2EE, XML, XSL, ASP, NSAPI, ISAPI, JDBC, ODBC	King of Prussia, PA
Sr. Software Developer		3–5 years	VB 6.0, C++, Sybase, WyStar, SQL	Rockville, MD

Lead Software Developer	BS MIS, CS, EE, Computer Engineering	5+ years	J2EE, XML, XSL, ASP, NSAPI, ISAPI	King of Prussia, PA
Systems Programmer I	BA/BS CS	2–4 years	Assembly language, voice mail, e-mail	Pittsburgh, PA
Sr. Applications A/P	BA/BS	3–5 years	COBOL, ENDEVOR, Mutual Fund experience	Westborough, MA

The Principal Financial Group

Fast Facts   Revenues: $8.885B (2000) Employees: 17,473 (2000) Founded: 1879
Public: PFG (NYSE)

Awards   Computerworld: 100 Best Places to Work in IT
Interactive Week: The Internet 500

Headquarters   711 High Street
Des Moines, IA 50392-0001
(515) 247-5111
http://www.principal.com

Job Title	Education	Experience	Skills	Location
IT Application Analyst	BA/BS		DB2, Oracle, SQL	Des Moines, IA
IT Application Associate	AAS		DB2, Oracle	Des Moines, IA
Summer Intern	BA/BS	Entry-level	COBOL, Java	Des Moines, IA

Prudential Financial

Fast Facts   Revenues: $26.544B (2000) Employees: 56,925 (2000)
Founded: 1875 Financial services; insurance (life) Mutual company

Awards   Computerworld: 100 Best Places to Work in IT
Information Week: 500 Top Technology Innovators

Headquarters   751 Broad Street
Newark, NJ 07102-3777
(973) 802-6000
http://www.prudential.com

Job Title	Education	Experience	Skills	Location
Business Continuity Specialist	BA/BS	1–3 years	LDRPS	Roseland, NJ
Distributed Server Support Analyst	AA/AS, MCSE, ASE	4–6 years	TCP/IP, NT, OPEN/Image	Roseland, NJ

Job Title	Education	Experience	Skills	Location
Oracle/Financials Developer		4–6 years	PVCS, PowerBuilder 6.5, Sybase, Smartstream, Java, accounting experience	Scottsdale, AZ
Sr. Web Integration Specialist		4–6 years	Java, ASP, IIS, COM, WebLogic, Jbuilder, Jdeveloper, Visual Café, Visual Age, EJB, AS/400	Philadelphia, PA
Systems Consulting Manager	BA/BS	7–9 years	NIS+, DNS, Veritas Volume Manager, Solaris	Livingston, NJ

Public Broadcasting Service (PBS)

Fast Facts Founded: 1969 Communications; radio stations Not-for-profit
Awards Computerworld: 100 Best Places to Work in IT
Headquarters 1320 Braddock Pl.
Alexandria, VA 22314
(703) 739-5000
http://www.pbs.org

Job Title	Education	Experience	Skills	Location
Web and Inline Editor	BA Journalism, English, Education, Child Development	3 years	HTML, MS Office, PhotoShop	Alexandria, VA
Sr. Associate	BA Education, Instructional Design	2–3 years	MS Office, NCTM, ISTE, listservs	Alexandria, VA

Publix Super Markets, Inc.

Fast Facts Revenues: $14.724B (2000) Employees: 126,000 (2000)
Founded: 1930 Retailer; grocery stores Private
Awards Fortune: 100 Best Companies to Work for in America
Fortune: Most Admired Companies
Headquarters 1936 George Jenkins Boulevard
Lakeland, FL 33815
(863) 688-1188
http://www.publix.com

Job Title	Education	Experience	Skills	Location

No IT jobs posted.

RadioShack Corporation

Fast Facts	Revenues: $4.795B (2000) Employees: 43,600 (2000) Founded: 1919 Retailer; consumer electronics Public: RSH (NYSE)
Awards	Computerworld: 100 Best Places to Work in IT Information Week: 500 Top Technology Innovators
Headquarters	100 Throckmorton Street, Suite 1800 Fort Worth, TX 76102 (817) 415-3700 http://www.tandy.com

Job Title	Education	Experience	Skills	Location
Sr. LAN Administrator	BS IS, MCSE or CNA	3+ years	MS SMS, Novell, NT/2000	Fort Worth, TX
Sr. Exchange Administrator	BA/BS or certification	3 years	MS Exchange, Lotus Notes	Fort Worth, TX
Sr. Lotus Notes Administrator	BA/BS or certification	3 years	Lotus Notes, MS Exchange	Fort Worth, TX

The Reader's Digest Association, Inc.

Fast Facts	Revenues: $2.518B (2001) Employees: 5,000 (2001) Founded: 1922 Publisher; magazines, books Public: RDA (NYSE)
Awards	Computerworld: 100 Best Places to Work in IT Information Week: Top 500 Technology Innovators
Headquarters	Reader's Digest Road Pleasantville, NY 10570-7000 (914) 238-1000 http://www.readersdigest.com

Job Title	Education	Experience	Skills	Location

No job listings on site. Submit resume.

Regions Financial Corporation

Fast Facts	Revenues: $3.836B (2000) Employees: 14,390 (2000) Founded: 1871 Financial services; banking Public: RGBK (Nasdaq)
Awards	Computerworld: 100 Best Places to Work in IT
Headquarters	417 N. 20th Street Birmingham, AL 35203 (205) 944-1300 http://www.regionsbank.com

Job Title	Education	Experience	Skills	Location
Hogan Programmer	BA/BS	3+ years	COBOL, JCL, Hogan	Montgomery, AL

Job Title	Education	Experience	Skills	Location
IS Auditor	BA/BS IS, Business, Finance, Accounting, CIA, CBA, CISA, CPA certification	3+ years	Audit experience	Montgomery, AL
IT Audit Analyst	BA/BS IS, Accounting, Business, Math	2+ years	Easytrieve, ACL, JCL	Montgomery, AL
SAS Programmer	BA/BS	1+ years	JCL, ETL, data warehouse	Montgomery, AL
Sr. IS Auditor	BA/BS IS, Business, Accounting, CIA, CBA, CISA, CPA certification	5+ years	Easytrieve Plus, PanAudit Plus, TSO	Memphis, TN

Recreational Equipment, Inc. (REI)

Fast Facts   Revenues: $698.3M (2000) Employees: 7,000 (2000) Founded: 1938
           Retailer; outdoor clothing and equipment Cooperative
Awards   Fortune: 100 Best Companies to Work for in America
Headquarters   6750 S. 228th Street
           Seattle, WA 98032
           (253) 395-3780
           http://www.rei.com

Job Title	Education	Experience	Skills	Location

No IT jobs posted.

Republic Bancorp Inc.

Fast Facts   Revenues: $419.2M (2000) Employees: 1,678 (2000) Founded: 1986
           Financial services; banking Public: RBNC (Nasdaq)
Awards   Fortune: 100 Best Companies to Work for in America
Headquarters   1070 E. Main Street
           Owosso, MI 48867
           (989) 725-7337
           www.republicbancorp.com

Job Title	Education	Experience	Skills	Location
IT Support Supervisor				Farmington Hills, MI
Systems Analyst				Farmington Hills, MI

R. J. Reynolds Tobacco Holdings, Inc.

Fast Facts   Revenues: $8.167B (2000) Employees: 9,100 (2000) Founded: 1875
                    Manufacturer; tobacco products Public: RJR (NYSE)
Awards   Fortune: 100 Best Companies to Work for in America
Headquarters   401 N. Main Street
                    Winston-Salem, NC 27102-2866
                    (336) 741-5500
                    http://www.rjrt.com

Job Title	Education	Experience	Skills	Location

No job openings at this time.

Roadway Corporation

Fast Facts   Revenues: $3.04B (2000) Employees: 28,000 (2000) Founded: 1930
                    Transportation; truck transport services Public: ROAD (Nasdaq)
Awards   Computerworld: 100 Best Places to Work in IT
                    Fortune: Most Admired Companies
Headquarters   1077 Gorge Boulevard
                    Akron, OH 44310
                    (330) 384-1717
                    http://www.roadway.com

Job Title	Education	Experience	Skills	Location

Technical Overview: C, C++, Java, SQL/ESQL, FoxPro, CICS, Oracle, Business Objects, UNIX/AIX shell, DB2, COBOL

No IT jobs posted.

Rockwell International

Fast Facts   Revenues: $7.151B (2000) Employees: 41,200 (2000) Founded: 1919
                    Manufacturer; industrial automation Public: ROK (NYSE)
Awards   Industry Week: 100 Best Managed Companies
                    PC Magazine: 100 Most Influential
Headquarters   777 E. Wisconsin Avenue, Suite 1400
                    Milwaukee, WI 53202
                    (414) 212-5200
                    http://www.rockwellautomation.com

Job Title	Education	Experience	Skills	Location
Manager, Information Technology	BA/BS CS, Business	5–7 years	Desktop shared services	Milwaukee, WI

Program Manager, IT	BA/BS Engineering, Business, MBA preferred	Several years	Project scheduling, cost accounting, recovery, KPI	Milwaukee, WI
Project Engineer, Software	BS or MS	8–12 years	C++, RSBatch, RSBizware Historian	Phoenix, AZ
Application Specialist	BS EE, Engineering Technology, Mechanical Engineering	5 years	Application or design of variable speed drives	Mequon, WI
Applications Specialist		7+ years	Cognos, Powerplay, Oracle, PeopleSoft, Convoy, MQSeries	Rotterdam, Netherlands

Rodale, Inc.

Fast Facts   Revenues: $500M (2000) Employees: 1,300 (2000) Founded: 1930
Publisher; magazines, books Private
Awards   Fortune: 100 Best Companies to Work for in America
Headquarters   33 E. Minor Street
Emmaus, PA 18098-0099
(610) 967-5171
http://www.rodale.com

Job Title	Education	Experience	Skills	Location

No IT jobs posted.

Rohm and Haas Company

Fast Facts   Revenues: $6.879B (2000) Employees: 18,474 (2000) Founded: 1907
Manufacturer; specialty chemicals Public: ROH (NYSE)
Awards   Industry Week: 100 Best Managed Companies
Information Week: Top 500 Technology Innovators
Headquarters   100 Independence Mall West
Philadelphia, PA 19106-2399
(215) 592-3000
http://www.rohmhaas.com

Job Title	Education	Experience	Skills	Location
Business Integrity Analyst		2 years	SAP/Financial, R/3	Philadelphia, PA
ABAP Development Team Lead			ABAP	Philadelphia, PA
HR Specialist		5+ years	SAP HR, SQL, Excel pivot tables	Philadelphia, PA

Royal Caribbean Cruises Ltd.

Fast Facts	Revenues: $2.866B (2000) Employees: 26,200 (2000) Founded: 1969 Transportation; luxury cruise ships Public: RCL(NYSE)
Awards	Computerworld: 100 Best Places to Work in IT
Headquarters	1050 Caribbean Way
	Miami, FL 33132
	(305) 539-6000
	http://www.rccl.com

Job Title	Education	Experience	Skills	Location

No IT jobs posted.

Sara Lee Bakery Group, Inc. (formerly Earthgrains)

Fast Facts	Revenues: $2.582B (2001) Employees: 25,400 (2001) Founded: 1925 Manufacturer; bakery products Business segment of Sara Lee
Awards	Computerworld: 100 Best Places to Work in IT
	Information Week: Top 500 Technology Innovators
Headquarters	8400 Maryland Avenue
	St. Louis, MO 63105
	(314) 259-7000
	http://www.earthgrains.com

Job Title	Education	Experience	Skills	Location

No IT jobs posted.

Schering-Plough Corporation

Fast Facts	Revenues: $9.815B (2000) Employees: 28,100 (2000) Founded: 1971 Manufacturer; drugs Public: SGP (NYSE)
Awards	Industry Week: 100 Best Managed Companies
	Fortune: Most Admired Companies
Headquarters	1 Giralda Farms
	Madison, NJ 07940-1010
	(973) 822-7000
	http://www.sch-plough.com

Job Title	Education	Experience	Skills	Location

No IT jobs posted.

The Charles Schwab Corporation

Fast Facts   Revenues: $7.139B (2000) Employees: 25,800 (2000) Founded: 1971
                      Financial services; discount brokerage Public: SCH (NYSE)
Awards   Computerworld: 100 Best Places to Work in IT
                      Fortune: 100 Best Companies to Work for in America
Headquarters   101 Montgomery Street
                      San Francisco, CA 94104
                      (415) 627-7000
                      http://www.schwab.com

Job Title	Education	Experience	Skills	Location
Divisional Technology Consultant	BA/BS	4+ years	Series 7, Advent, Centerpiece	Jersey City, NJ; Northbrook, IL
Divisional Support Manager	BA/BS	6+ years	Series 7, 63, 8, RIA, brokerage, trust experience	Jersey City, NJ
Sr. Technical Support Services	BA/BS	6+ years	NT, Novell, Citrix, telephony, ISP	Charlotte, NC

Sears, Roebuck and Co.

Fast Facts   Revenues: $40.937B (2000) Employees: 323,000 (2000)
                      Founded: 1886 Retailer; general consumer goods, clothing Public: S
                          (NYSE)
Awards   Computerworld: 100 Best Places to Work in IT
                      Information Week: Top 500 Technology Innovators
Headquarters   3333 Beverly Road
                      Hoffman Estates, IL 60179
                      (847) 286-2500
                      http://www.sears.com

Job Title	Education	Experience	Skills	Location

No jobs available.

Securities Industry Automation Corporation

Fast Facts   Founded: 1972 Financial services; technology arm
                      Jointly-owned subsidiary: NYSE, AMEX
Awards   Computerworld: 100 Best Places to Work in IT
Headquarters   New York, NY
                      Email: Webmaster@siac.com
                      http://www.siac.com

Job Title	Education	Experience	Skills	Location

Submit resume online.

SEI Investments Company

Fast Facts	Revenues: $598.8M (2000) Employees: 1,800 (2000) Founded: 1968
	Financial svcs; asset management, software Public: SEIC (Nasdaq)
Awards	Fortune: 100 Best Companies to Work for in America
Headquarters	1 Freedom Valley Drive
	Oaks, PA 19456-1100
	(610) 676-1000
	http://www.seic.com

Job Title	Education	Experience	Skills	Location
Technical Services Unit Business Analyst Lead		7 years	Trust 3000	Oaks, PA
Trust Product Manager			Trust 3000, trust industry experience	Oaks, PA
Technical Services Unit Business Analyst		3–5 years	Trust 3000	Oaks, PA

Sigma-Aldrich Corporation

Fast Facts	Revenues: $1.096B (2000) Employees: 6,218 (2000) Founded: 1935
	Manufacturer; specialty chemicals Public: SIAL (Nasdaq)
Awards	Computerworld: 100 Best Places to Work in IT
Headquarters	3050 Spruce Street
	St. Louis, MO 63103
	(314) 771-5765
	http://www.sigma-aldrich.com

Job Title	Education	Experience	Skills	Location
Sr. Functional Analyst		5 years	SAP Production Planning, Warehouse Management, SD	St. Louis, MO

Southwest Airlines Co.

Fast Facts	Revenues: $5.65B (2000) Employees: 29,274 (2000) Founded: 1971
	Transportation; airline Public: LUV (NYSE)
Awards	Fortune: 100 Best Companies to Work for in America
	Computerworld: 100 Best Places to Work in IT
Headquarters	2702 Love Field Drive
	Dallas, TX 75235
	(214) 792-4000
	http://www.southwest.com

Job Title	Education	Experience	Skills	Location
Systems Analyst II (Project Manager)	BA/BS	7–9 years	SDLC, airline industry experience	Dallas, TX
Systems Engineer I	BA/BS	5–7 years	Java, Websphere, MQ Series, Oracle	Dallas, TX
Systems Engineer II	BA/BS	7–9 years	Java, EJB, Java servlets, JSP	Dallas, TX

Staples, Inc.

Fast Facts Revenues: $10.674B (2001) Employees: 48,458 (2001)
Founded: 1986 Retailer; home office supplies Public: SPLS (Nasdaq)

Awards Computerworld: 100 Best Places to Work in IT
Interactive Week: The Internet 500

Headquarters 500 Staples Drive
Framingham, MA 01702
(508) 253-5000
http://www.staples.com

Job Title	Education	Experience	Skills	Location
IS Manager	BA/BS CS, MIS	8 years	Oracle 8, VB, ASP, COM, Ariba, BRIO	Framingham, MA
Operations Analyst	BS CS	5 years	HPUX, AIX, VMS, Solaris, NT, AS/400, Omniback, Tivoli Storage Manager, BRFMS, Orsyp Dollar Universe	Marlboro, MA
E-Commerce Sr. Systems Marketing Manager	BA/BS Info. Systems Technology	5+ years	DSS tools, AS/400, Staples.com business	Framingham, MA
Operations Analyst	BA/BS CS	5 years	AS/400, HPUX, AIX, Omniback, Tivoli, BRMS	Marlboro, MA
Remote PC/LAN Technician		2 years	MS Office, Ethernet, TCP/IP	Philadelphia, PA

State Street Corporation

Fast Facts Revenues: $5.921B (2000) Employees: 17,604 (2000) Founded: 1792
Financial services; banking Public: STT (NYSE)

Awards Computerworld: 100 Best Places to Work in IT

Headquarters   225 Franklin Street
Boston, MA 02110
(617) 786-3000
http://www.statestreet.com

Job Title	Education	Experience	Skills	Location
Information Security Admin	BA/BS MIS, Business	3–5 years	OS/390, Notes, Tandem, DEC	Quincy, MA
Programmer Analyst		3+ years	PL/I, COBOL, Sungard Global Plus, financial services experience	Quincy, MA
DBA Associate	BA/BS		Oracle, Sybase, MS SQL	Boston, MA
Design Analyst	BA/BS Business, Software Engineering	5 years	Front Office, portfolio management, accounting, insurance experience	Princeton, NJ
Sr. Application Developer	BA/BS	5 years	C++, Visual C++, UNIX, NT	Newport Beach, CA

Steelcase Inc.

Fast Facts   Revenues: $3.886B (2001) Employees: 21,000 (2001) Founded: 1912
Manufacturer; office furniture Public: SCS (NYSE)
Awards   Industry Week: 100 Best Managed Companies
Headquarters   901 44th Street
Grand Rapids, MI 49508
(616) 247-2710
http://www.steelcase.com

Job Title	Education	Experience	Skills	Location
Associate Operations Analyst			Desktop software, corporate quality	Grand Rapids, MI

Sunoco, Inc.

Fast Facts   Revenues: $12.426B (2000) Employees: 12,300 (2000)
Founded: 1886 Energy; oil refinery Public: SUN (NYSE)
Awards   Computerworld: 100 Best Places to Work in IT

Headquarters   10 Penn Center, 1801 Market Street
                     Philadelphia, PA 19103-1699
                     (215) 977-3000
                     http://www.sunocoinc.com

Job Title	Education	Experience	Skills	Location

No IT jobs posted.

SUPERVALU INC.

Fast Facts   Revenues: $23.194B (2001) Employees: 62,100 (2001)
                   Founded: 1870 Wholesaler; groceries Public: SVU (NYSE)
Awards   Computerworld: 100 Best Places to Work in IT
                   Information Week: Top 500 Technology Innovators
Headquarters   11840 Valley View Rd.
                   Eden Prairie, MN 55344
                   (952) 828-4000
                   http://www.supervalu.com

Job Title	Education	Experience	Skills	Location
Representative job category: Sr. Systems Analyst			O/O Designer, Java, distributed applications	Eden Prairie, MN

Synovus Financial Corporation

Fast Facts   Revenues: $1.931B (2000) Employees: 9,672 (2000) Founded: 1888
                   Financial services; banking Public: SNV (NYSE)
Awards   Fortune: 100 Best Companies to Work for in America
Headquarters   1 Arsenal Place, 901 Front Avenue, Suite 301
                   Columbus, GA 31901
                   (706) 649-5220
                   http://www.synovus.com

Job Title	Education	Experience	Skills	Location

No IT jobs posted.

TDIndustries, Ltd.

Fast Facts   Revenues: $204M (2000) Employees: 1,500 (2000) Founded: 1946
                   Services; heating, ventilation, and air-conditioning Private
Awards   Fortune: 100 Best Companies to Work For in America

Headquarters	13850 Diplomat Drive Dallas, TX 75234 (972) 888-9500 http://www.tdindustries.com

Job Title	Education	Experience	Skills	Location
No IT jobs posted.				

TECO Energy, Inc.

Fast Facts	Revenues: $2.295B (2000) Employees: 5,872 (2000) Founded: 1899 Utility; electricity Public: TE (NYSE)
Awards	Computerworld: 100 Best Places to Work in IT
Headquarters	TECO Plaza, 702 N. Franklin Street Tampa, FL 33602 (813) 228-4111 http://www.teco.net

Job Title	Education	Experience	Skills	Location
Payroll IS Analyst	BA/BS IS, Accounting, Finance, Business	3 years	SAP, accounting and payroll experience	Tampa, FL
Business Analyst	BA/BS Finance, Accounting, Business, Marketing	3–5 years	Financial models for infrastructure projects, competitive market analysis of IT, telecom services	Ybor Data Center

Textron Inc.

Fast Facts	Revenues: $13.09B (2000) Employees: 71,000 (2000) Founded: 1923 Manufacturer; textiles, industrial products Public: TXT (NYSE)
Awards	Industry Week: 100 Best Managed Companies Information Week: Top 500 Technology Innovators
Headquarters	40 Westminster Street Providence, RI 02903-2596 (401) 421-2800 http://www.textron.com

Job Title	Education	Experience	Skills	Location
Embedded Software Engineer	BS, advanced degree preferred	10 years	TI's TMS320, Nuclous, C, DSP assembly, C++, FFTs, Beamforming, Tracking Filters	Wilmington, MA

Job Title	Education	Experience	Skills	Location
Sr. CNC Programmer		3–5 years	Unigraphics, Compact 11, 2,3,4,5-axis CNC mills and lathes	Valencia, CA
Sr. Algorithm Developer	BA/BS Math, CS, EE		TBMD, MFBD, Maui High Performance Computing System	Maui, HI
Systems Analyst	Master's	3+ years	VxWorks, C++, sh, csh, Maui Space Surveillance Site, work at 10,000 feet	Maui, HI
MAS System Specialist	BA/BS CS	5 years	Oracle, VB6, 1388 2-B, ASP, SGML, SQL, DTDs	Fort Worth, TX

Third Federal Savings & Loan

Fast Facts   Employees: 928 (1999) Founded: 1938
Financial services; banking Private

Awards   Fortune: 100 Best Companies to Work for in America
Computerworld: 100 Best Places to Work in IT

Headquarters   7007 Broadway Avenue
Cleveland, OH 44105
(216) 441-6000
http://www.thirdfederal.com

Job Title	Education	Experience	Skills	Location

No IT jobs posted.

The Timberland Company

Fast Facts   Revenues: $1.092B (2000) Employees: 5,400 (2000) Founded: 1952
Retailer; outdoor clothing, shoes Public: TBL (NYSE)

Awards   Fortune: 100 Best Companies to Work for in America

Headquarters   200 Domain Drive
Stratham, NH 03885
(603) 772-9500
www.timberland.com

Job Title	Education	Experience	Skills	Location
Telecommunications Engineer	BA/BS CS, IS	3–5 years	Rolm PBX, Voice mail, call processing, video conferencing, Dytel messaging	Finance & Administration Dept.
Computer Operator II	AA/AS	2 years	BPCS, IP, Infinium, TBS, AS/400, RS/6000	Finance & Administration Dept.

Towers Perrin

Fast Facts Revenues: $1.5B (2000) Employees: 9,000 (2000) Founded: 1934
Professional services; health care and HR consulting Private

Awards Computerworld: 100 Best Places to Work in IT
Information Week: Top 500 Technology Innovators

Headquarters 335 Madison Avenue
New York, NY 10017-4605
(212) 309-3400
http://www.towers.com

Job Title	Education	Experience	Skills	Location
IT Sr. Specialist	BA/BS	3+ years	QA, small to medium IT projects	Philadelphia, PA
IT Specialist	BA/BS MIS, CS, Math, Actuarial Science, Risk Mgt.	3+ years	DB Module, defined benefits experience	Philadelphia, PA
Pension Calculator Project Manager	BA/BS	5+ years	Web programming, defined benefit experience	Boston, MA
UNIX System Administrator			HP/UX, Oracle, Clarify, FileNet	Voorhees
IT Associate		2+ years	Novell NetWare 4.11, NT Server	Voorhees

Trinity Industries, Inc.

Fast Facts Revenues: $1.904B (2001) Employees: 15,300 (2001) Founded: 1933
Manufacturer; rail cars Public: TRN (NYSE)

Awards Industry Week: 100 Best Managed Companies
Computerworld: 100 Best Places to Work in IT

Headquarters	2525 Stemmons Freeway Dallas, TX 75207-2401 (214) 631-4420 http://www.trin.net

Job Title	Education	Experience	Skills	Location
Server Infrastructure Manager	BA/BS CS, IT, CNE, MCSE preferred	6–7 years	GroupWise, NT, Novell, UNIX, ARCSERVE	Dallas, TX
Sr. Network Design Analyst	BS CS, Engineering	3–5 years	ISDN, T1, WAN, Cisco IOS routers, Novell, IPX	Dallas, TX

T. Rowe Price Group, Inc.

Fast Facts	Revenues: $1.212B (2000) Employees: 4,000 (2000) Founded: 1937 Financial services; mutual funds Public: TROW (Nasdaq)
Awards	Computerworld: 100 Best Places to Work in IT
Headquarters	100 E. Pratt Street Baltimore, MD 21202 (410) 345-2000 http://www.troweprice.com

Job Title	Education	Experience	Skills	Location

No IT jobs posted.

Tyco Capital
(formerly The CIT Group)

Fast Facts	Revenues: $6.16B (2000) Employees: 7,355 (2000) Founded: 1908 Financial services; commercial financing Public: CIT (NYSE)
Awards	Computerworld: 100 Best Places to Work in IT Information Week: Top 500 Technology Innovators
Headquarters	1211 Avenue of the Americas New York, NY 10036 (212) 536-1390 http://www.citgroup.com

Job Title	Education	Experience	Skills	Location

No IT jobs posted.

Ukrop's Super Markets, Inc.

Fast Facts	Revenues: $575M (2000) Employees: 5,600 (2000) Founded: 1937 Retailer; grocery stores Private
Awards	Fortune: 100 Best Companies to Work for in America

Headquarters	600 Southlake Boulevard Richmond, VA 23236 (804) 379-7300 http://www.ukrops.com

Job Title	Education	Experience	Skills	Location

No IT jobs listed.

UNICOR
(Federal Prison Industries, Inc.)

Fast Facts	Revenues: $566.2M (1999) Employees: 20,966 (1999) Founded: 1930 Manufacturer; services; Government-owned
Awards	Computerworld: 100 Best Places to Work in IT
Headquarters	320 1st Street N.W. Washington, D.C. 20534 (202) 305-3500 http://www.unicor.gov

Job Title	Education	Experience	Skills	Location

No job listings on site.

UnitedHealth Group Incorporated

Fast Facts	Revenues: $20.89B (2000) Employees: 30,000 (2000) Founded: 1974 Health maintenance organization Public: UNH (NYSE)
Awards	Computerworld: 100 Best Places to Work in IT Information Week: Top 500 Technology Innovators
Headquarters	UnitedHealth Group Center, 9900 Bren Rd. East Minnetonka, MN 55343 (952) 936-1300 http://www.unitedhealthgroup.com

Job Title	Education	Experience	Skills	Location
Applications Development Consultant	MA/MS or equivalent experience		Actuate, VB, JAD	Minneapolis, MN
Sr. Project Analyst	BA/BS Business		Project management, Visio	Fort Washington, PA
Sr. Applications Development Consultant	BA/BS CS	5 years	Oracle PL/SQL Developer/ Designer 2000, Crystal Reports, health care industry experience	Phoenix, AZ

Business Analyst/	BA/BS	3–5 years	Lucent, Avaya	Hartford, CT
Sr. Business Analyst			ACD, MS Project, health/managed care experience	
IS Quality Assurance Analyst	BA/BS CS, CSTE, QAA certification	6 years	SQL, ERGO, Rational SQA Robot, Seque Silk Test, Mercury Win Runner, Sybase, Oracle	Golden Valley, MN

United Parcel Service, Inc.

Fast Facts Revenues: $29.771B (2000) Employees: 359,000 (2000)
Founded: 1907 Services; package delivery Public: UPS (NYSE)

Awards Computerworld: 100 Best Places to Work in IT
Red Herring: 100 Top Companies of the Electronic Age

Headquarters 55 Glenlake Parkway, N.E.
Atlanta, GA 30328
(404) 828-6000
http://www.ups.com

Job Title	Education	Experience	Skills	Location
Lead Programmer Analyst	BA/BS CS	8+ years	Solaris, Netscape iPlanet, WebLogic, Socket/RMI Servers, Oracle, Java, C, Perl	Timonium, MD
Applications Development Manager	BA/BS IT		JavaScript, HTML, ASP, SQL server, Davox Predictive Dialer	Newport News, VA
Programmer Analyst	AA/AS CS		COBOL, CICS, DB2	Morristown, NJ
Sr. Consultant— Supply Chain	BA/BS or MA/ MS/MBA Finance, Operations, OR, Industrial Engineering, Transportation, IT	8–12 years	Big 5, or Booz, McKinsey, BCG experience	Atlanta, Georgia
Oracle DBA	BA/BS CIS	5+ years	Oracle, Hub 2000	Louisville, KY

United Stationers Inc.

Fast Facts Revenues: $3.945B (2000) Employees: 8,350 (2000) Founded: 1922
Wholesaler; office supplies Public: USTR (Nasdaq)

Awards Computerworld: 100 Best Places to Work in IT
Information Week: Top 500 Technology Innovators

Headquarters   2200 E. Golf Road
Des Plaines, IL 60016-1267
(847) 699-5000
http://www.unitedstationers.com

Job Title	Education	Experience	Skills	Location

No job listings online.

USAA

Fast Facts   Revenues: $8.55B (2000) Employees: 22,000 (2000) Founded: 1922
Financial services; insurance (property/casualty) Mutual company

Awards   Fortune: 100 Best Companies to Work for in America
Computerworld: 100 Best Places to Work in IT

Headquarters   9800 Fredericksburg Rd., USAA Bldg.
San Antonio, TX 78288
(210) 498-2211
http://www.usaa.com

Job Title	Education	Experience	Skills	Location

No IT jobs posted.

Valassis

Fast Facts   Revenues: $835.3M (2000) Employees: 1,400 (2000) Founded: 1970
Direct marketer; newspaper inserts, coupons Public: VCI (NYSE)

Awards   Fortune: 100 Best Companies to Work for in America

Headquarters   19975 Victor Parkway
Livonia, MI 48152
(734) 591-3000
http://www.valassis.com

Job Title	Education	Experience	Skills	Location
Client Support Rep.			UNIX, vi editor, Spanish language	Shelton, CT
Quality Assurance Specialist	BS CS, Engineering	2 years	C++, RDBMS	Shelton, CT

Valero Energy Corporation

Fast Facts   Revenues: $14.671B (2000) Employees: 3,180 (2000) Founded: 1980
Energy; oil and gas refineries Public: VLO (NYSE)

Awards   Fortune: 100 Best Companies to Work for in America
Industry Week: 100 Best Managed Companies

Headquarters One Valero Place
San Antonio, TX 78212-3186
(210) 370-2000
http://www.valero.com

Job Title	Education	Experience	Skills	Location
Systems Specialist	BA/BS MIS, CS	5 years	SQL, VB, C++, oil industry experience	San Antonio, TX
Lead Systems Specialist	BA/BS CS	8 years	Active X, OpenVMS, Linux, UNIX, DCS, Fortran, refinery experience	Benicia, CA

The Vanguard Group, Inc.

Fast Facts Revenues: $1.6B est. (2000) Employees: 11,000 (2000)
Founded: 1975 Financial services; mutual funds Private

Awards Fortune: 100 Best Companies to Work for in America
Information Week: Top 500 Technology Innovators

Headquarters 100 Vanguard Boulevard
Malvern, PA 19355
(610) 648-6000
http://www.vanguard.com

Job Title	Education	Experience	Skills	Location
Web Interface Designer	BA/BS Computer Engineering, Software Engineering	5 years	User interface design	Valley Forge, PA
Audit Supervisor, IT	BA/BS Accounting, Finance, CS, Master's IT, CISA, CPA	3–5 years	UNIX, TSO, ISPF, JCL, Easytrieve, MS Office	Valley Forge, PA
College IT	BA/BS CS, Computer Engineering	Entry-level, 3.0+ GPA	Software developer, systems tester, dba, user interface designer	February and June 2002, Valley Forge, PA

VF Corporation

Fast Facts Revenues: $5.748B (2000) Employees: 75,000 (2000) Founded: 1899
Manufacturer; clothing Public: VFC (NYSE)

Awards Industry Week: 100 Best Managed Companies
Fortune: Most Admired Companies

Headquarters	628 Green Valley Rd., Suite 500 Greensboro, NC 27408 (336) 547-6000 http://www.vfc.com

Job Title	Education	Experience	Skills	Location

No IT jobs posted.

VHA Inc.

Fast Facts	Revenues: $442M (2000) Employees: 1,200 (2000) Founded: 1977 Health care; hospitals Cooperative
Awards	Fortune: 100 Best Companies to Work for in America
Headquarters	220 E. Las Colinas Boulevard Irving, TX 75039-5500 (972) 830-0000 http://www.vha.com

Job Title	Education	Experience	Skills	Location

No IT jobs posted.

Vision Service Plan

Fast Facts	Revenues: $1.322B (1999) Employees: 2,212 (1999) Founded: 1955 Health care; vision services Not-for-profit
Awards	Fortune: 100 Best Companies to Work for in America
Headquarters	3333 Quality Drive Rancho Cordova, CA 95670 (916) 851-4854 http://www.vsp.com

Job Title	Education	Experience	Skills	Location
Manager, Information Management	BA/BS Business, CS, pre-employment substance abuse testing	5 years	Data warehouse	Rancho Cordova, CA
Manager, IS Enterprise Architecture Group	BA/BS Business, CS, pre-employment substance abuse testing	8 years	Project development tracking, customer relationships	Rancho Cordova, CA
Programmer Analyst III	BA/BS CS, pre-employment substance abuse testing	5 years	VB, Java ASP, LiveLink, J2EE	Rancho Cordova, CA

| Programmer Analyst III | BA/BS CS, pre-employment substance abuse testing | 5 years | COBOL, CICS, PROS, VB, FoxPro, SAS, OOA, Crystal | Rancho Cordova, CA |
| Strategic Planning Analyst— e-Business | Master's preferred, pre-employment substance abuse testing | 3–5 years | Organizational effectiveness, capacity utilization, mergers and acquisitions | Rancho Cordova, CA |

Vulcan Materials Company

Fast Facts	Revenues: $2.492B (2000) Employees: 9,315 (2000) Founded: 1916 Manufacturer; construction materials (crushed stone) Public: VMC (NYSE)
Awards	Industry Week: 100 Best Managed Companies Fortune: Most Admired Companies
Headquarters	1200 Urban Center Drive Birmingham, AL 35242 (205) 298-3000 http://www.vulcanmaterials.com

Job Title	Education	Experience	Skills	Location

No IT jobs posted.

Wal-Mart Stores, Inc.

Fast Facts	Revenues: $191.329B (2001) Employees: 1,244,000 (2001) Founded: 1945 Retailer; household goods Public: WMT (NYSE)
Awards	Fortune: 100 Best Companies to Work for in America Computerworld: 100 Best Places to Work in IT
Headquarters	702 S.W. Eighth Street Bentonville, AR 72716 (501) 273-4000 http://www.walmartstores.com

Job Title	Education	Experience	Skills	Location
International Strategy Manager (Mexico)			Strategic planning, business analysis	Bentonville, AR
International Business Analyst (Germany)			Detailed function specifications	Bentonville, AR
International Director (Americas)			IT security, disaster recovery, architecture	Bentonville, AR

Operations Engineer (Walmart.com)		2 years	Apache, Oracle Linux, firewalls, load balancers	Brisbane, CA
Sr. Manager of Information Architecture (Walmart.com)	BA/BS or Master's Human Computer Interaction, Information/ Library Science	5+ years	MS Office, Visio, Illustrator, Photoshop, Quark Express, HTML	Brisbane, CA

Wegman's Food Markets, Inc.

Fast Facts   Revenues: $2.67B (2000) Employees: 28,766 (2000) Founded: 1916
Retailer; grocery stores Private

Awards   Fortune: 100 Best Companies to Work for in America

Headquarters   1500 Brooks Avenue
Rochester, NY 14603-0844
(716) 328-2550
http://www.wegmans.com

Job Title	Education	Experience	Skills	Location

No IT jobs posted.

West Group

Fast Facts   Founded: 1804 Publisher; law books, online legal research
Subsidiary: Thomson Corporation

Awards   Computerworld: 100 Best Places to Work in IT

Headquarters   610 Opperman Drive
St. Paul, MN 55123
(651) 687-7000
http://www.westgroup.com

Job Title	Education	Experience	Skills	Location
Architect—Global Online	BS CS, graduate degree a plus	8 years	XML, DOM, SAX, Fluency in a second language is an advantage	Eagan, MN
EPS Coordinator	AA/AS, BA/BS preferred	3–5 years	WESTLAW databases	Rochester, NY
SAP/Basis Technical Lead	BA/BS CS	7+ years	SAP/Basis, AIX, UDB	Eagan, MN
Technical Product Specialist	BA/BS	2–3 years	HTML, Java, JavaScript, ActiveX	Eagan, MN
Sr. Associate, Strategic	MBA preferred	2–3+ years	Strategy and business development	Eagan, MN

Whole Foods Market, Inc.

Fast Facts	Revenues: $1.839B (2000) Employees: 18,500 (2000) Founded: 1980
	Retailer; grocery stores Public: WFMI (Nasdaq)
Awards	Fortune: 100 Best Companies to Work for in America
Headquarters	601 N. Lamar, Suite 300
	Austin, TX 78703
	(512) 477-4455
	http://www.wholefoodsmarket.com

Job Title	Education	Experience	Skills	Location

No IT jobs posted.

Wisconsin Energy Corporation

Fast Facts	Revenues: $3.355B (2000) Employees: 10,191 (2000) Founded: 1896
	Utility; electricity Public: WEC (NYSE)
Awards	Computerworld: 100 Best Places to Work in IT
Headquarters	231 W. Michigan Street
	Milwaukee, WI 53201
	(414) 221-2345
	http://www.wisenergy.com

Job Title	Education	Experience	Skills	Location

No IT jobs posted.

W. L. Gore & Associates, Inc.

Fast Facts	Revenues: $1.35B (2000) Employees: 5,888 (2000) Founded: 1958
	Manufacturer; specialty fabric (GORE-TEX), clothing Private
Awards	Fortune: 100 Best Companies to Work for in America
	Computerworld: 100 Best Places to Work in IT
Headquarters	555 Paper Mill Road
	Newark, DE 19711
	(302) 738-4880
	http://www.gore.com

Job Title	Education	Experience	Skills	Location
SAS Programmer	MA/MS CS, Statistics, SAS Institute certification	2 years	SAS macro coding, graphics, MS Office, clinical trial data, pharmaceutical experience	Flagstaff, AZ

Clinical Database Developer Programmer	BA/BS CIS, MIS, CS, MCP, MCSD certification	3–5 years	SAS, regulatory submissions	Flagstaff, AZ
Analog Mixed-Signal IC Designer	BS EE or advanced degree	3+ years	BiCMOS analog/ mixed-signal high speed design	Elkton, MD
VCSEL Research Scientist	Ph.D EE, Materials Engineering, Physics		Device simulation, VCSEL, C, C++	Lompoc, CA
Software QA	BS EE, Math, CIS, CS	3 years	VB, Oracle, Relsys, Documentum, FlowStream	Flagstaff, AZ

Wm. Wrigley Jr. Company

Fast Facts Revenues: $2.146B (2000) Employees: 9,800 (2000) Founded: 1891
Manufacturer; chewing gum Public: WWY(NYSE)
Awards Industry Week: 100 Best Managed Companies
Headquarters 410 N. Michigan Avenue
Chicago, IL 60611
(312) 644-2121
http://www.wrigley.com

Job Title	Education	Experience	Skills	Location
Consumer Database Administrator			Consumer Research Study Designs	Chicago, IL

Chapter Four

Tekhound*, FlipDog*, and Monster, Oh My**

This chapter describes other resources for job-hunters. Resources for getting a job in techie-land abound. Online recruiting and employee referrals are the top recruiting methods for most companies, although creative hiring managers have tried everything. Some have put billboards near their competitors' offices. Some have raided techies from competitors at trade shows. Some have sent spiders over the Internet to find resumes with targeted skills. This chapter describes the advantages and disadvantages for employers and candidates of the most popular methods of recruiting. In-depth profiles in Chapters Two and Three show the percentage of candidates found through each method for profiled companies.

*Tekhound has been bought by techies.com. FlipDog has been bought by TMP, the parent company for monster.com. ** With apologies to The Wizard of Oz.

Online Recruiting

The hottest news in job hunting for the last couple of years has been the Internet. Some employers use it as a screening device. In this category, we are including both internal online recruiting, through the company's own web site, and third party online recruiting, as found at such sites as monster.com and techies.com. In using online recruiting employers reason that since techies hang out on the Internet all the time the most attractive candidates can be found there. As with all other assumptions, this method has its flaws. But, first, let's look at the advantages to employers:

- It is far cheaper for employers than any alternative except employee referrals.
- It reaches the right target audience—those who are comfortable with technology.
- It can target candidates geographically and by skill set.
- It is easy and fast, generating responses within seconds.

With all these advantages, why would an employer use anything else?

- It does not qualify candidates, as agencies and employee referrals do.
- It does not reach passive candidates, only those who are actively looking.
- It may be too successful, overwhelming a company's resources to process resumes.
- It reaches geographically undesirable candidates, for which a company may have to pay re-location fees.

- There are now more than 2,000 online sites, and this number is growing every day.

What are its advantages to candidates looking for a new job?

- Job opportunities can be found during non-work hours.
- Automatic job searching techniques find jobs matching a candidate's requested profile, on a regular basis, without additional work.
- It is easy to search in a target city, without having to travel to the city first.
- It is easy to search for information about an employer before applying for a job.

What are its disadvantages for candidates?

- Popular skills such as C++ or Java may draw thousands of responses.
- Many corporate sites have hundreds of job listings, with little way to drill down to the specific ones that are appropriate.
- Often there are separate return email addresses for jobs of interest at the same company.
- Care must be exercised if a candidate wants the job search to be confidential; many boards post a candidate's resume publicly, which their current employer may find.
- Many companies cross-list on dozens of job boards; it may not be easy to find out which of the job opportunities are duplicates.
- Searching is, in general, by keyword, and that generally means by hardware and software name (i.e., C++, PeopleSoft, Oracle). Soft skills, like managing 100 people or a $25 million program, may be harder for search engines to identify.
- It is rare to find an entry-level job this way (see Chapter Five for more information about finding an entry-level position).

Employee Referrals

One of the most popular methods companies have for finding new employees is asking their current employees to refer colleagues. During the tight technical job market of the last couple of years, most companies instituted a policy of offering bonuses for employees who referred candidates. For a period of time, they even offered additional incentives such as drawings for cars and other prizes. Sixty-eight of *Fortune*'s 100 Best Companies to Work For in America offer employee referral bonuses. The advantages to the employer in identifying candidates through employee referrals are:

- The candidate is pre-selected by someone who knows them and is an immediate reference.
- This method is cheaper, even with bonuses, than almost any other method.
- Candidates are likely to be a better fit, since they are already familiar with the company culture.
- It is a good way to find passive candidates, intrigued by an employee's description of the company and their job.

Are there any disadvantages?

- Employees generally don't know enough people in the industry to supply all of a company's staffing needs. This method must be supplemented by others.
- Employees generally only know of openings in their immediate area, not the rest of the company.

What are the advantages to candidates?

- They know someone who can answer tough questions, those that cannot be asked in an interview.
- They can often talk directly to a hiring manager first, shortening the application process.
- Employees often know of jobs being created that are not yet publicly listed.

Why might a candidate not use this method?

- They may not know anyone in the company they want to work for.
- Their friends may not know of any job openings.

Employment Agencies

These are traditional recruiters, who will interview candidates and pre-screen them for employers. They coach candidates on what an employer is looking for, aggressively search out jobs, and steer candidates to the best fit or quickest match between their skills and interests and an employer's needs and willingness to pay. They earn a hefty commission each time they are successful, at the employer's expense. This is the most expensive recruiting option for employers. They typically use it for the following reasons:

- They want to staff up quickly.
- They don't want to hire their own internal recruiting staff.
- They are supplementing this method with others, for difficult-to-find skills.

What are the advantages for candidates? There are some reasons that using an employment agency can really pay off for candidates.

- They spend minimum time in their job search.
- They get a coach for interviews and sometimes a second interview if the first one goes poorly.
- They get access to jobs that are not on the open market.
- Soft skills, like analysis and project management, get more attention.

On the other hand, candidates may find:

- Agents may try to place them too quickly.
- They may not get top dollar in salary requests.
- As with all other methods, popular skills get the most offers.
- Some companies never use agencies.
- Some agents may not understand the value of rare technical skills.

Advertising

Until the Internet, this was one of the most popular methods for recruiting. Now, while advertisements continue to be placed in local newspapers and trade publications, most companies use them simply to duplicate their online job descriptions. While they report that few candidates come from this source, it is difficult to know how successful this method is in driving candidates to a company's own web site, where they then apply.

What are the advantages to companies using this method?

- It is tightly geographically focused.
- It reaches candidates with specific skills and interests, through targeted trade publications.

What are the disadvantages?

- It is much more expensive than most online recruiting fees.
- It is static. It cannot lead candidates to more information about the company, such as a linked corporate home page or profile.

What are the advantages to candidates?

- It is confidential. Employers do not know candidates are looking for other jobs.
- It is geographically based or targeted to a technical area of interest.
- It allows for serendipitous scanning of a number of jobs quickly.

What are the disadvantages?

- It requires extra steps to send in a resume or research the company.
- Response to a resume is delayed.

Job Fairs, Campus Recruiting, and Networking

Hiring managers use a number of other methods to find candidates. They host their own job fairs. They attend third-party job fairs. They hold regularly scheduled campus recruiting trips. They use their own personal networks in the industry. They talk to companies that are laying people off. They respond to unsolicited resumes. These methods are all open-ended. That is, they are not tied to a specific job description. They can all be good avenues into a company. A candidate may not know which specific job in a company is best suited to them or they may want to work for a particular company, but have not seen a job opening tailored to their skills.

Companies vary in their approach to hiring. They may hire good candidates when they run across them or they may only hire in response to a specific job description. They may consider candidates with related experience in the industry, or they may only respond to those with resumes that have an exact technical fit with the company's environment. Candidates cannot know in advance which kind of company they are dealing with unless they have a personal connection with someone in the company. In general, candidates have a better chance at a job they are applying for if they structure their resume to show how their skills match those listed in a job description they are responding to. For open-ended channels, as described above, a general-purpose resume, highlighting the candidate's deepest or most recent technical experience in a quick paragraph at the head of the resume will find the best response.

Summary

In the year 2000, employers were looking for candidates in the tightest labor market in decades. Employers traveled to Russia, Australia, and India to find candidates. They cultivated high school students. They petitioned Congress to raise the number of H1-B visas allowed. In 2001, the economy tightened sharply and the job outlook changed. Industries such as telecommunications and the Internet consolidated. Most industries have been affected by the recession. Before September 11, 2001, the strongest industries, and those whose companies continued to hire, were financial services and biotechnology, and, through the Spring of 2001, energy. Housing sales have remained strong. Since September 11, 2001, resources are being aimed at companies in the military sector, security, and bio-technology/pharmaceuticals, with selected sectors, such as grocery stores, remaining strong. A security clearance has become a prized commodity.

But, while the companies hiring has changed, the way they hire has not. Candidates should remember to tailor their resume to match the skills requested in a job description, literally. The resume may be screened by resume-scanning software. It will probably be reviewed by a technical recruiter before a hiring manager sees it. In either case, reviewers may not be able to make the logical connections that techies assume leap off the page. Be specific. Know what you want and what you can offer. Employers want to know how you can help their business. Candidates want to know where the technically-challenging jobs are. The company profiles in this guide will help you find each other.

Chapter Five

The Entry-Level Dilemma

The traditional dilemma for entry-level candidates is that you can not get a job without experience and can not get experience without a job. However, in the tight labor market of 2000, companies were bending the rules. They even recruited high school students who had demonstrated they were crack programmers. For their part, candidates were helping themselves look more experienced with professionally-oriented summer jobs, college classes, and their own, personal work on computers. Starting in the Spring of 2001, the rules changed. Many soon-to-be college graduates had their offers rescinded weeks before they were to start working.

For the school year 2001–2002, many companies have cut back or eliminated their college recruiting programs. But, this simply means we are back to normal. Getting an entry-level job in the computer industry is difficult, but not impossible. Many companies still offer summer intern or co-op programs and expect to get most of their entry-level professionals through these programs. We will examine some of the traditional paths into the computer industry.

Gateways

There are several ways to get a first job in the computer industry.

- Earn a degree in a technical field.
- Take a programmer's aptitude test at a hiring company.
- Enter a company's training program.
- Transfer internally.
- Earn a diploma or certification at a technical school.

We will look at each option.

Earn a technical degree.

Students majoring in Computer Science, Computer Engineering, Engineering, Management Information Systems, or Computer Information Systems are the top candidates for most companies that hire entry-level candidates. Companies send hiring managers to campuses around the country to interview seniors in these degreed programs. Most of these students will have several offers to choose from before they graduate. However, many companies have stiff requirements. It is common to require a Grade Point Average of 3.0 or 3.5. Managers may ask students to describe projects they have worked on to gauge hands-on experience. They are also listening for a candidate's ability to communicate complex, technical issues. They may ask for a sample of code, or even a sample of writing. Companies prefer candidates that already have some professional experience, such as by working in the school's computer support department or working as a summer intern in a technical role. Many companies also ask about a candidate's participation in campus activities, and whether they took a leadership role. Some companies regard participation in activities or community service as evidence of a well-rounded, balanced approach to work and life. A few look for the determination that comes from working your way through school.

Take a programmer's aptitude test

Before technical degrees were widespread, many companies used a programmer's aptitude test to determine whether candidates had the logical and analytical skills necessary for programming. A large part of the test consists of pattern-recognition questions, designed to determine whether candidates have the eye for detail required in programming and the analytical skills to apply that precision. These tests are still used by some companies to uncover candidates who might otherwise not be considered, especially if they have a degree in something other than a technical field. Liberal arts, music, and foreign language backgrounds are often favored, when paired with a high score on the programmer's aptitude test. It is generally considered not possible to study for this test since there are no facts to memorize. However, it is possible to prepare for it by reviewing sample questions in books found in the public library.

Company training program

Some companies have found that experience in their industry is a better indicator of success than a technical background. Others have found that candidates who understand business issues and how important they are in applying technology to business problems are more compatible to their culture than candidates who have focused solely on technology. Some have found that bright candidates who learn well can be taught technical skills regardless of their educational focus or professional background.

These companies generally provide an extensive training program for entry-level candidates. It is not uncommon for them to require that candidates stay with the company two to three years to re-coup their training costs. The training program may vary from rotating candidates through different assignments in various technical areas to a university-type full-time one to six-month classroom experience. Qualifying for these programs is generally based on a combination of interviews, grades, and possibly tests, such as the programmer's aptitude test. A technical degree is not generally required. Other traits are considered as important or more important than a technical background. Paul LeForte, CIO of United Healthcare Group, discovered this when polling his company's technical hiring managers. Good communication skills and teamwork were cited as more important than existing technical skills. As a result, United Healthcare instituted a formal training program that provides a selection of college courses, interactive video conferencing, and online courses to the technical and non-technical candidates they hire.

Internal Transfers

This opportunity is generally only available at companies that have a formal internal training program. Some companies encourage employees with an interest in computers to transfer to an entry-level technical role. Jeff Marshall, of The Men's Warehouse, illustrates this approach. Says Marshall, "Let's say a wardrobe consultant wants to get into IT. Rather than say he's not an IT guy, we say, he's a PC guy with retail experience."

Technical schools

There have always been vocational schools for technical professionals. The Computer Learning Center and DeVry Institute are two of the most well known. They teach programming, networking, and PC support skills, in keeping with the hot skills of the day. Some employers prefer graduates of these programs to those with university degrees, because these schools favor a hands-on approach and their graduates are ready to contribute from their first day on the job. Candidates may prefer this approach because it is faster than getting a two-year or four-year university degree. Further, the courses are more targeted. They include only a technical curriculum. University programs, by contrast, demand a broader approach for their graduates, incorporating requirements for English and other non-technical course material.

More recently, there has been intense competition for certified professionals. Cisco, Microsoft, and Sun Microsystems provide training and certification for their products. While some employers shy away from certified candidates with no hands-on experience, others willingly recruit these candidates. This training, however, can be very expensive. When evaluating programs, candidates should ask what percentage of graduates get technical jobs within a year after graduation and how much help is provided in connecting graduates to potential employers.

Job Categories

Entry-level jobs fall into several major categories, depending on the type of employer. The web sites of companies that routinely hire entry-level professionals often direct candidates to a separate college graduate section for job openings or campus visit schedules. The following list shows the most common entry-level positions.

- Customer Support Representative
- PC/Desktop Support
- LAN/Systems Administrator
- Entry-level Programmer/Software Developer
- Associate Business Analyst
- Tester
- Trainer.

We will look at each one in turn.

Customer Support Representative.

Software and hardware vendors typically hire customer service representatives to help field questions about their products, by answering telephone or email inquiries. Internet Service Providers were recently among the hottest employers for customer service representatives, because of their phenomenal growth. Seventy percent of Earthlink's technical professionals, for instance, are call center personnel. In 2000, it was not uncommon for them to open a call center with 200 employees, and grow it to 800 within six months. Some of the most sophisticated software today is being developed for call centers, to queue and route calls, and to provide customer histories to representatives.

This can be a very good way to get into the industry, but employees should also be looking for opportunities to move up in the organization. This may be through supervising, through moving into pre- or post-sales engineering support, or through tackling more difficult support levels. Support is gauged to be Level 1 for simple problems, Level 2 for more complex issues, Level 3 for software conflict issues, and Level 4 for complex design issues that can only be resolved by the product designers themselves.

PC/Desktop Support

Most companies, large and small, dedicate one or more employees to the installation, upgrade, and maintenance of desktop software. Certification, such as that for Microsoft products, helps validate various levels of expertise.

One sector, automobile dealerships, routinely converts a power user who takes on the responsibility for learning about PCs into the sole technical representative for the company. As the dealership grows, this person's role can become a substantial, full-time position, with the complexities of a rich, varied hardware and software environment. Various automobile manufacturers, for instance, use different software packages for their products. Dealerships responsible for more than one manufacturer must learn the variations in these packages and interface them to their own internal systems. For dealerships that control a chain of other dealers, the central office may set standards for the rest.

Employees should look for additional responsibilities to further career growth. In many large companies, this position is a springboard into LAN administration. Other natural growth paths include trouble-shooting for more complex hardware and providing pre- and post-sales support for hardware or software vendors.

LAN or Systems Administrator

LAN or Systems Administrators manage a company's local area network. For small LANs, this position may be filled by an entry-level professional. Training is largely on-the-job. Career growth is generally measured by the number of nodes on the LAN. Increased complexity is added for Wide Area Networks (WANs), or Metropolitan Area Networks (MANs). Certification in vendor-specific network equipment, such as Novell's NetWare, or Cisco's routers and switches, is prized. Training is expensive so look for companies that offer this as part of their professional development package.

Entry-Level Programmer/Software Developer

Candidates with technical degrees are often qualified for positions in writing code since their coursework has generally introduced them to programming already. Typical majors would include Computer Science and Computer Engineering. Entry-level jobs generally entail modifying existing programs or generating simple reports. This gives candidates an opportunity to see how others have written programs and learn the style used by their employer. Employers may or may not offer an initial training program. Training is generally offered throughout a programmer's career, as companies bring in new software products and train their staff on the new products.

The programming career path generally leads to Senior, Lead, and Principal Programmer or Software Engineer. Then, options split between technical and management positions. On the technical side, programming typically leads into specialization, such as database administration. The most senior technical position is Chief Technical Officer. A few companies have a Fellow position for very senior technical staff. The management track generally starts with Project Lead, then Program Manager, then Director and Vice President/Chief Information Officer. A Technical Fellow is generally comparable to a Director or Vice President on the management track.

Associate Business Analyst

Business Analysts bridge the worlds of business and technology. They determine how a business operates and translate this knowledge into technical terms that can be used to develop software. Typical majors for this career path include Management Information System, Information Systems, or Business with an emphasis on Computers. Good communication skills, both written and verbal, are required for these positions. Excellent analytical skills are also required. Understanding the processes that underlie business operations and explaining them to a non-business-oriented technologist is a talent in its own right. While Analysts generally do not write software, they may have started out as Programmers.

Business Analysts are commonly found in consulting companies. Most of the work in these companies revolves around understanding a customer's environment and translating that information into technical requirements. In addition, software companies that customize their product for each customer represent a growing opportunity for Business Analysts. TenFold Corporation is one of these companies. Glen Mella, Senior Vice President, Marketing, describes candidates for these positions as professionals "with a consulting orientation. They should be analytical thinkers who write well and can speak with senior managers at some of the largest companies in the world." This position is also closely related to a more senior position, Systems Analyst. The career path for Analysts is typically Associate, Analyst, and Senior Analyst and may include either systems or business analysis.

Tester

Software product testers determine where a product's flaws are by trying to break it. There is a disciplined approach to testing products so that various features of the software are exercised. Regression testing exercises the product with a control set of data and transactions to be sure that no new errors have been introduced.

Testing is a good route into software development. Testers can see where software breaks and what kinds of errors are common. The style of different coders is evident and makes it easier to learn how to write code that can be fixed easily, or more importantly, that is stable.

Trainer

Trainers are given an opportunity to learn a company's products then teach them to customers. The ability to explain complex terms in simple language, relate well to a wide variety of people, and speak easily in public are all valuable traits in a skilled trainer. For entry-level trainers, materials are already prepared for the trainer to learn. As they move up in the training track, they will have to learn to prepare training materials themselves. Trainers have to keep up with the latest releases of technical products, integrate these advancements into their training and look for real-world examples of how the products are used in the students' environment. A Business, Liberal Arts, or teaching background with an emphasis on Computers is a good background for a trainer.

Summary

There are several, well-defined routes into a technical career and companies know that they need a pipeline of bright, energetic candidates. The computer industry offers good compensation and an exciting career path. While today's economic conditions have changed the easy availability of entry-level jobs, companies still need to hire their next generation of leaders.

Chapter Six

There Has to Be a Job Here Somewhere

This chapter describes the top online recruiting resources for techies. While Chapter Four described the advantages and disadvantages of various job-searching methods, this chapter narrows its focus to online sites. It is divided into two sections—online recruiting sites and online corporate sites.

Online Recruiting Sites

Online sites differ in their approach. Some of these differences include:

- Resumes may be open to searches by any employer or confidential.
- Job listings may be open or available only after a registration process.
- Jobs may include all careers, or be techie-specific.
- Sites may earn all their fees from job postings, or be affiliated with other organizations, such as career-counselors, recruiters, or software and consulting services vendors for corporate web hiring tools.
- Jobs listed may be only those contracted for by the site, or from a scraping of jobs posted across the web.

Just as with newspapers, half or more of the jobs listed may be with recruiting agencies. Many are for contract or temporary positions only. We will look at some of the most popular sites.

General job search

careerbuilder.com aggregates newspaper listings into a single online site. A tedious search highlighting approximately a dozen variations of technical positions (Engineer/software, IT, e-commerce) turned up 1,000 hits for the Virginia-metro DC area in a February, 2002 search. Many of these were for data entry clerks. More significantly, a search of software engineering positions turned up 209 hits, all directly with hiring companies. Further, each company has a detailed company profile. careerbuilder.com recently acquired headhunter.net.

hotjobs.com does not show many technical job categories and its geographic search could only be restricted to the Washington, D.C. metro area, which included Baltimore, Maryland. A February, 2002 search turned up 1,000 jobs, but some of these were for sales positions. Interestingly, most of its positions were for direct hires, including for the U.S. government and many were senior software engineering positions.

monster.com is the largest job site on the web. Candidates may post resumes and look at job openings through any of a number of filters, including geographic and career-specific. Candidates report that most technical positions cluster in the network and technical support areas and that they have not been able to keep their employers from seeing their posted resumes. monster.com is owned by the Yellow Pages advertising company, TMP Worldwide Inc., which also owns an executive search firm. A February, 2002 search for technical jobs in Northern Virginia turned up more than 600 hits, with a wide range of technical levels, but many of these were for TMP, acting as a recruiter for an unnamed client, or for other recruiting companies.

Techie-specific

computerjobs.com shows listings openly. They showed almost 900 technical jobs in a February, 2002 search. The geographic boundary, however, ranged from Washington, D.C. to Richmond, Virginia, Baltimore, Maryland, and Delaware and could not be further restricted. Nearly half of the listings were with recruiting agencies or for contract positions. But, there were also many direct hires, including a position with Microsoft. The best part about this site is that jobs are divided into technical specialties, ranging from ERP and e-Commerce to Legacy and AS/400. Further, jobs can be requested specifically for start-ups, entry-level positions, or telecommuting.

dice.com lists the most number of technical jobs on its site. Its job listings include full-time positions, as well as contract and temporary positions. One of its most useful features is the area-code metro search to narrow a target geographic boundary.

techies.com concentrates on technical positions. Headquartered in Minnesota, it still has more jobs in the Midwest than the rest of the country. However, a February, 2002 search for technical positions in the Northern Virginia area turned up almost 500 hits, including a significant number for one company that has announced plans to hire 1,000 people in the next three years. All levels of positions are posted, as well as a number of articles to help techies in the job search. Perhaps more interesting, techies.com hosts an online job fair, and publishes booklets with company profiles for specific geographic regions, since its acquisition of Tekhound.

Web scrapes

flipdog.com was the first of the web-scraping sites. It looks for all jobs posted on corporate sites every night and posts them. Its business model includes encouraging companies to post jobs with them directly as well as paying a fee to enhance the listings that flipdog's spiders find. Probably its most interesting feature is the unusual jobs it finds and highlights. However, these are rarely technical jobs and do not include their geographic location until you drill down to the job description, unlike all its other postings. flipdog.com has been acquired by TMP, the parent company of monster.com.

grassisgreener.com requires that candidates register in order to capture a profile. Candidates are alerted when matching jobs come available and can block their resumes from selected employers. This site, like flipdog.com, sends spiders out over the web nightly to find all the jobs posted on the web.

Corporate online sites

Nearly all corporate sites now include a section aimed at helping candidates apply on-line. They vary significantly in their ability to attract top technical candidates. Some of the best sites:

- Provide an email for a "corporate buddy" that candidates can contact directly for specific questions about the company.
- Give a technical overview of the company.
- Separate technical positions from other categories of jobs at the company.
- Provide an email alert system to let candidates know when matching positions come open.
- Let candidates submit resumes to multiple positions with a single response.
- Keep resumes to compare to upcoming job openings.
- Provide an umbrella area for decentralized company recruiting sections.
- Describe a "day in the life" of a typical operational employee.

Probably the most intriguing feature that candidates have reported is putting a riddle on the site for candidates to solve before the interview. Many are familiar with Microsoft's interview question: "How many piano tuners are there in the United States?" Riddles are a similar qualifier. Though some companies require that candidates come to the interview with the answer, many are looking for how candidates reason, a necessary skill in the technology industry. Similarly, hiring managers may ask questions such as, "Describe a difficult problem you faced and how you handled it" to determine how candidates think their way through tough situations. Probably no one knows how many piano tuners there are in the United States, or how many man-hole covers, but candidates stand out when they present an intriguing approach to solving these problems and hiring managers look for candidates who are not only well-prepared for the interview, but smart.

This is where your research on the company ahead of time makes you stand out!

Methodology

Companies that agreed to be interviewed have long profiles at the beginning of Chapters Two and Three. Short profiles follow in each of these chapters.

Companies were selected based on their inclusion on one of three lists:

- *Fortune*: 100 Best Companies to Work for in America
- *Computerworld*: 100 Best Places to Work in IT
- *Industry Week*: 100 Best Managed Companies

Six companies were named on all three lists: Harley-Davidson, Hewlett-Packard, Intel, Merck, Sun Microsystems, and Texas Instruments.

Since the initial research for this guide began in 2000, companies from several other lists that were initially profiled in the early stages of research have also been included. They were selected because they were named on one of the following lists:

- *PC Magazine*: 100 Most Influential
- *Interactive Week*: The Internet 500
- *Information Week*: Top 500 Technology Innovators
- *Red Herring*: 100 Top Companies of the Electronic Age
- *Computer Business Review*: Top 50 Software Vendors
- *PC Week*: Fast-Track 500
- *Fortune*: America's Most Admired Companies

In all cases, the assumption was that excellent companies have excellent jobs. Dot-coms typically did not make these lists because they are weighted, indirectly, toward Fortune 500 companies.

Fortune selects from among companies with at least 250 employees. *Industry Week* selects from among manufacturers. Both *Fortune* and *Computerworld* selected companies based on their benefits, training, and promotion policies. *Industry Week* selected companies based on their ability to grow sales and profits, invest in their employees, and contribute to the community. *Computerworld* also selected companies for their record on diversity. All of its selection criteria relate to IT employees specifically.

Our web site (http://www.20minutesfromhome.com) identifies additional lists of companies that are good targets for candidates, including emerging companies. Lists are divided according to whether companies were selected because of their technology, business, or culture.

Process

For long profiles, we conducted telephone interviews with technology and human resource executives and technical recruiters. Long profiles were developed for a fee from the companies. The opportunity to describe their technical environment in detail is designed to more efficiently draw candidates that best fit their needs. Companies supplied additional materials, such as fact sheets, benefits summary forms, or company backgrounders. We asked for materials that would typically be supplied to a new hire. We conducted additional research at the company's web site, read annual reports, and researched relevant articles about the company, its products, and customers. All companies were asked the same questions, responding to a structured telephone interview based on a four-page questionnaire.

Short profiles were developed from public information on the Internet and at the companies' own sites. Awards were gathered from the named professional publications.

All job descriptions, except where noted, were either taken directly from company web sites between the fourth week of September and the second week of November, 2001 or confirmed as representative of job listings posted during that period.

Product/Company Cross-Reference

This list has been compiled to help candidates find companies that need their particular skills. These are typically the buzzwords—the tools, languages, and applications software—that recruiters and automated resume scanning software look for on candidates' resumes. Be sure to list them explicitly, when appropriate, with the correct spelling. Automated software cannot infer a language or tool from the vendor's name or related software. Use the following product names to differentiate yourself with your resume by making sure that a company knows when you have skills that match their environment.

A few software tools, languages, and vendors are so common they have not been included here, as almost every company uses techies with these skills. These include C, C++, Visual Basic, Java, MS-Office, Windows, UNIX, HTML, SQL, Cisco and Sun. You should still include them on your resume, if you have experience with these vendors. Not all vendors and products from the profiles are listed, just those considered the most popular, rare, or significant for resumes. Where possible, techies should always highlight the skills on their resumes listed on a job description.

The author takes complete responsibility for any errors. Where techies realize that products in a job listing are misspelled, they should be sure to spell them correctly on their resumes. All technical products shown below have been referenced in a company's recent job listings or described in interviews. For editing reasons, they may not have been included in this guide's short or long profiles.

ABAP	46–47, 54, 57, 72–73, 140–141, 156–157, 182, 190, 207	Apache	19–22, 31–34, 42–43, 51–52, 56, 113–116, 147–148, 206–207
Ab Initio	35–36	Apex	23–26
ACD	81–84, 146–147, 166, 201–202	APO	152–153
		AppleGlot	36
Active X	31–34, 77–80, 183, 203–204, 207	Arbor	37–38, 53
		Arc/Info	23–26, 64
Actuate	45–46, 101–104, 201–202	Ariba	27–30, 194
Ada	23–26, 150	ASP	23–26, 31–34, 43, 45, 49, 56,
ADABAS	77–80, 133–134		71–72, 72, 77–80, 85–88,
ADO	38–39, 183		89–92, 125–128, 131,
AIX	7–10, 19–22, 27–30, 45–46, 97–100, 130–131, 135–136, 138, 143–144, 156–157, 177–178, 189, 194, 207		133–134, 135–136, 147–148, 151, 155–156, 163–164, 174, 176–177, 182, 183, 64, 185–186, 194, 197–198, 202, 205–206
Alpha	15–18		
Analog Artist Design	71	Assembler	19–22, 49–50, 52–53, 58–59, 62, 71–72, 77–80, 81–84,

Industry/Company Cross-Reference

Energy
American Electric Power
Edison International
FPL Group
Peoples Energy
Sunoco
TECO Energy
Valero Energy
Wisconsin Energy

Entertainment
Harrah's Entertainment
Home Shopping Network
Royal Caribbean Cruises

Financial Services
Banking
Citigroup
Comerica
First Tennessee National
Fannie Mae
Fifth Third Bancorp
FleetBoston Financial
Freddie Mac
Goldman Sachs
Household International
Mellon Financial
National City
PNC Financial Services Group
Regions Financial
Republic Bancorp
State Street
Synovus Financial
Third Federal Savings & Loan
Brokerage/Investment
A.G. Edwards
American Century Investments
Edward Jones
Frank Russell
Merrill Lynch
MFS Investment Management

Schwab (Charles)
Securities Industry Automation
SEI Investments
T. Rowe Price
Vanguard
Credit Card
American Express
Capital One Financial
Equifax
MBNA
Insurance
Aetna
AFLAC
Allstate
American Family Insurance
American Skandia
AXA Financial
Cigna
Cincinnati Financial.
Harleysville Group
John Hancock Financial Services
Metropolitan Life Insurance
Minnesota Mutual
MONY Group
Nationwide Financial Services
New York Life Insurance
Principal Financial Group
Prudential Financial
State Farm Insurance
UnitedHealth Group
USAA
Leasing/Financing
GATX
Tyco Capital

Health Care
Products
Alcon Laboratories
Amgen
Baxter International
Becton, Dickinson

Bristol-Myers Squibb
Eli Lilly
Genentech
Guidant
Immunex
Johnson & Johnson
Medtronic
Merck
Millennium Pharmaceuticals
Pfizer
Schering-Plough
Services
East Alabama Medical Center
Griffin Hospital
HCA
VHA
Vision Service Plan

Manufacturing
Computers/Hardware
3Com
Agilent Technologies
Analog Devices
Apple Computer
Applied Materials
Cisco Systems
Dell Computer
EMC
Gateway
Hewlett-Packard
Honeywell International.
IBM
Intel
Kingston Technology
Lexmark
Motorola
National Instruments
National Semiconductor
NCR
Network Appliance
QUALCOMM
Scientific-Atlanta
Silicon Graphics
Solectron
Sun Microsystems
Teradyne
Texas Instruments
Unisys
Xilinx
Computers/Software
Adobe Systems
Autodesk
Candle

Cerner
Computer Associates International
EPIQ Systems
Galileo International
Interwoven
Manugistics Group
Mercury Interactive
Microsoft
MicroStrategy
Oracle
SAS Institute
WRQ
Industrial
3M
Alcoa
ACIPCO
BorgWarner
Bowater
Cabot
Caterpillar
Corning
Dana
Deer
DuPont
Eastman Chemical
Eaton
Emerson
Engelhard
General Dynamics
Georgia-Pacific
Granite Rock
Illinois Tool Works
Ingersoll-Rand
International Truck and Engine
Johnson Controls
Lear
Lockheed Martin
PACCAR
Parker Hannafin
Rockwell International
Rohm and Haas
Sigma-Aldrich
TDIndustries
Textron
Trinity Industries
Vulcan Materials
W. L. Gore & Associates
Consumer
Anheuser-Busch
Avon Products
Bose
Colgate-Palmolive
Coors (Adolph)

General Electric
General Mills
Herman Miller
Hershey Foods
HON Industries
J. M. Smucker
Maytag
Mohawk Industries
Pella
R. J. Reynolds Tobacco
Sara Lee Bakery Group
Steelcase
UNICOR
VF
Wm. Wrigley Jr.

Publishing/Media
Gartner
International Data Group
Nielsen Media Research
Public Broadcasting Service (PBS)
Reader's Digest Association (The)
Rodale
Valassis
West Group

Retail/Wholesale
Computer
Arrow Electronics
Avnet
CDW Computer Centers
Comark
Consumer
Ace Hardware
Best Buy
Brinker International
Burlington Coat Factory Warehouse
Container Store
Hannaford Bros.
Harley-Davidson
Home Depot
J. C. Penney
JM Family Enterprises
Lands' End
LensCrafters
Liz Claiborne
Lost Arrow
Men's Wearhouse
Nordstrom
Office Depot
Publix Super Markets
RadioShack
REI

Sears, Roebuck
Staples
SUPERVALU
Timberland
Ukrop's Super Markets
United Stationers
Wal-Mart Stores
Wegman's Food Markets
Whole Foods Market

Services
Internet
EarthLink
Genuity
Other
Barton Protective Services (Security)
Beck Group (Construction)
Bright Horizons Family Solutions (Day care centers)
David Weekly Homes (Construction)
DPR Construction
Ecolab (Commercial cleaning)
FedEx (Package delivery)
Kinko's (Photocopying)
Marriott International (Hotels)
United Parcel Service (Package delivery)
Professional/Computer
Acxiom
American Management Systems
Analysts International
Andersen
@stake
BORN
BV Solutions Group
Deloitte Touche Tohmatsu
Electronic Data Systems
Ernst & Young
Forsythe Technology
Kelly Services
KPMG Consulting
Litton PRC
Lockheed Martin Management & Data Systems
PricewaterhouseCoopers
Robert Half International
SRA International
Systems & Computer Technology
TechieGold.com
TRW Systems and IT Group
Ventera
Professional
Alston & Bird
Battelle Memorial Institute

Brobeck, Phleger & Harrison
Fenwick & West
Hewitt Associates
McCutchen, Doyle, Brown & Enersen,
Plante & Moran
Towers Perrin

Telecommunications
AT&T
BellSouth

Lucent Technologies
Sprint
Tellabs

Transportation
Continental Airlines
Duncan Aviation
J. B. Hunt Transport Services
Roadway
Southwest Airlines

State/Company Cross-Reference

Companies are either headquartered in the listed states or offer jobs there. Job locations are either shown in this guide or taken from recent company web postings. No attempt was made to ensure that all states were represented, only that representative technologies and career paths were noted.

Alabama (AL)
ACIPCO
BellSouth
East Alabama Medical Center
JM Family Enterprises
Regions Financial
Vulcan Materials

Alaska (AK)
None

Arizona (AZ)
American Express
Avnet
General Dynamics
Honeywell
Lockheed Martin Mgt. & Data Systems
Prudential Financial
Robert Half International
Rockwell International
UnitedHealth Group
W. L. Gore & Associates

Arkansas (AR)
Acxiom
J.B. Hunt Transport Services
Wal-Mart Stores

California (CA)
3Com
Adobe Systems
Agilent Technologies
Amgen
Apple Computer
Applied Materials
Arrow Electronics
@stake

Autodesk
Baxter International
Becton, Dickinson
Brobeck, Phleger & Harrison
Candle
Caterpillar
Cisco Systems
DPR Construction
EarthLink
Edison International
Fenwick & West
Gateway
Genentech
Granite Rock
Hewlett-Packard
Household International
Intel
International Data Group
Interwoven
Kelly
Kinko's
Kingston Technology
KPMG Consulting
Liz Claiborne
Lockheed Martin
Lost Arrow
McCutchen, Doyle, Brown & Enersen
Mercury Interactive
Metropolitan Life Insurance
National Semiconductor
NCR
Network Appliance
Oracle
Qualcomm
Pfizer
Robert Half International
SAS Institute

Schwab
Silicon Graphics
Solectron
State Street
Sun Microsystems
TechieGold.com
Teradyne
Textron
Valero Energy
Vision Service Plan
Wal-Mart Stores
W. L. Gore & Associates
Xilinx

Colorado (CO)
Amgen
Arrow Electronics
Coors
Galileo International
Gateway
IBM
National Semiconductor

Connecticut (CT)
Aetna
American Skandia
Cigna
Citigroup
Gartner
General Electric
Griffin Hospital
Ingersoll-Rand
National Semiconductor
Pfizer
TechieGold.com
UnitedHealth Group
Valassis

Delaware (DE)
DuPont
MBNA
W. L. Gore & Associates

District of Columbia (DC)
Fannie Mae
IBM
KPMG Consulting
UNICOR

Florida (FL)
Baxter International
Citigroup
FPL Group
Home Shopping Network

JM Family Enterprises
John Hancock Financial Services
Johnson & Johnson
Lockheed Martin
Nielsen Media Research
Office Depot
Publix Super Markets
Royal Caribbean Cruises
TECO Energy

Georgia (GA)
AFLAC
Allstate
Alston & Bird
Andersen
Barton Protective Services
BellSouth
EarthLink
Ernst & Young
Equifax
Gartner
General Electric
Georgia-Pacific
Home Depot
IBM
JM Family Enterprises
Lucent Technologies
Mohawk Industries
PricewaterhouseCoopers
Scientific-Atlanta
Synovus Financial
TechieGold.com
United Parcel Service

Hawaii (HI)
Analysts International
Sprint
Textron

Idaho (ID)
Capital One Financial
Hewlett-Packard

Illinois (IL)
3Com
Ace Hardware
Acxiom
Allstate
Andersen
Baxter International
BorgWarner
Candle
Caterpillar
CDW Computer Centers

Citigroup
Comark
Dana
Deere
Deloitte Touche Tohmatsu
Equifax
Forsythe Technology
Galileo International
GATX
Harrah's Entertainment
Hewitt Associates
Household International
Illinois Tool Works
International Truck and Engine
Manugistics Group
Microsoft
Motorola
Peoples Energy
SAS Institute
Schwab
Sears, Roebuck
State Farm Insurance
Tellabs
United Stationers
Wm. Wrigley Jr.

Indiana (IN)
Bristol-Myers Squibb
Eaton
Eli Lilly
Guidant
Ingersoll-Rand

Iowa (IA)
Deere
HON Industries
Maytag
Pella
Principal Financial Group
Robert Half International

Kansas (KS)
BV Solutions Group
EPIQ Systems
Sprint

Kentucky (KY)
Electronic Data Systems
General Electric
Lexmark
United Parcel Service

Louisiana (LA)
None

Maine (ME)
Candle
Hannaford Bros.
National Semiconductor

Maryland (MD)
AT&T
General Dynamics
Lockheed Martin
Manugistics Group
Marriott International
NCR
PNC Financial Services Group
PRC
SRA International
T. Rowe Price
United Parcel Service
W. L. Gore & Associates

Massachusetts (MA)
Analog Devices
Arrow Electronics
@stake
Bose
Bright Horizons
Cabot
Candle
Electronic Data Systems
EMC
FleetBoston
General Dynamics
Genuity
Intel
International Data Group
John Hancock Financial Services
MFS Investment Management
Millennium Pharmaceuticals
Motorola
Oracle
PNC Financial Services Group
PricewaterhouseCoopers
Staples
State Street
TechieGold.com
Tellabs
Teradyne
Textron
Towers Perrin

Michigan (MI)
Autodesk
BV Solutions Group
Comerica
Herman Miller

Kelly
Lear
Lockheed Martin
Pfizer
Plante & Moran
Republic Bancorp
Robert Half International
Steelcase
Valassis

Minnesota (MN)
Adobe Systems
Analysts International
AT&T
Best Buy
BORN
Ecolab
General Mills
Guidant
Medtronic
3M
Minnesota Mutual
Silicon Graphics
Supervalu
UnitedHealth Group
West Group

Mississippi (MS)
None

Missouri (MO)
A. G. Edwards
American Century Investments
Anheuser-Busch
Battelle Memorial Institute
Cerner
Edward Jones
Emerson
General Electric
Robert Half International
Sara Lee Bakery
SAS Institute
Sigma-Aldrich
Sprint
Unisys

Montana (MT)
None

Nebraska (NE)
Duncan Aviation

Nevada (NV)
Harrah's Entertainment

New Hampshire (NH)
Timberland

New Jersey (NJ)
AT&T
Becton, Dickinson
Bristol-Myers Squibb
Burlington Coat Factory Warehouse
Cisco Systems
Engelhard
FleetBoston
Honeywell
Ingersoll-Rand
Johnson & Johnson
Liz Claiborne
Lucent Technologies
Merck
Prudential Financial
Schering-Plough
Schwab
State Street
TechieGold.com
United Parcel Service

New Mexico (NM)
None

New York (NY)
Acxiom
Arrow Electronics
American Express
AT&T
Avon Products
AXA Financial
Bristol-Myers Squibb
Candle
Citigroup
Colgate-Palmolive
Computer Associates International
Corning
Deloitte Touche Tohmatsu
Ernst & Young
FleetBoston
General Electric
Goldman Sachs
IBM
Kelly
KPMG Consulting
Liz Claiborne
Lockheed Martin
Merrill Lynch
Metropolitan Life Insurance
MONY Group
New York Life Insurance

Pfizer
PricewaterhouseCoopers
Reader's Digest Association
Securities Industry Automation
TechieGold.com
Towers Perrin
Tyco Capital
Wegman's Food Markets
West Group

North Carolina (NC)
Analog Devices
BV Solutions Group
Eaton
Ingersoll-Rand
Lucent Technologies
NCR
R. J. Reynolds Tobacco
SAS Institute
Schwab
VF

North Dakota (ND)
Ecolab
Ingersoll-Rand

Ohio (OH)
Acxiom
American Electric Power
Battelle Memorial Institute
Cincinnati Financial
Dana
Eaton
Ernst & Young
Fifth Third Bancorp
General Electric
J. M. Smucker
Johnson Controls
Kelly
LensCrafters
National City
Nationwide Financial Services
NCR
Parker Hannafin
Roadway
Robert Half International
Third Federal Savings & Loan

Oklahoma (OK)
None

Oregon (OR)
Applied Materials
Intel
SAS Institute

Pennsylvania (PA)
3Com
Aetna
Alcoa
Cigna
EarthLink
Harleysville Group
Hershey Foods
Lockheed Martin Mgt. & Data Systems
Mellon Financial
Merck
Metropolitan Life Insurance
PNC Financial Services Group
Prudential Financial
Robert Half International
Rodale
Rohm and Haas
SEI Investments
Staples
Sunoco
Systems & Computer Technology
Towers Perrin
Unisys
UnitedHealth Group
Vanguard

Rhode Island (RI)
FleetBoston
Immunex
Textron

South Carolina (SC)
Alcoa
Bowater

South Dakota (SD)
None

Tennessee (TN)
Caterpillar
Deloitte Touche Tohmatsu
Eastman Chemical
FedEx
First Tennessee
Harrah's Entertainment
HCA
Regions Financial
Solectron

Texas (TX)
Alcon Laboratories
Analysts International
Applied Materials
Beck Group

Brinker International
Capital One Financial
Container Store
Continental Airlines
David Weekly Homes
Dell Computer
DuPont
Electronic Data Systems
First Tennessee
General Dynamics
Genuity
J. C. Penney
Interwoven
Lockheed Martin
Mellon Financial
Men's Wearhouse
Motorola
National Instruments
PACCAR
RadioShack
SAS Institute
Southwest Airlines
TDIndustries
Teradyne
Texas Instruments
Textron
Trinity Industries
USAA
Valero Energy
VHA
Whole Foods Market

Utah (UT)
3Com
Unisys

Vermont (VT)
None

Virginia (VA)
American Management Systems
AT&T
Candle
Capital One Financial
Coors
EMC
Fannie Mae
Freddie Mac
General Dynamics
Kelly
KPMG Consulting
Lockheed Martin Mgt. & Data Systems
Microstrategy

PRC
Public Broadcasting Service
Silicon Graphics
Sprint
SRA International
TRW Systems and IT Group
Ukrop's Super Markets
Unisys
United Parcel Service
Ventera

Washington (WA)
Adobe Systems
Frank Russell
Immunex
Microsoft
Nordstrom
PACCAR
REI
WRQ

West Virginia (WV)
General Electric

Wisconsin (WI)
American Family Insurance
Comark
Eaton
Harley-Davidson
Johnson Controls
Lands' End
Rockwell International
Silicon Graphics
Wisconsin Energy

Wyoming (WY)
None

Overseas

Australia
PricewaterhouseCooopers

Canada
Deloitte Touche Tohmatsu
Electronic Data Systems

China (People's Republic)
Apple Computer
KPMG Consulting
Motorola
Qualcomm
Teradyne

Denmark
Analog Devices

France
Hewlett-Packard

Germany
American Management Systems
Manugistics Group

India
Oracle

Ireland
PricewaterhouseCoopers

Italy
Cisco Systems

Malaysia
Agilent Technologies

Mexico
Hewlett-Packard

Netherlands
Agilent Technologies
American Management Systems
General Electric
Rockwell International

Romania
Motorola

Slovenia
Deloitte Touche Tohmatsu

Spain
DuPont

Switzerland
American Management Systems
Autodesk

United Kingdom (Great Britain)
Andersen
Manugistics Group
Qualcomm

Product/Vendor Cross-Reference

This list has been compiled to give credit to vendors for their products. Both hardware and software vendors are included. Products are listed first, alphabetically. Vendors follow, sometimes with an extended name or alternate name for their products. We have made every attempt to identify vendors of listed products. Where possible, we have expanded acronyms. We take sole responsibility for any errors or omissions.

While this list is intended to protect the copyright and trade names of the respective vendors, it also includes several other categories of acronyms or names to help the reader. Generic names, open source software names, and functional names are included as well as product names. Where the technical concept has been implemented by several vendors, this is noted.

All registered trademarks, trademarks, and service marks are the property of their respective owners. Where companies have been bought out or renamed, the current owner/name of the company is listed last, in parentheses. This convention is also followed for open source products where an organization is responsible for the product.

2003	IBM Corp.
3090	IBM Corp.
3270	IBM Corp.
9672	IBM Corp.
ABAP	SAP AG
ABI	Intel Corp., Applications Binary Interface
Ab Initio	Ab Initio Software Corp.
Access	Microsoft Corp., also MS-Access
ACD	Lucent Technologies, Inc., Automated Call Distribution
ActiveX	Microsoft Corp.
Actuate	Actuate Corp.
Ada	Programming language. U.S. Department of Defense
ADABAS	Software AG
ADO	Standard, Active Data Objects
AIX	IBM Corp., Advanced Interactive eXecutive
Alpha	Digital Equipment Corporation/DEC (Compaq Computer Corp.)
Alias|wavefront	Silicon Graphics, Inc.
ALLTEL Financials	ALLTEL Information Services
Analog Artist Design	Cadence Design Systems, Inc.
Apache	Open source (The Apache Software Foundation)
Apex	Rational Software Corp.
APO	SAP AG, Advanced Planning Optimizer
Apple	Apple Computer, Inc.
AppleGlot	Apple Computer, Inc.
AppTrieve	WRQ, Inc.

AppWorx	AppWorx Corp.
Arbor	Hyperion Solutions Corp.
Arc/Info	ESRI Inc.
Ariba	Ariba, Inc.
ASCII	Standard, American Standard Code for Information Interchange
ASP	Microsoft Corp., Active Server Pages
Assembler	Programming language, machine-dependent (IBM Corp.)
AS/400	IBM Corp., Application System/400
ATM	Standard, Asynchronous Transfer Mode
Austin-Hayne	Austin-Hayne Corp.
AutoCAD	Autodesk, Inc., Computer Aided Design
Automod	Auto Simulations, Inc. (Brooks Automation, Inc.)
Avanti	avanti technology, inc.
Avaya	Avaya Inc.
Baan	Baan
BAL	IBM Corp., Basic Assembler Language
Bandwidth Manager	Sun Microsystems, Inc.
BAPI	SAP AG, Business Application Programming Interface
Bay Networks	Nortel Networks Ltd.
BEST/1	BMC Software, Inc.
Blue Martini	Blue Martini Software, Inc.
BMC	BMC Software, Inc.
BoundsChecker	Compuware Corp.
BPCS	SSA Global Technologies, Inc., Business Planning and Control Systems
Biosym	Molecular Simulations, Inc.
BLAST	BLAST, Inc.
Bourne shell	sh, UNIX command processor interface, developed at AT&T, Author Stephen Bourne
Brio	Brio Software, Inc.
Broadbase	Broadbase Software (KANA Inc.)
BroadVision	BroadVision, Inc.
Business Objects	Business Objects S.A.
Business Warehouse	SAP AG, BW
C	Open source, developed at AT&T Bell Labs, Authors Ken Thompson, Dennis Ritchie
C++	Open source, developed at AT&T Bell Labs, Author Bjarne Stroustrup
CA-ADSO	Computer Associates International, Inc.
Cadence	Cadence Design Systems, Inc.
CA-KBM	Computer Associates International, Inc.
CA-MANMAN	Computer Associates International, Inc.
Candle	Candle Corp.
CAS	Channel Associated Signaling; Column Address Strobe
Casbah	Open source application framework (Prosthetic Monkey)
CCC/Harvest	Computer Associates International, Inc.
CE	Microsoft Corp.
CGI	Standard, Common Graphical Interface
CICS	IBM Corp., Customer Information Control System
Cirent	Cirent Semiconductor (Agere Systems)
Cisco	Cisco Systems, Inc.
Cisco Works	Cisco Systems, Inc.
Citrix	Citrix Systems, Inc.
Clarify	Clarify Inc.
Claris	Claris Corp.

ClearCase	Rational Software Corp.
CMS	IBM Corp., Conversational Monitor System
CMOS	IBM Corp., Complementary Metal Oxide Semiconductor
COBOL	Open source, IBM, Hewlett-Packard; Common Business-Oriented Language
Cocoa	Apple Computer, Inc.
CodeWarrior	Metrowerks (Motorola, Inc.)
Cognos	Cognos Inc.
ColdFusion	Allaire Corp.
COM/DCOM	Microsoft Corp., Component Object Model/Distributed Component Object Model
Commerce One	Commerce One, Inc.
Commerce Server	Microsoft Corp.
Compaq	Compaq Computer Corp.
Compuware	Compuware Corp.
COMTI	Microsoft Corp., Component Object Model Transaction Integrator
Constellar	Constellar Corp. (DataMirror Corp.)
COOL:2E	Sterling Software, Inc. (Computer Associates International, Inc.), also Synon/COOL: 2E
CORBA	Standard, Object Management Group, Common Object Request Broker Architecture
Cost Accounting	Proamics Corp. (Niku Corp.)
CRM	Generic, Customer Relationship Management
CrossWorlds	CrossWorlds Software Inc.
Crystal Reports	Seagate, Inc.
csh	Berkeley C shell, UNIX command-oriented shell
CSS	Standard, Cascading Style Sheets
cXML	Standard, Commerce XML
DB2	IBM Corp., Database 2
DEC	Digital Equipment Corporation (Compaq Computer Corp.)
Decision Stream	Cognos, Inc.
Developer 2000	Oracle Corp.
DHTML	Standard, Dynamic HTML
Direct (NDM)	Sterling Software (Computer Associates International, Inc.)
Discern Explorer	Cerner Corp.
DKSystems	DKSystems Inc.
DNA	Microsoft Corp., Digital Network Architecture
Documentum	Documentum, Inc.
Domino	Lotus (IBM Corp.)
DOS	IBM Corp., Disk Operating System
Dreamweaver	Macromedia, Inc.
DSL	Generic, Digital Subscriber Line
DSU	Data Service Unit
Dynamo	Art Technology Group, Inc.
Easytrieve	Computer Associates International, Inc.
EBCDIC	Standard, IBM Corp., Extended Binary Coded Decimal Interchange Code
EcoTOOLS	Compuware Corp.
EDI	Standard, Electronic Data Interchange (Sterling Software)
EJB	Sun Microsystems, Inc., Enterprise Java Beans
EMC	EMC Corp.
Endevor	Computer Associates International, Inc.
Entera	Borland Inprise Corp.

Entrust	Entrust, Inc.
ER*win*	Computer Associates International, Inc., Entity Relationship
ES9000	IBM Corp.
Essbase	Hyperion Solutions Corp.
Ethernet	Standard
ETL	Generic, Extract, Transform, and Load
eVision Workbench	TIE Commerce (TIE Holding NV)
Expense Management	Concur Technologies, Inc.
FileNet	FileNet Corp.
Financials	Oracle Corp.; PeopleSoft, Inc.
Flexi	Computer Associates International, Inc.
Flowcharter	Micrografx, Inc.
Forté	Forté (Sun Microsystems, Inc.)
FORTRAN	Formula Translator programming language, developed at IBM Corp., Author Johyn Backus
Fourth Shift	Fourth Shift Corp.
FoxPro	Microsoft Corp.
Front Page	Microsoft Corp.
GDB	Open source, the GNU Debugger
GDS	Standard, Global Directory Service
General Ledger	Walker Interactive Systems; PeopleSoft, Inc.
Genesys	Genesys Software Systems, Inc.; Genesys Testware, Inc.
Gentran	Sterling Commerce (SBC Communications, Inc.)
Ghost	Norton (Symantec Corp.)
Gmake	GNU Make (Free Software Foundation)
GNU	Free Software Foundation
Haushahn	Haushahn Systems and Engineers (Provia Software Inc.)
Harvest	Computer Associates International, Inc.
Hitachi	Hitachi, Ltd.
HP 3000	Hewlett-Packard Co.
HP 9000	Hewlett-Packard Co.
HP/UX	Hewlett-Packard Co.
HTML	Standard, Hypertext Markup Language
HTTP	Standard, Hypertext Transfer Protocol
Human Resouces	PeopleSoft, Inc.; Lawson Software
Hyperion	Hyperion Solutions Corp.
i2	i2 Technologies, Inc.
iAS	Sun Microsystems, Inc., iPlanet Application Server
ICE	Information and Content Exchange; In-Circuit Emulator
IDEF1X	Standard, Integration Definition for Functional Modeling, Nat'l Institute of Standards and Technology (NIST)
IDMS	Computer Associates International, Inc., also CA-IDMS, Integrated Database Management System
IIS	Microsoft Corp., Internet Security Systems
IMAGINE	ERDAS, Inc.
IMAP	Standard, Internet Message Access Protocol
Impromptu	Cognos, Inc.
IMS	IBM Corp., Information Management System
Incyte	Incyte Pharamaceuticals, Inc. (Incyte Genomics, Inc.)
Informatica	Informatica Corp.
Informix	Informix Software, Inc.
Ingres	Computer Associates International, Inc.
Insight Manager	Compaq Computer Corp.

Internet Explorer	Microsoft Corp.
InTouch	Wonderware Corp.
IOS	Microsoft Corp., Input/Output Supervisor
IP	Standard, Internet Protocol
iPlanet	Sun Microsystems, Inc.
ISDN	Standard, Integrated Services Digital Network
ISPF/DMS	IBM Corp., Interactive System Productivity Facility
ISS	Portal
IVR	Generic, Interactive Voice Response
J2EE	Sun Microsystems, Inc., Java 2 Enterprise Edition
Java	Sun Microsystems, Inc.
JavaBeans	Sun Microsystems, Inc.
JavaScript	Sun Microsystems, Inc.
Java Swing	Sun Microsystems, Inc.
J-Builder	Candle Corp.
JDBC	Standard, Java Database Connectivity
J.D. Edwards	J.D. Edwards & Company
JDK	Java Development Kit, Sun Microsystems, Inc.; Microsoft Corp.
JMS	Tibco Software Inc., Java Message Service
Journada	Hewlett-Packard Co.
JOVIAL	U. S. Air Force, Jules Own Version of the International Algorithmic Language
JSP	Sun Microsystems, Inc., Java Server Pages
Kintana	Kintana, Inc.
Kronos	Kronos Inc.
ksh	Korn shell, UNIX command-oriented shell
LAN	Generic, Local Area Network
Larscom	Larscom, Inc.
Lawson	Lawson Software
LDAP	Standard, Lightweight Directory Access Protocol
Lingo	Macromedia, Inc.
Linux	Open source, Red Hat Software, Inc.; VA Linux Systems, Inc.
LISP	List Processor, AI programming language, developed at Dartmouth, MIT, Author, John McCarthy,
L0pht	L0pht Heavy Industries (@Stake, Inc.)
LoadRunner	Mercury Interactive Corp.
Lotus Notes	Lotus (IBM Corp.)
MacApp	Apple Computer, Inc.
Macintosh	Apple Computer, Inc.
Maestro NFS	Hummingbird Ltd. (also NFS Maestro)
MAN	Generic, Metropolitan Area Network
Manugistics	Manugistics Group Inc.
Mapics	Mapics, Inc.
Matlab	The Mathworks, Inc.
McCormack & Dodge	McCormack & Dodge (Dun & Bradstreet Software/ Geac Computer Corp. Ltd.)
MES	Generic, Manufacturing Execution Systems
MFC	Microsoft Corp., Microsoft Foundation Classes
MFG/PRO	QAD Inc.
Micron	Micron Technology, Inc.
MicroStrategy	MicroStrategy Inc.
Model 204	Computer Corporation of America
MOTIF	Graphical user interface for UNIX

MQSeries	IBM Corp.
MS-Access	Microsoft Corp.
MSI	Micro-Star International Co., Ltd.
MTS	MTS Systems Corp.
MVS	IBM Corp., Multiple Virtual Storage
My Eureka!	IQ Objects (Computer Associates International, Inc.)
NAS	NetObjects, Inc. (Website Pros) NetObjects Authoring Server; generic, Network Attached Storage
Natural	Software AG
Navigator	Netscape Communications Corp.
NDM	Sterling Software, Network Data Mover
NDS	Novell, Inc., Novell Directory Services
NEON	New Era of Networks, Inc. (Sybase, Inc.)
Nessus	Open source, Author Renaud Deraison
.Net	Microsoft Corp.
Netbeui	Protocol, NetBios Enhanced User Interface. Developed by IBM, with extensions by Microsoft and Novell.
NetIQ	NetIQ Corp.
NetObjects	NetObjects, Inc. (Website Pros)
Net/OP	Internet/Open Pages
Netscape Server	Netscape Communications Corp.
NetView	Tivoli (IBM Corp.)
NetWare	Novell, Inc.
Network Health	Concord Communications, Inc.
Nextlink	NEXTLINK Communications, Inc.
NNTP	Standard, Network News Transport Protocol (Academ Consulting Services)
Nortel	Nortel Networks Ltd.
Notes	Lotus (IBM Corp.)
NT	Microsoft Corp.
Numetrics	Numetrics Management Systems, Inc.
ObjectARX	Autodesk, Inc.
OBI	Open Buying on the Internet (OBI Consortium)
OC12	Standard, Optical Carrier (SONET; 622.08 Mbps)
OC48	Standard, Optical Carrier (SONET; 2.488 Gbps)
OctelNet	Lucent Technologies, Inc.
ODBC	Standard, Open Database Connectivity
OEM	Generic, Original Equipment Manufacturer
Office	Microsoft Corp., also MS-Office
OLAP	Standard, Online Analytical Processing
OLTP	Standard, Online Transaction Processing
OMEGAMON	Candle Corp.
OneWorld	J. D. Edwards & Co.
OpenView	Hewlett-Packard Co., also HP OpenView
Optimizeit	VMGEAR
Oracle	Oracle Corp.
Oracle Financials	Oracle Corp.
Orcad	Cadence Design Systems, Inc.
OS/390	IBM Corp., Operating System/390
Palm Pilot	3Com Corp.
Pantera SDK	Pantera, Software Development Kit
Pascal	Programming language, Author, Niklaus Wirth
Patrol	BMC Software Inc.

Payroll	Lawson Software
PC	Generic, Personal Computer (IBM, Compaq, HP, Dell, Micron)
PCAnywhere	Symantec Corp.
PCMCIA	Standard, Personal Computer Memory Card International Association
PeopleSoft	PeopleSoft Inc.
Perl	Open source, Practical Extraction and Report Language, Author, Larry Wall
Personic	Personic, Inc.
PHP	Generic, Personal Home Page
PL/I	IBM Corp., Programming Language/One
PL/SQL	Oracle Corp., Procedural Language/Structured Query Language
POP3	Standard, Post Office Protocol
POS	Generic, Point-of-Sale
PowerBuilder	Sybase, Inc.
PowerPlay	Cognos, Inc.
PPPoA	Standard, Point-to-Point Protocol over ATM
PPPoE	Standard, Point-to-Point Protocol over Ethernet
Primavera	Primavera Systems, Inc.
Probes	NetScout Systems, Inc.
ProEngineer	Parametric Technologies Corp.
Project	Oracle Corp., Microsoft Corp.
ProVision	ProVision, Inc. (Box21, Inc.)
PTC	Parametric Technologies Corp.
Purify	Rational Software Corp.
QAD	QAD Inc.
Quantify	Rational Software Corp.
QuarkXPress	Quark, Inc.
QUEST	Deneb Robotics, Inc. (Delmia Corp.)
Rational Rose	Rational Software Corp.
Redback	Redback Networks Inc.
Red Brick	Informix Software, Inc.
Reflections	WRQ, Inc.
Remedy	Remedy Corp.
Rendezvous	Tibco Software Inc.
Resource Management	Niku Corp.
Resumix	Resumix, Inc. (HotJobs Software)
Rexx	IBM Corp., Restructured Extended Executor Language; Author, Michael Cowlishaw
RF	Generic, Radio Frequency
RISC 6000	IBM Corp., Reduced Instruction Set Computer, also RS/6000
ROAP	Standard, Remote Object Proxy Engine Protocol
RPG	IBM Corp., Report Program Generator
RUMBA	NetManage, Inc.
SAA Gateways	IBM Corp., System Application Architecture
SAN	Generic, Storage Area Network
SAP	SAP AG
Sapient Framework	Sapient Corp.
SAS	SAS Institute Inc.
Saville	ADC
SCP	Standard, Simple Control Protocol
SDLC	System Development Life Cycle
SeeBeyond	SeeBeyond Technology Corp.
Sequent	Sequent Computer Systems, Inc.

SGI	Silicon Graphics Inc.
Shiva	Intel Corp.
ShowCase STRATEGY	ShowCase Corp. (SPSS Inc.)
Siebel Systems	Siebel Systems, Inc.
Silk	Segue Software Inc.
Silk-Performer	Segue Software Inc.
SilverStream	SilverStream Software, Inc.
SL	Hitachi, Ltd.
Smalltalk	Xerox Corp. (ParcPlace Systems, Inc.)
SMTP	Standard, Simple Mail Transfer Protocol
SNA	IBM Corp., Systems Network Architecture
Sniffer	Network Associates Technology, Inc.
Snoop	Pearl Software, Inc., Cyber Snoop
Snort	Open source, Network Intrusion Detection System
SOAP	Standard, Simple Object Access Protocol
SoftICE	Compuware Corp.
Solaris	Sun Microsystems, Inc.
SolidWorks	SolidWorks Corp.
SourceSafe	Microsoft Corp., Visual SourceSafe
SP	IBM Corp., Symmetric Processor
SPARC	Sun Microsystems, Inc., Scalable Processor Architecture
SPICE	Standard, Software Process Improvement and Capability dEtermination
SPSS	SPSS Inc.
SQA	Software Quality Assurance
SQL	Standard, Structured Query Language (IBM, Microsoft, Oracle)
SQL Anywhere	Sybase, Inc.
SQL Server	Microsoft Corp., Sybase, Inc.
SQL-Time	Structured Query Language - Time Class
SQR	Structured Query Report Writer
STC	Storage Technology Corp.
Sterling Software	Sterling Software (Computer Associates International, Inc.)
STK	StorageTek, Storage Technology Corp.
Story Server	Vignette Corp.
Sun	Sun Microsystems, Inc.
Sybase	Sybase, Inc.
Symix	Symix Systems, Inc. (FrontStep, Inc.)
Synapse	Integrated Business Systems & Services, Inc.
Synon/COOL:2E	Synon Corp. (Sterling Software/Computer Associates International, Inc.)
Synopsys	Synopsys, Inc.
Sysplex	IBM Corp.
Tandem	Tandem (Compaq Computer Corp.)
Tcl/Tk	Tool Command Language, Author John Ousterhout
TCP/IP	standard, Transaction Control Protocol/Internet Protocol
TCS	TCS Management Group, Inc. (Aspect Communications Corp.)
TeamSite	Interwoven, Inc.
Telemate	Telemate, Net Software, Inc.
Telxon	Telxon Corp.
TenFold	TenFold Corp.
Teradata	Teradata (NCR Corp.)
Terminal Server	Microsoft Corp.
TestDirector	Mercury Interactive Corp.

Tivoli	Tivoli (IBM Corp.)
Tool Chain	GNU (Free Software Foundation)
TowerJ	Tower Technology Corp.
TPF	IBM Corp., Transaction Processing Facility
Trilogy	Trilogy, Inc.
Tripos	Tripos, Inc.
TSO	IBM Corp., Time Sharing Option
Tuxedo	BEA Systems, Inc.
UDB	IBM Corp., Universal Database
UDDI	Microsoft Corp., Universal Description, Discovery, and Integration
Ultrix	Digital Equipment Corporation/DEC, (Compaq Computer Corp.)
UML	Unified Modeling Language (Object Management Group)
Uniface	Compuware Corp.
Unisphere	Unisphere Networks, Inc.
Unisys	Unisys Corp.
UNIX	Open source (X/Open Company Limited)
Vantive	Vantive Corp. (PeopleSoft, Inc.)
VAX	Digital Equipment Corporation (Compaq Computer Corp.), Virtual Address eXtension
Vectra	Hewlett Packard Co.
Verilog	Standard, Hardware Description Language (Cadence Design Systems, Inc./Open Verilog International)
Verity	Verity, Inc.
Vignette	Vignette Corp.
VISE Installer	MindVision Software, Installer VISE
Visible Advantage	Visible Advantage Corp.
Visio	Microsoft Corp.
VisualAge	IBM Corp.
Visual Basic	Microsoft Corp., Visual Beginners' All-Purpose Symbolic Instruction Code
Visual C++	Microsoft Corp.
VisualCafé	Symantec Corp. (WebGain, Inc.)
Visual InterDev	Microsoft Corp.
Visual SourceSafe	Microsoft Corp.
Visual Studio	Microsoft Corp.
Vitria	Vitria Technology, Inc.
VM	IBM Corp., Virtual Machine
VMS	Digital Equipment Corporation (Compaq Computer Corp.), Virtual Memory System
VoIP	Voice over Internet Protocol
VPN	Generic, Virtual Private Network
VSAM	IBM Corp., Virtual Storage Access Method
VTAM	IBM Corp., Virtual Telecommunications Access Method
VxWorks	Wind River Systems, Inc.
Wall Data	Wall Data, Inc.
WAN	Generic, Wide Area Network
WAP	Standard, Wireless Application Protocol
WebEx	WebEx Communications, Inc.
WebLogic	BEA Systems, Inc., also WebLogic Server
webMethods	webMethods, Inc.
Webserver	Netscape Communications Corp.
WebSphere	IBM Corp.
WebSystems	Alteon WebSystems (Nortel Networks Ltd.)

Windows 98	Microsoft Corp.
Windows 2000	Microsoft Corp.
Windows NT	Microsoft Corp.
Winframe	Citrix Systems, Inc.
WinRunner	Mercury Interactive Corp.
Wise	Wise Solutions, Inc.
WML	Standard, Wireless Markup Language
Wonderware	Wonderware Corp.
Workstream	Workstream, Inc.
WySTAR	PNC Financials Corp.
Xbox	Microsoft Corp.
XGL	Standard, Extensible Graphics Language
XML	Standard, Extensible Markup Language
XSLT	Standard, Extensible Stylesheet LanguageTransformations
Yourdon	Yourdon methodology, Author, Ed Yourdon

Bibliography

The author used several Internet sites for most research. These include:

- The web site of each company profiled
- http://www.hoovers.com, for a business overview
- http://www.webopedia.com, for product terms and vendors
- http://www.yahoo.com, for general searches
- http://netlingo.com, for Internet terms
- http://whatis.techtarget.com, for computer terms

Long profiles, as discussed under Methodology, were supplemented by interviews with company representatives, as well as additional company materials. In addition, the following articles were referenced.

BV Solutions Group, Inc.
- Computerworld, "Construction Firm Builds on Tech Prowess,'" January 31, 2000
- Computerworld, "Cultivating the IT Staff," May 8, 2000

Candle Corp.
- Computerworld, "Candle Updates, Refines Its Web Site Monitoring Tool," June 19, 2000
- Information Week, "Companies See Gold in Outside Data Analysis," March 20, 2000
- PCWeek, "Candle to Host B2B Integration Service," March 27, 2000

EarthLink, Inc.
- Technology Review, "Profiles: Sky Dayton," November/December, 1999
- Wall Street Journal, "EarthLink's Loss Widens as Marketing Costs Rise," April 20, 2000

Interwoven, Inc.
- Computer Reseller News, "Interwoven Unveils TeamSite 4.0," December 13, 1999
- Interactive Week, "Interwoven's TeamSite Tackles Content Management," December 13, 1999

Kelly Services, Inc.
- Information Week, "Kelly Gets Y2K on Schedule," May 10, 1999
- Information Week, "IT Puts the Right People in the Right Place," September 27, 1999

National Semiconductor, Inc.
- CNET News.com, "National Targets Net Devices Boom with Low-Power Chip," April 11, 2000
- CNET News.com, "National Semi, Liberate Team on Set-Tops," May 9, 2000
- Information Week, "Tapping the Pipeline," March 15, 1999
- NetworkWorld, "What Went Wrong with ASPs?" October 29, 2001

Robert Half International, Inc.
- Computerworld, "Where the Best Jobs Are," May 29, 2000

AFLAC, Inc.
- The Wall Street Transcript (www.twst.com/info53.htm)
- NAIC Better Investing/Investor News, April, 2000
- Forbes, "Forbes Platinum 400/Industry Buzz," Carrie Coolidge, January 8, 2001 (www.forbes.com)

Bose Corp.
- Technology Review, "At Bose the Challenges Don't Always Involve Stereo Systems," advertisement, May/June, 2000

Citigroup Inc.
- Computerworld, "Citigroup Tests Wireless Services in Japan," June 12, 2000
- Computerworld, "Citigroup Unveils Wireless Banking Plans, August 12, 1999
- The Industry Standard, "Citigroup, Commerce One to Create Portal," February 17, 2000
- Wired, "The Future of Money," October, 1996

First Tennessee National Corp.
- Computerworld, "Profile: Response Networks, Tracking Web App Performance," November 13, 2000
- Computerworld, "Users Tell Their Java Tales," May 18, 1998
- Fortune, "America's Top Employers," January 8, 2001

Freddie Mac
- Computerworld, "Hire Callings," September 24, 2001
- Interactive Week, "Freddie, Fannie Agree to XML Standard,"June 18, 2001
- Washingtonian, "Great Places to Work," October, 2001
- Washington Post, "Coaxing Staffers to Aim Hire," December 7, 1999
- Washington Post, "Freddie Mac Giving Employees a Chance to Change Fields," April 8, 2001
- The Wall Street Journal, "Why Big Lenders Are So Afraid of Fannie Mae and Freddie Mac," April 5, 2001

Hannaford Bros. Co.
- Reuters Online News, "FTC OKs Delhaize America-Hannaford Deal," July 25, 2000
- Washington Post, "Food Lion Outbids Ahold for Hannaford," August 19, 1999

Ingersoll-Rand Co.
- Business Wire, "Ingersoll-Rand Forms E-Business Sector," March 24, 2000
- Forbes, "Ingersoll-Rand Gets a Makeover," September 6, 1999

- Information Week, "A Company Merges Its Many Units—Successfully," May 8, 2000
- Wall Street Journal, "Ingersoll-Rand Uses 'IR' as a Way to Play New-Image Name Game," August 22, 2000

Lands' End Inc.
- Computerworld, "Service Needs Drive Tech Decisions at Lands' End," December 20, 1999
- Computerworld, "Lands' End Tailors to Corporate Clients," March 20, 2000
- Computerworld, "Clash of the Killers Ps," June 19, 2000
- Context, "Fashion Forward," April/May 2000
- Information Week, "Lands' End Looks Beyond Consumers," March 20, 2000
- Information Week, "Boom Times for the Class of 2000," May 22, 2000
- Information Week, "E-Retail Customer Service: It's More than Just E-Mail," September 25, 2000

Mellon Financial Corp.
- PR Newswire, "Mellon's e-Commerce Solutions Make the Grade at eschoolmall. com(tm)," April 3, 2000
- PR Newswire, "Mellon to Pilot Voice-Guided ATMs," April 4, 2000

Millennium Pharmaceuticals, Inc.
- Business Week, "A Pharma Star is Born?" September 25, 2000
- Fortune, "Blessings from the Book of Life," March 6, 2000
- Fortune, "Hatching a DNA Giant," May 24, 1999
- Red Herring, "Millennium Pharmaceuticals Exploits the Big Opportunity in Genomics," April, 2000

New York Life Insurance Co.
- Business Wire, "AppWorx Partners with AnswerThink to Automate Backend Processes for eBusiness," March 16, 2000
- Computerworld, "The CIO/CTO Balancing Act," June 19, 2000

Nielsen Media Research
- The Industry Standard, "Playing for Keeps," May 14, 2001

State Farm Life Insurance Cos.
- Computerworld, "Fish" (June 18, 2001)
- Computerworld, "Retention: To Have and To Hold" (June 12, 2000)
- Business Week, "State Farm: What's Happening to the Good Neighbor?" (November 8, 1999)

Where Do They Do That?

1. **Who has a Halloween costume party for their employees' children?**
   BV Solutions Group, Candle

2. **Who offers free beepers for expectant parents?**
   Freddie Mac

3. **Who pays overtime?**
   BV Solutions Group, Robert Half International

4. **Who pays employees to van pool?**
   EarthLink

5. **Who has a company-sponsored skeet team?**
   BV Solutions Group

6. **Where can you sell back vacation days?**
   Candle

7. **Who has on-site dry cleaning pickup?**
   Freddie Mac, Candle, National Semiconductor

8. **Who organizes deep-sea fishing trips?**
   EarthLink

9. **Who offers free bagels?**
   Candle

10. **Where can you wear jeans or shorts?**
    EarthLink, Millenium Pharmaceuticals, Nielsen Media Research

11. **Who offers free housecleaning?**
    Interwoven

12. Who offers free fruit?
   Candle

13. Who is working on wearable computers?
   State Farm Insurance

14. Who organizes whale-watching trips?
   Candle

15. Whose company fitness trainer is a world-class triathlete?
   Interwoven

16. Who organizes paint ball outings?
   EarthLink, Millennium Pharmaceuticals

17. Where might you get a rose for your birthday?
   State Farm Insurance

18. Who offers on-site massages?
   Interwoven, National Semiconductor

19. Who gives you a balloon on your birthday?
   AFLAC

20. Who offers on-site film drop-off?
   Freddie Mac

21. Who offers on-site dental services?
   National Semiconductor

22. Who offers free apples?
   Lands' End

23. Whose address is The Mountain?
   Bose

24. Where do you get your birthday off?
   National Semiconductor

25. Who offers white-water rafting trips?
   Interwoven, National Semiconductor

26. Who pays employees to van pool?
EarthLink

27. Who has a rock-climbing team?
Millennium Pharamaceuticals

28. Who has a toll-free line for helping employees' children with their homework?
Lands' End

29. Whose founder is still a professor at MIT?
Bose

30. Who offers on-site car wash and oil change?
National Semiconductor

31. Who has an Olympic-sized swimming pool?
Lands' End

32. Where is the average commute 10 minutes?
AFLAC, Hannaford Bros.

33. Where can you get discount tickets to Disneyland?
National Semiconductor, Bose

INDEX